IMAGES
of America

African Americans in Culpeper, Orange, Madison, and Rappahannock Counties

On the Cover: The home economics class of the Culpeper Training School included, from left to right, Jacqueline Madden, Laverne Smith, Ross Lee Payne, Evelyn Jackson, Georgine Payne, Grace Nibblins, Edna Alexander, Susie Scott, Rena Johnson, Pauline Vivian Green, Jean Brock, and Betty Sanchez. Several of these young women attended Virginia College for Negroes (later Virginia State University) and returned to Culpeper as schoolteachers. This photograph was taken in 1943. (Terry Miller.)

IMAGES
of America

AFRICAN AMERICANS IN CULPEPER, ORANGE, MADISON, AND RAPPAHANNOCK COUNTIES

Terry L. Miller

ARCADIA
PUBLISHING

ISBN 978-1-4671-2994-7

Published by Arcadia Publishing
Charleston, South Carolina

Printed in the United States of America

Library of Congress Control Number: 2018940251

For all general information, please contact Arcadia Publishing:
Telephone 843-853-2070
Fax 843-853-0044
E-mail sales@arcadiapublishing.com
For customer service and orders:
Toll-Free 1-888-313-2665

Visit us on the Internet at www.arcadiapublishing.com

To Dad, Mom, Robert, and Pia

Contents

ACKNOWLEDGMENTS

I am grateful for the kindness and unselfish information shared by many people. Special appreciation goes to Bonnie Utz and Susan Keller, head librarians for Madison and Culpeper Counties, respectively. In addition, Laura Thompson, executive director of The Arts Center in Orange, and Morgan Pierce, Gloria Cooper, and Pam Stewart of the Museum of Culpeper History graciously allowed me to exhibit to the public some of the research contained here. The collections in the Orange County Historical Association contributed to my understanding of the context of that county within the region.

My editors at Arcadia Publishing, Angel Hisnanick and Sara Miller, provided patient encouragement to ensure this project was the best that my talents could produce.

My first entry to the region came from Dr. Hortense Hinton-Jackson, who introduced me to people who became my hosts, guides, and friends: Michelle Jameson and her husband, Charles; William Lewis; Jane Pollard; Myra Williams; and Rebecca Coleman. Special appreciation is extended to an extraordinary community historian, Angela J. Chapman, for her insight, ephemera, and encouragement. The eight of them were invaluable to me in ways too many to count.

Archives continually surprise and none as brightly as those of Virginia State University in Petersburg, Virginia. As one of the only accessible higher education institutions available to Virginia's African Americans during the time period of this book (1855 to 1955), the depth of the university's collections of photographs and speeches significantly contributed to this content. All that I needed was generously provided by the university's historical archivist, Francine Archer.

Finally, my family kept me focused by asking, "Who are you looking for this time?" This book could not have been completed without their support. To all, I simply say, "Thank you."

Introduction

Cameras are now democratized. Once the prized possession of a few people, everyone now has the ability to take photographs to share with others. Books like this one, which features the faces and lives of rural people of color, are difficult to compose, because the choice between buying a camera and/or paying for a portrait or purchasing food for the family was a real one.

Rather than looking at this as a history book, imagine it as a treasured glimpse at the time period from 1855 to 1955. This book shows some faces of people of color in Culpeper, Orange, Madison, and Rappahannock Counties. These four counties were chosen because they now represent a region that regularly works together to solve common problems, although the character of each county is distinct.

The first chapter gives context on the landscape in which people lived. The second chapter focuses on the scores of men and women who shaped the area through their military service, and there is an appreciation for those who served in conflicts from the Revolutionary War through the Korean War. Because land is a crucial resource, the entire third chapter is devoted to those whose primary means of sustenance was farming. When wives and mothers were not helping to farm, they were coordinating chores and organizing a home for families that sometimes included up to 16 children. At times, the sheer exhaustion is glaring from their faces. The fourth chapter includes the wives of farmers, and those married to men in other professions, who had a role in keeping house that was just as critical to peace at night. Chapter five shows that not everyone chose farming. Some questions addressed in the chapter include, "What other skills could they use to make a living?" and "Where else could they go to do so?" Chapter six demonstrates how people tried to educate themselves and their children. This walk through time ends with the different ways that churches and those who gather for religious purposes are actually supported.

Two cautionary notes: First, the oldest available photographs were sought so that readers could reflect and see on their own faces the vestiges of the emotional and physical journey traveled by their ancestors. Second, this is a book about people of color, and thus, I do not always specify that within each caption. Because the region has a strong legacy of slaveholding and Native American inhabitation, in addition to genuine tenderness between men and women of all races, the spectrum of color and facial features is broad. All representations of those colors are found in these pages.

One

Where They Lived

The people shown in this book were born in, worked in, and/or lived in one of four contiguous counties in upper central Virginia comprising approximately 1,321 square miles.

Whether they lived in valleys, on the sides of mountains, near the Rapidan or Rappahannock Rivers or at the banks of one of the streams that run throughout the region, inside or outside of the rim of a plantation, they called it home.

The first county established was Orange, in 1734, and after 1865, this county's African American population seemed more progressive than those of Culpeper, Madison, and Rappahannock, as evidenced by its education system. Minority children had the benefit of high school education in Orange long before 1948, which was when George Washington Carver Regional High School opened in Culpeper. As will be shown in chapter six, Carver Regional High School was built for minority students who lived in all four counties.

Culpeper was established in 1749, and its highest peak is approximately 600 feet. It, like all the counties, is rich in farmland. Culpeper was the last county in Virginia to integrate its schools.

Madison was established in 1792 and contains 322 square miles. It is characterized by a population that has remained relatively stable at 13,000 largely due to familial ties. Its farmland is best served by dairy and egg farming, as is the farmland in Rappahannock. Between 1900 and 1950, more than 34 percent of Rappahannock's population relocated.

The land continues to be rural, scenic, and agricultural in nature. Still, it was home.

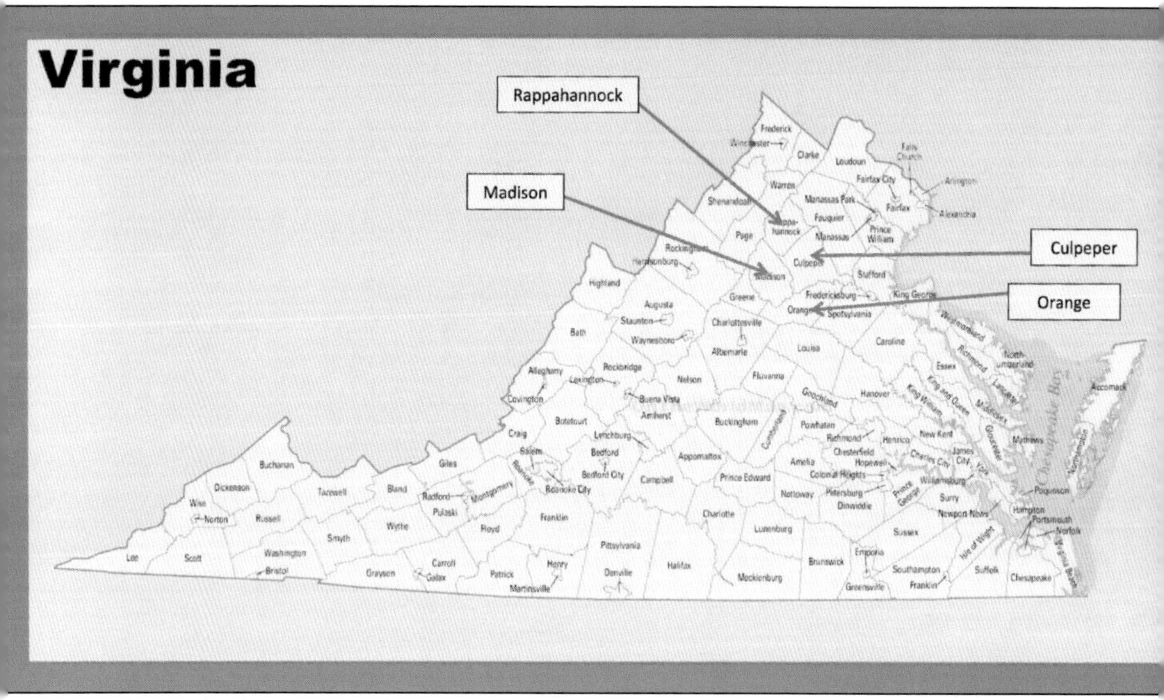

The marked portion of this map shows the counties of Culpeper, Orange, Madison, and Rappahannock and their locations in the Upper Piedmont region of Virginia. (Virginia Department of Transportation.)

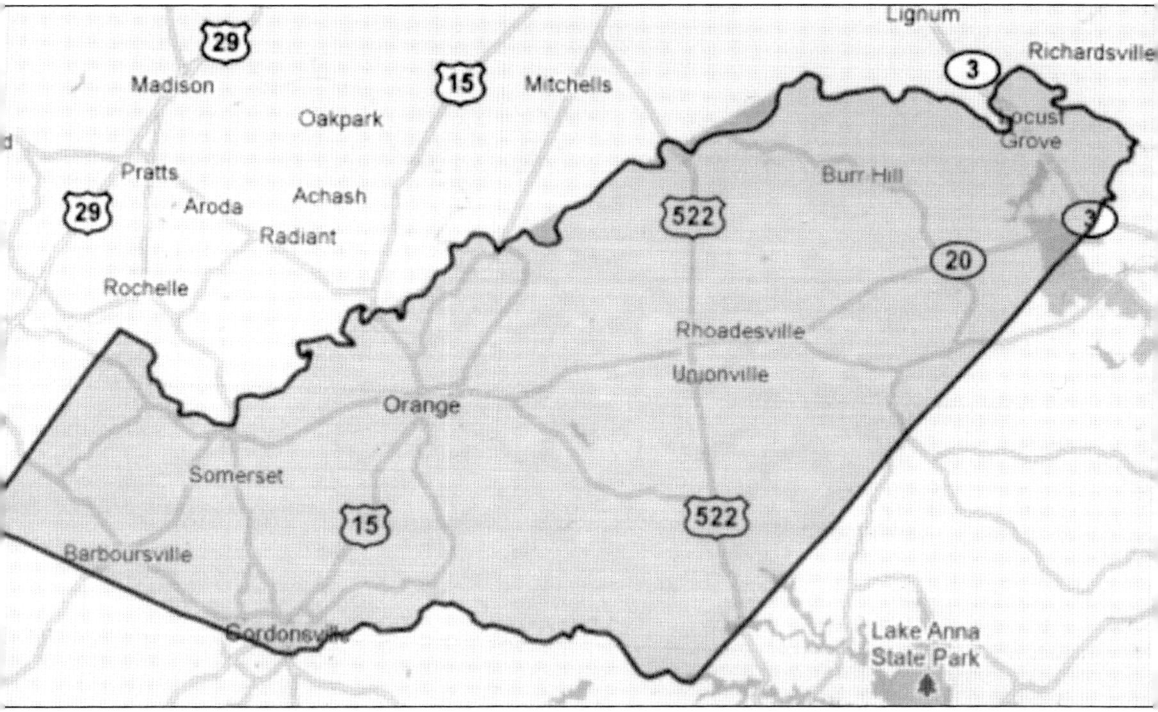

Orange County dates from 1734, making it the first to be established among this group of four counties. It is the home of two US presidents. James Madison, the fourth president, has been called the "Father of the Constitution." He served two terms from 1809 to 1817. His second cousin Zachary Taylor was the 12th president and served from 1848 until his death in office in 1850. Orange is rich in both farmland and mineral deposits, including iron ore. (Orange County Visitors Bureau.)

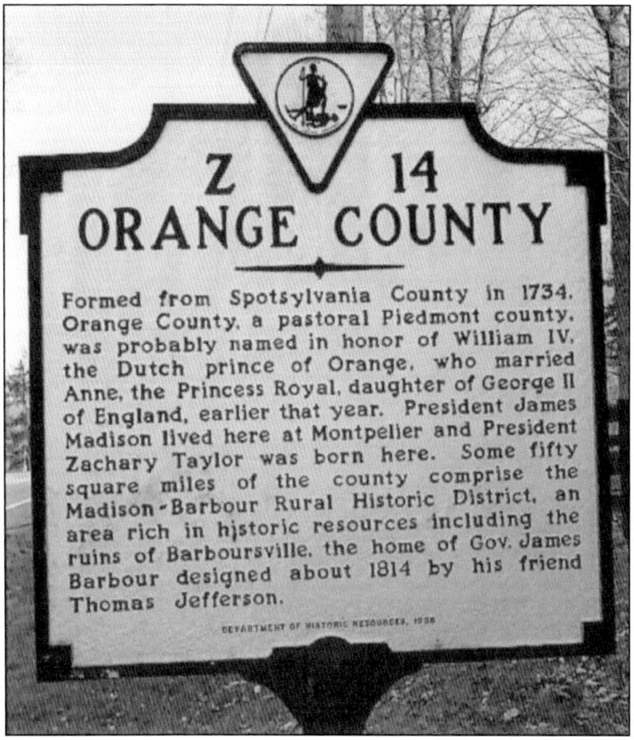

A vibrant African American community thrived in the town of Gordonsville, which was on a popular travel route from the Shenandoah Valley to Richmond. It thrived because of this route, and the African American population, especially women, developed successful businesses at the railroad tracks. As early as the Civil War, during train stops at the depot, women balancing trays of fried chicken and carrying baskets of rolls sold their wares to train passengers who reached from the windows. The local government began licensing and taxing them as "snack vendors" in 1879. Their businesses continued until the mid-1900s, when increased regulations became too cumbersome. (Left, Virginia Department of Historic Resources; below, the Exchange Hotel Civil War Medical Museum.)

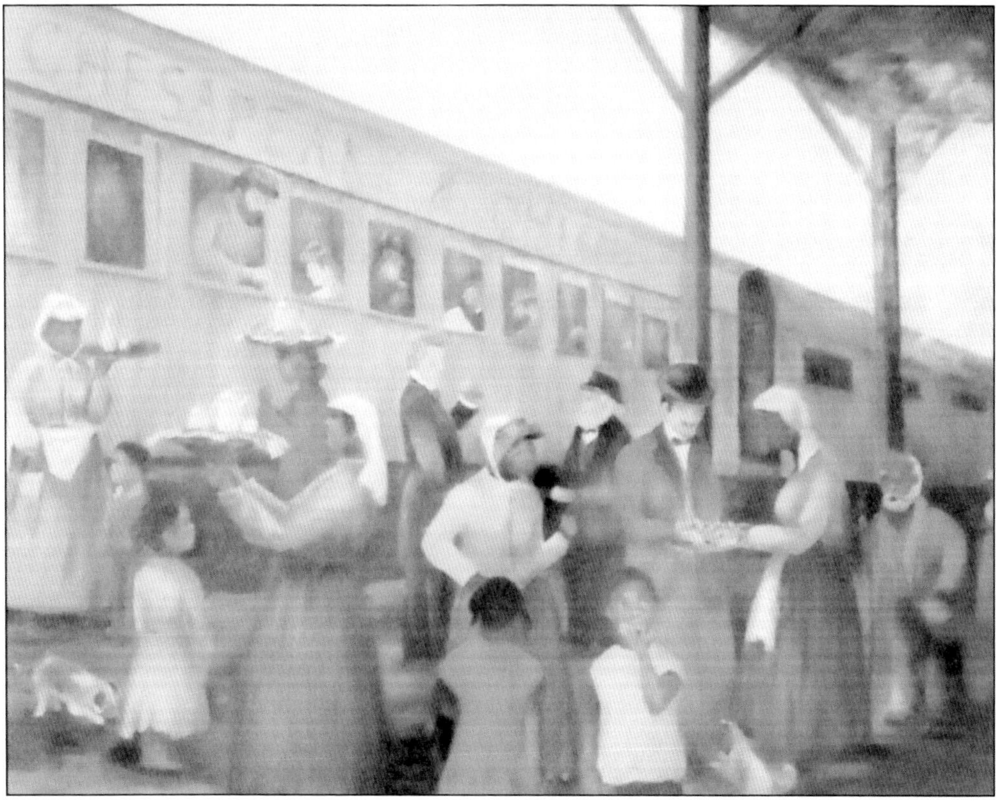

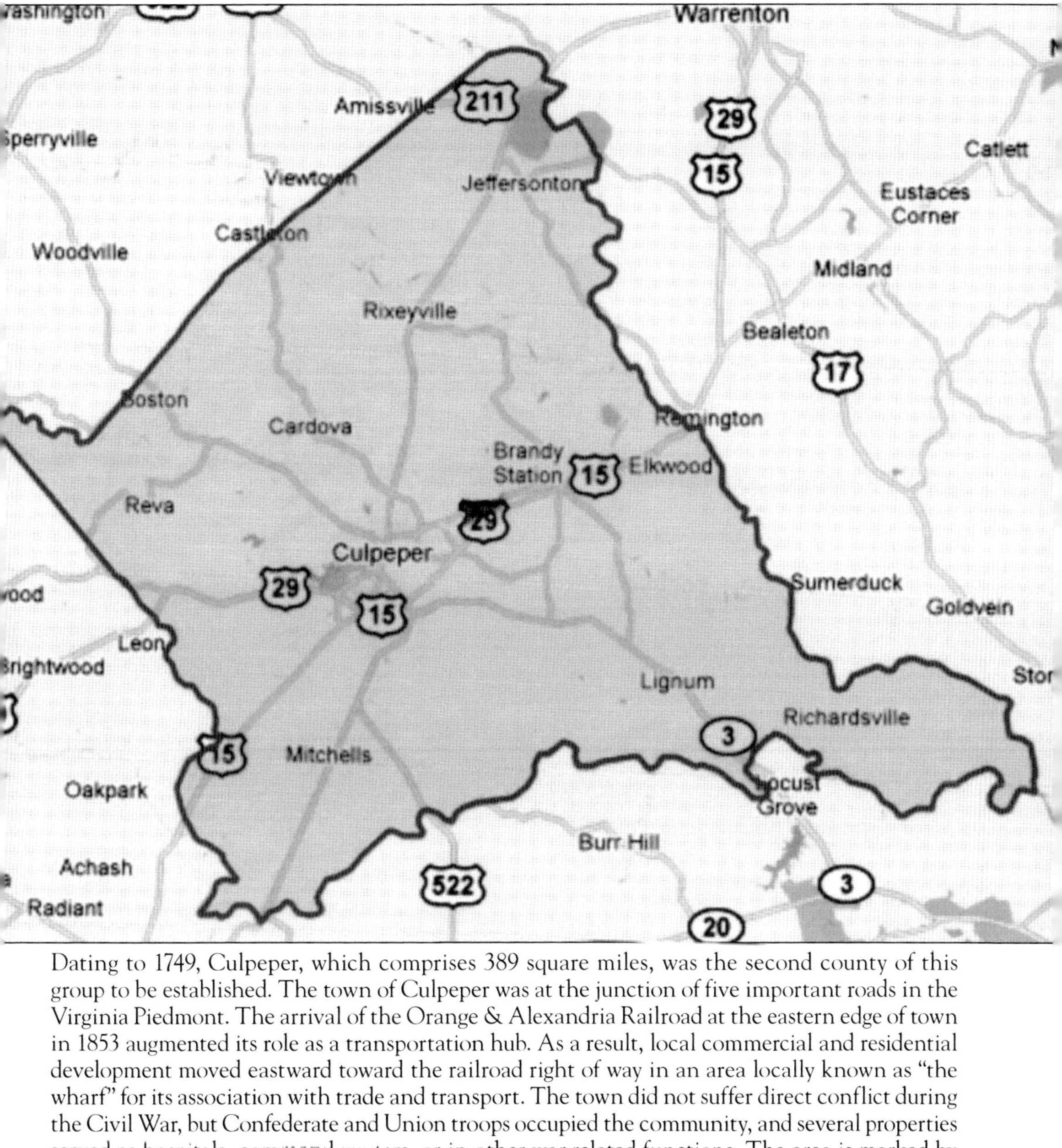

Dating to 1749, Culpeper, which comprises 389 square miles, was the second county of this group to be established. The town of Culpeper was at the junction of five important roads in the Virginia Piedmont. The arrival of the Orange & Alexandria Railroad at the eastern edge of town in 1853 augmented its role as a transportation hub. As a result, local commercial and residential development moved eastward toward the railroad right of way in an area locally known as "the wharf" for its association with trade and transport. The town did not suffer direct conflict during the Civil War, but Confederate and Union troops occupied the community, and several properties served as hospitals, command centers, or in other war-related functions. The area is marked by two military engagements: the Battle of Cedar Mountain (1862) and Brandy Station (1863). Many residents—tavern owner Willis Madden is an example—suffered significant property loss. They sought and often received restitution from the federal government, although it did not make them whole. (Culpeper County Clerk's Office.)

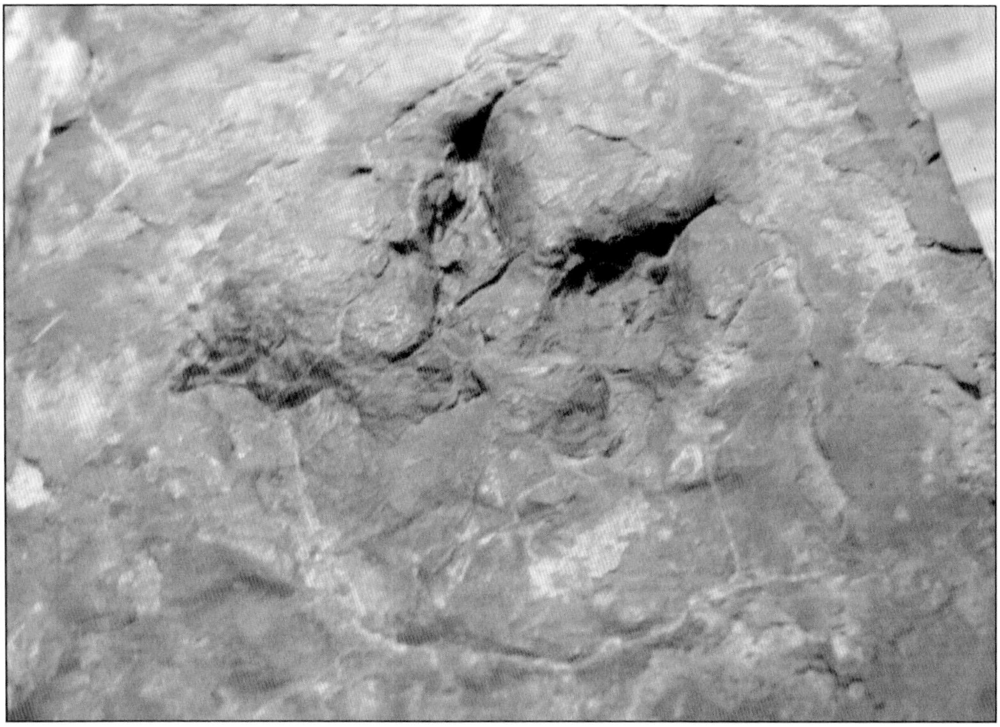

In the Stevensburg area of Culpeper is a rock quarry that descends 250 feet. It was once the site of a lakeshore or floodplain. In that quarry, Triassic-era dinosaur tracks were found. This means that the tracks are at least 215 million years old. Owned by the Luck Stone Company (below) since May 2002, the quarry's dinosaur tracks are still visible, and some have been transferred to both the Smithsonian Institution and the Museum of Culpeper History. The quarry is located on State Route 3 a few miles southeast of Culpeper. (Above, Museum of Culpeper History; below, Terry Miller.)

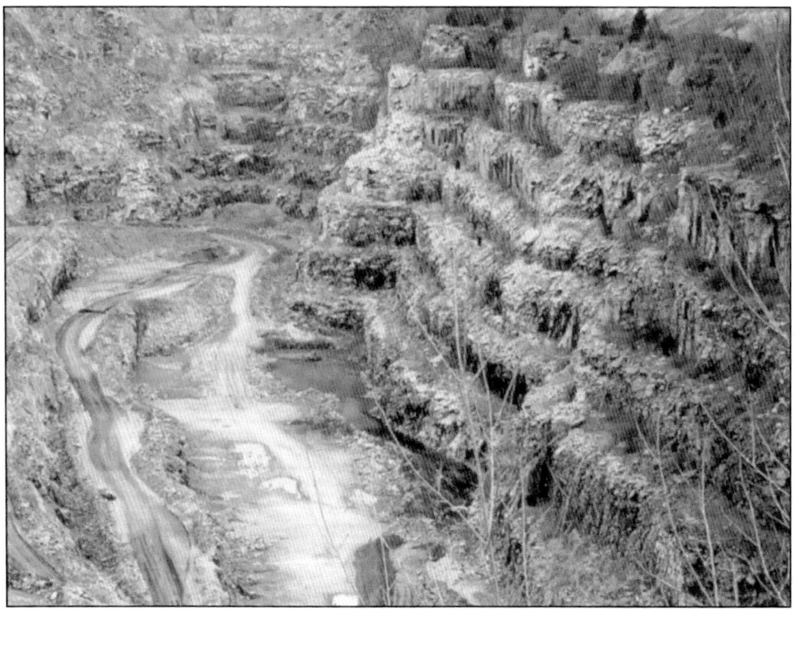

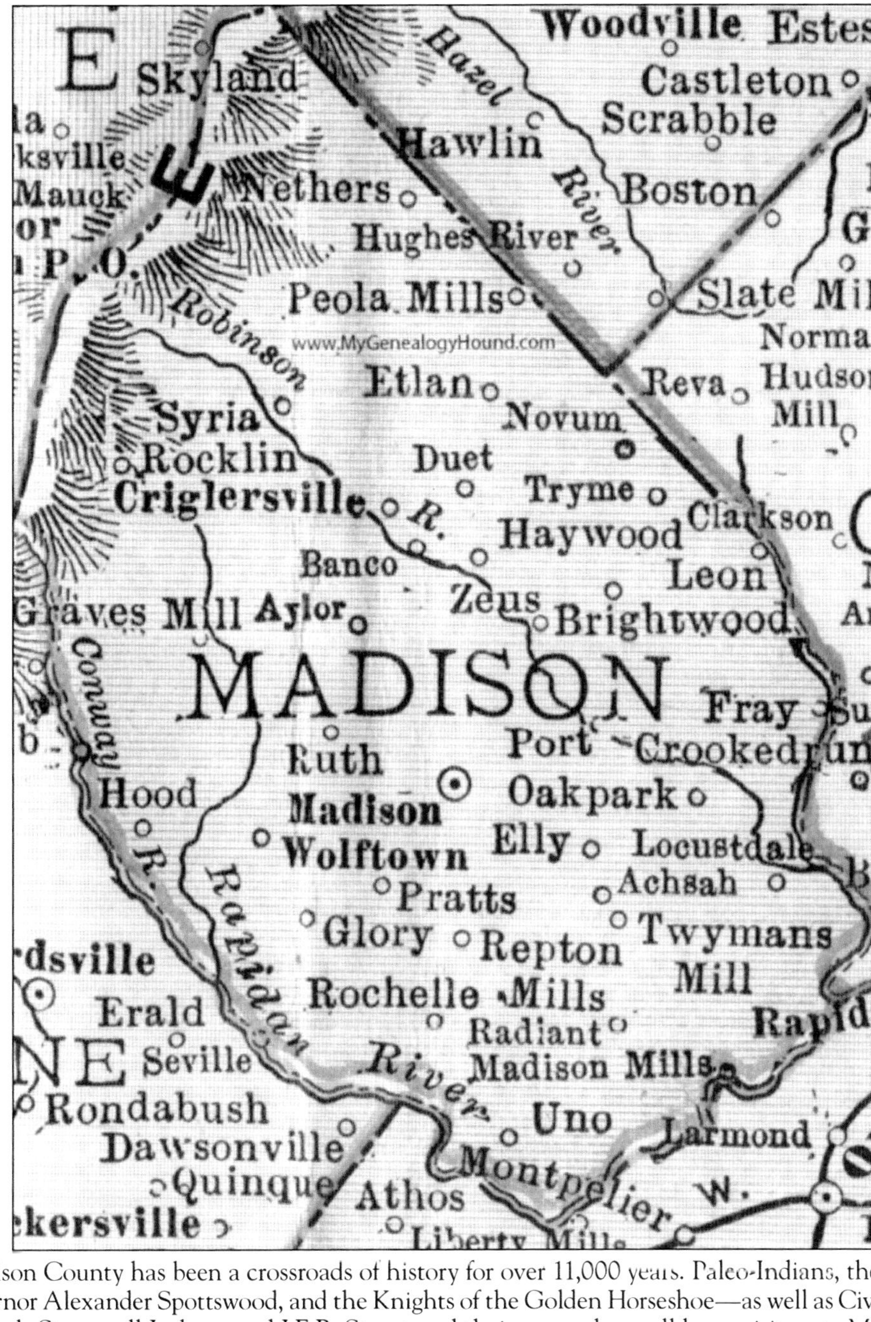

Madison County has been a crossroads of history for over 11,000 years. Paleo-Indians, the royal governor Alexander Spottswood, and the Knights of the Golden Horseshoe—as well as Civil War generals Stonewall Jackson and J.E.B. Stuart and their men—have all been visitors to Madison County. Trails and early roads led through the Piedmont area of Madison and up into the Blue Ridge Mountains, allowing 18th- and 19th-century travelers to enter the Shenandoah Valley. Early settlers in the 18th century included German, English, and Scots-Irish families. Descendants of these families still live in Madison. In the 1850 census, there were 4,608 free residents of the county; only 147 (three percent) were free persons of color. The most recent census data show that of the total population of 13,700, nine percent are African American. (Madison County Chamber of Commerce.)

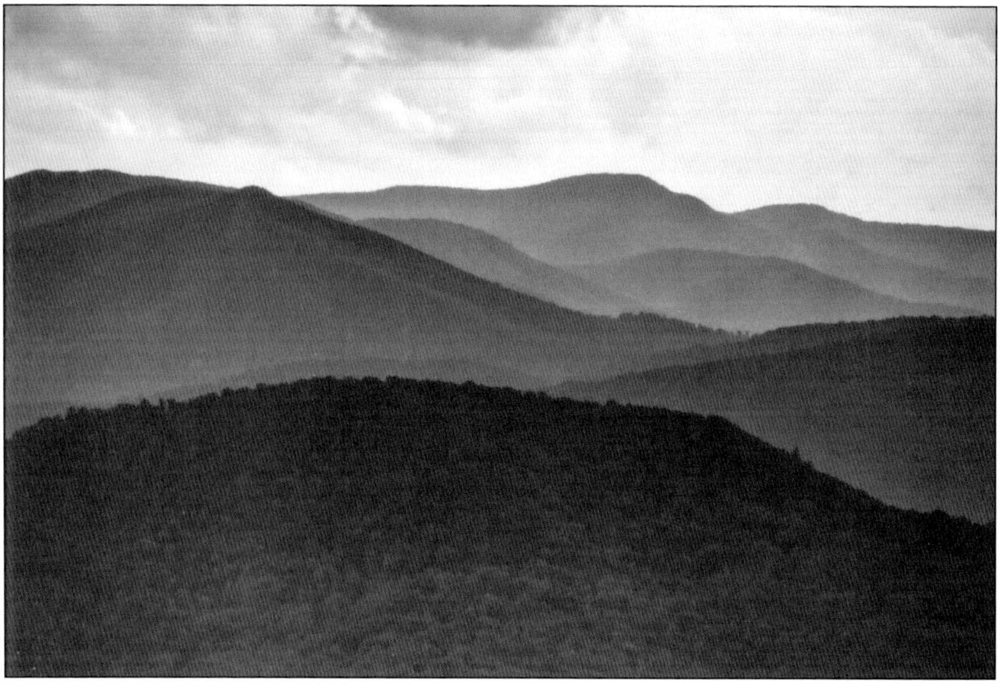

The Blue Ridge Mountains cast a shadow of mystery around Madison County, home to a portion of Shenandoah National Park. In the 1800s and 1900s, some enslaved men and women escaped to the mountains for safety and made their homes there, sometimes living among Native Americans. Today, within the park on Doubletop Mountain is Rapidan Camp, the retreat of Herbert Hoover, who served as the nation's 31st president from 1929 to 1933. Two springs join within the camp to form the Rapidan River. (Terry Miller.)

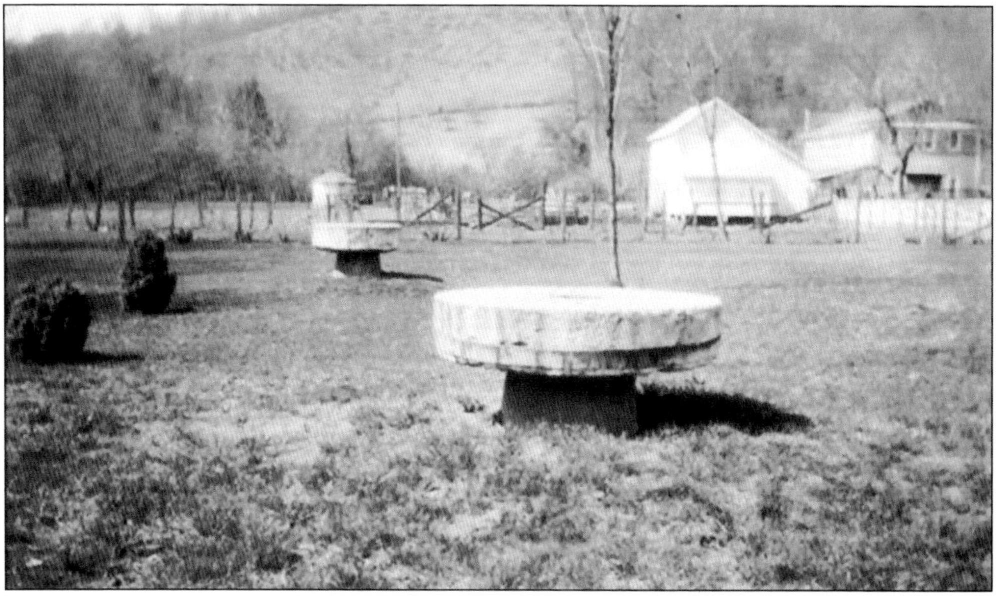

In the 1930s, photographer Evelyn W. Tunison was tasked with recording life in rural counties throughout Virginia for the Works Progress Administration. She photographed a pair of millstones in Madison that were used to grind wheat and other grains. (Library of Virginia.)

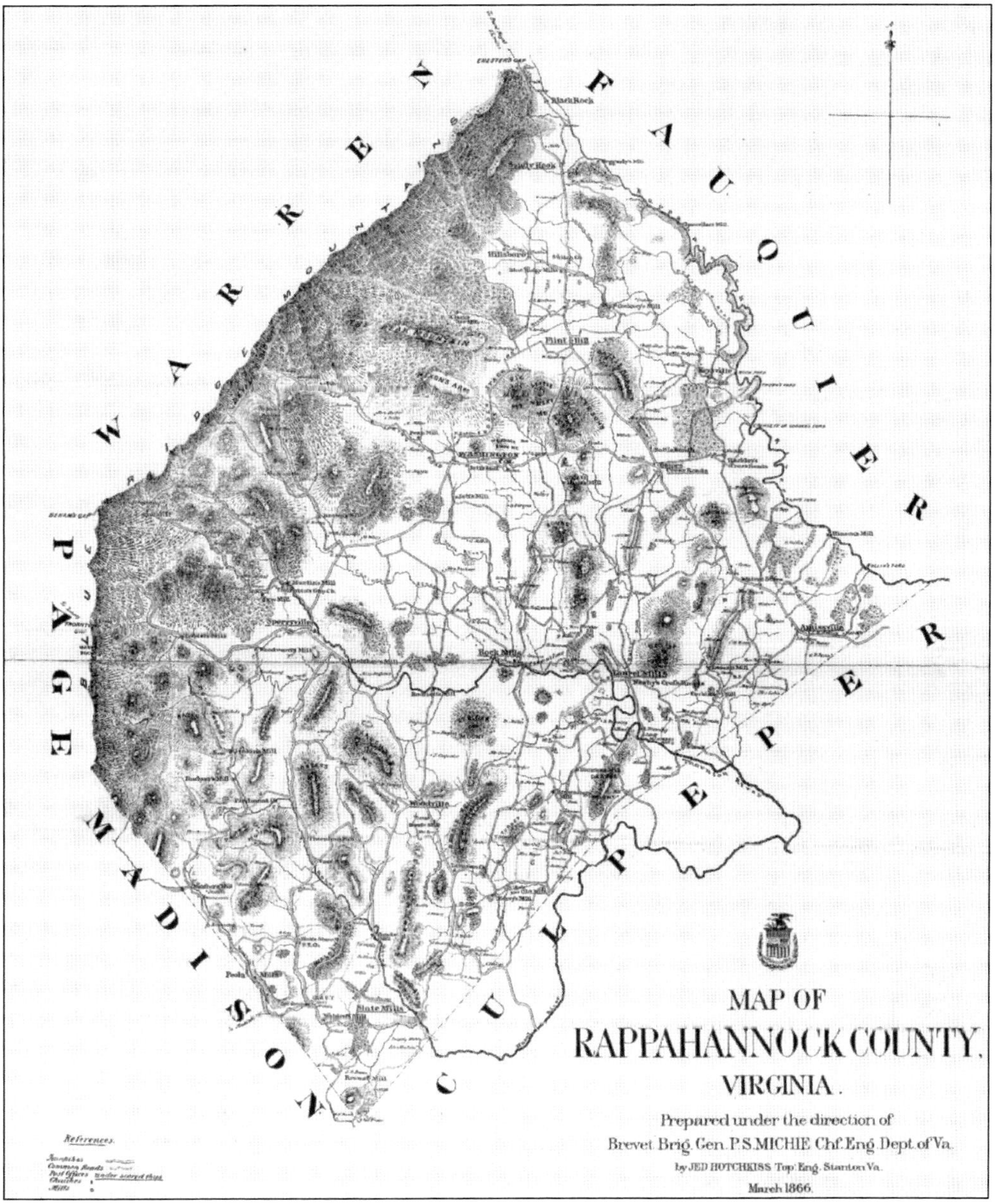

The last county to be established in this group of four is Rappahannock, although the town of Washington was surveyed and platted by George Washington in 1749. Organized in 1833 and comprised of 267 square miles, the county still holds much of its rural character in the midst of progress. In 1860, there were some 3,520 slaves and 312 free blacks in Rappahannock. A number of well-preserved slave quarters are extant and stand as monuments to those who were important to local history. Among the 2016 population of 7,400, fewer than five percent of residents are African American. (Library of Virginia.)

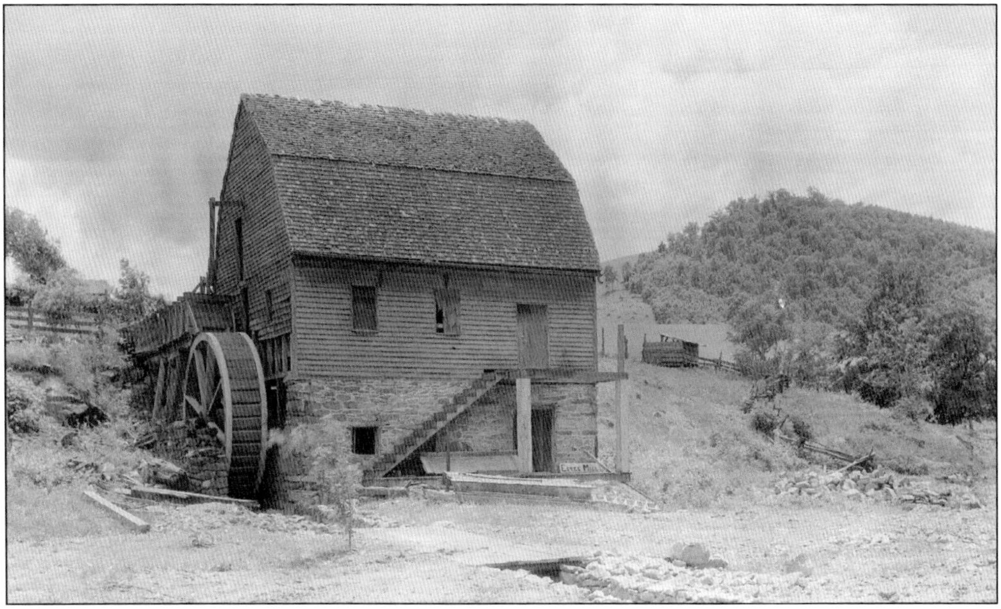

Mills are a feature of the Rappahannock landscape. Fed by the nearby Thornton River on US 211 and State Road 667 is the Estes Mill (formerly called Woodard's Mill), built around 1836. In 1900, the Estes family purchased it and renamed it in their honor. Most of the original parts of the mill have been donated to the Smithsonian Institution. (Library of Congress.)

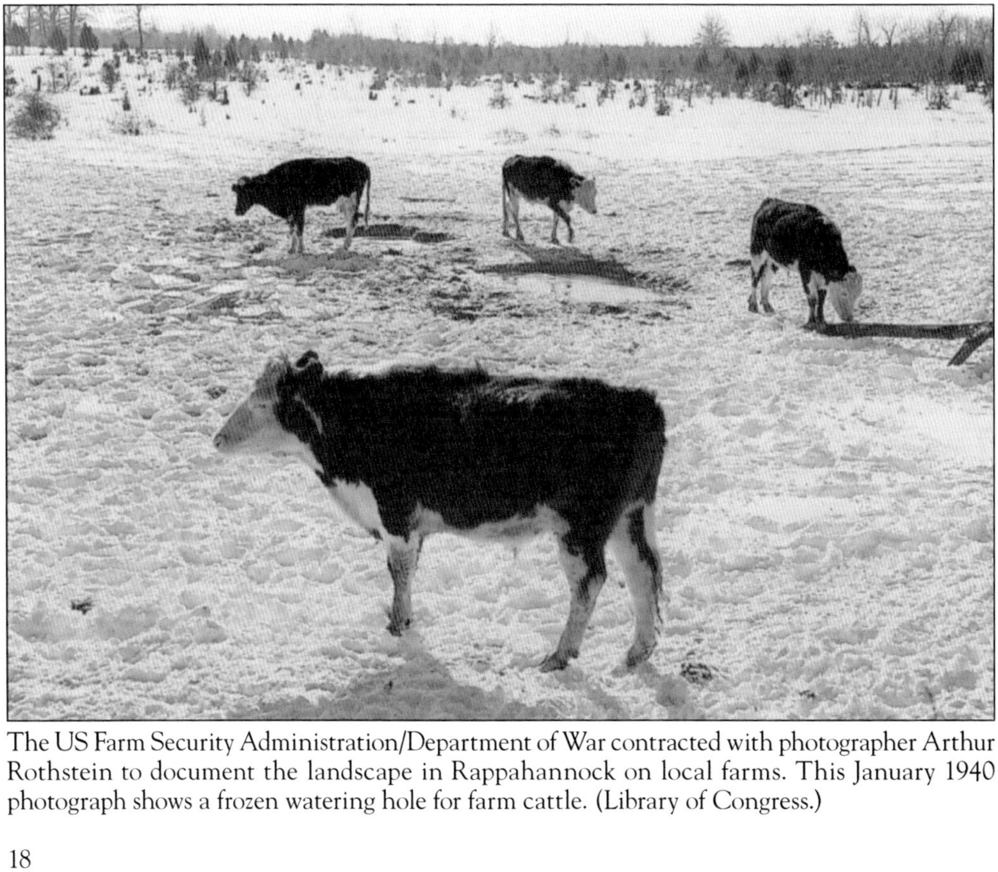

The US Farm Security Administration/Department of War contracted with photographer Arthur Rothstein to document the landscape in Rappahannock on local farms. This January 1940 photograph shows a frozen watering hole for farm cattle. (Library of Congress.)

Two

When They Fought

Leaders can always find a cause to fight for militarily. The Revolutionary War was fought for independence from Britain. In the War of 1812, the United States wanted to stop the British navy from ramming its ships, taking American sailors as captives, and forcing them to work for the British navy. The Civil War was fought over slavery. The Indian Wars were fought to conquer the land for western expansion. World War I was over dissolving European alliances, imperialism, and an increase in militarism and nationalism—resulting in the assassination of Archduke Franz Ferdinand of Austria-Hungary. World War II was the result of unresolved conflicts from the peace talks of the First World War. The Korean War was the result of the invasion of North Korea into South Korea. Regardless of the reason, enlisted men and women, and the families they left behind, sacrificed their lives for the freedom of all American citizens.

This chapter represents each of the wars mentioned above, thus, it is the longest chapter in the book. Often, military service for African Americans meant a way to prove their worth as full citizens of the United States. The first two reasons given by the great abolitionist Frederick Douglass in his 1863 essay "Why Should a Colored Man Enlist?" state:

> "1. You are a man, although a colored man . . . He who looks upon a conflict between right and wrong and does not help the right against the wrong, despises and insults his own nature, and invites the contempt of mankind.
>
> 2. You are however, not only a man, but an American citizen, so declared by the highest legal adviser of the Government, and you have hitherto expressed in various ways not only your willingness but your earnest desire to fulfill any and every obligation which the relation of citizenship imposes."

On July 26, 1948, Pres. Harry Truman signed Executive Order No. 9981 that abolished racial discrimination in the US Armed Forces, which eventually led to desegregation. The chapter ends with newly graduated Carver Regional High School students who served in the Korean War and experienced some of the benefits of a desegregated armed services and the promises of a better life.

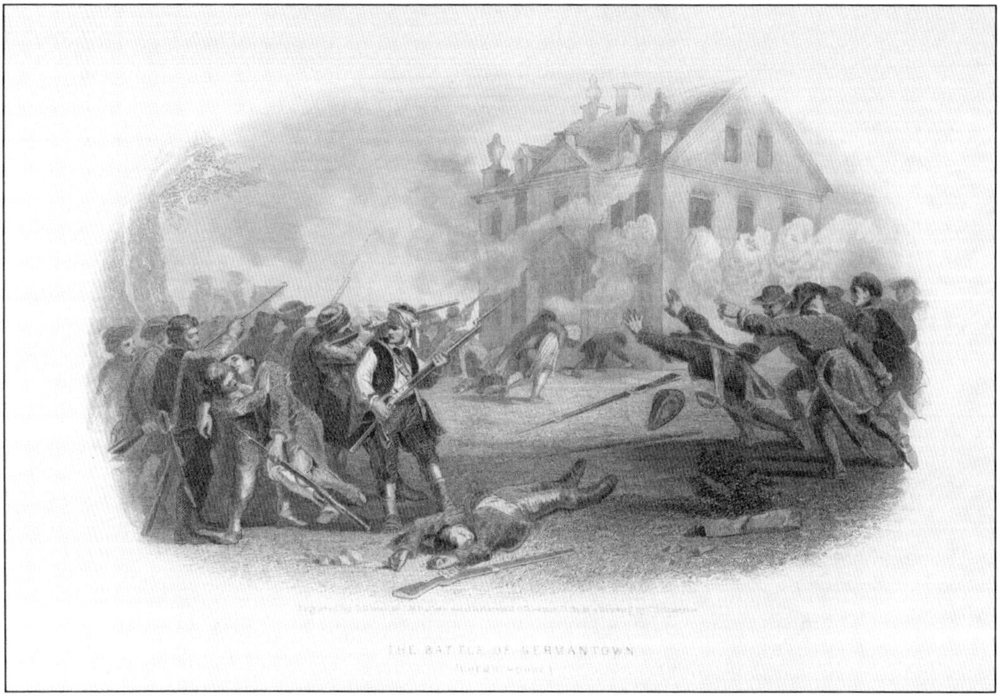

Drafted from Culpeper as servant soldier to Capt. Thomas Welles at the start of the Revolutionary War, William Clarke remained for two terms, during which he was at the Battle of Germantown (shown) on October 4, 1777, and later at the Battle of Monmouth, New Jersey, in June 28, 1778. (Library of Congress.)

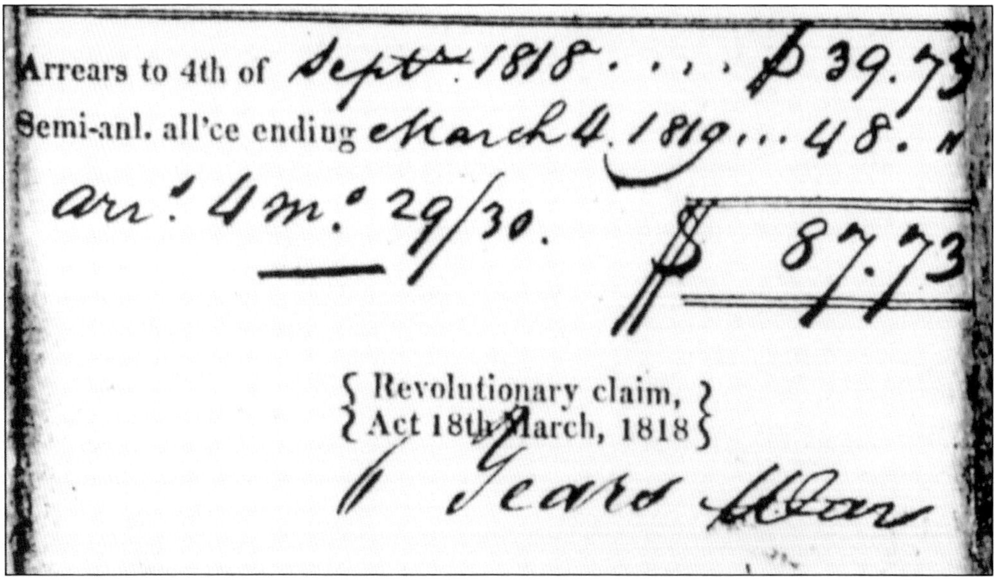

Arrears to 4th of Sept. 1818 . . . $ 39.73
Semi-anl. all'ce ending March 4. 1819 . . . 48.
arr. 4 mo. 29/30. $ 87.73

Revolutionary claim,
Act 18th March, 1818

William Clarke's second three-year term was to Col. John Jameson (who later served as clerk of Culpeper), who did not submit Clarke's discharge papers, and thus, Clarke had difficulty receiving a pension. His application was accepted in 1818. After his death on December 8, 1827, his widow, Hannah Peters Clarke, benefited until her death. (National Archives and Records Administration.)

African American descendants of the Culpeper Minute Men live, thrive, and are valued contributors throughout the region. Two of them, Charles Jameson and Michael Dennis, have been inducted into the local chapter of the Sons of the American Revolution. (Terry Miller.)

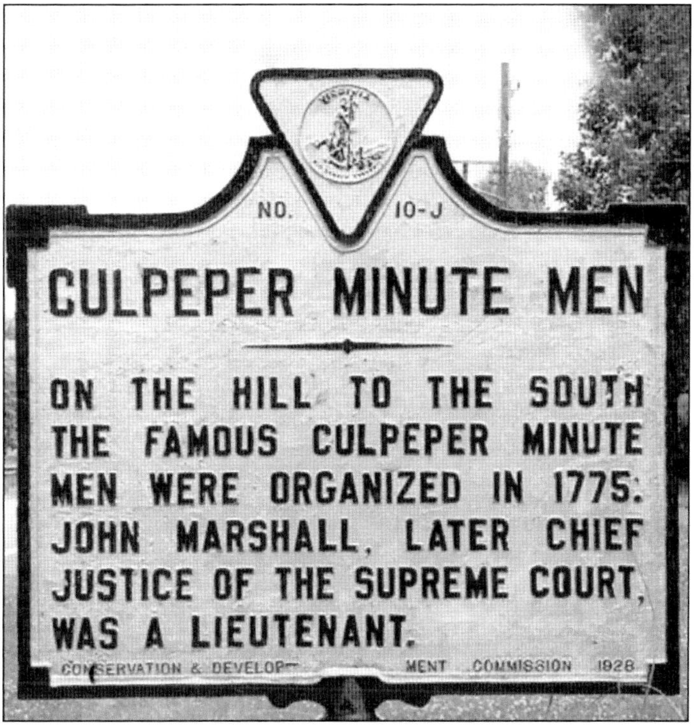

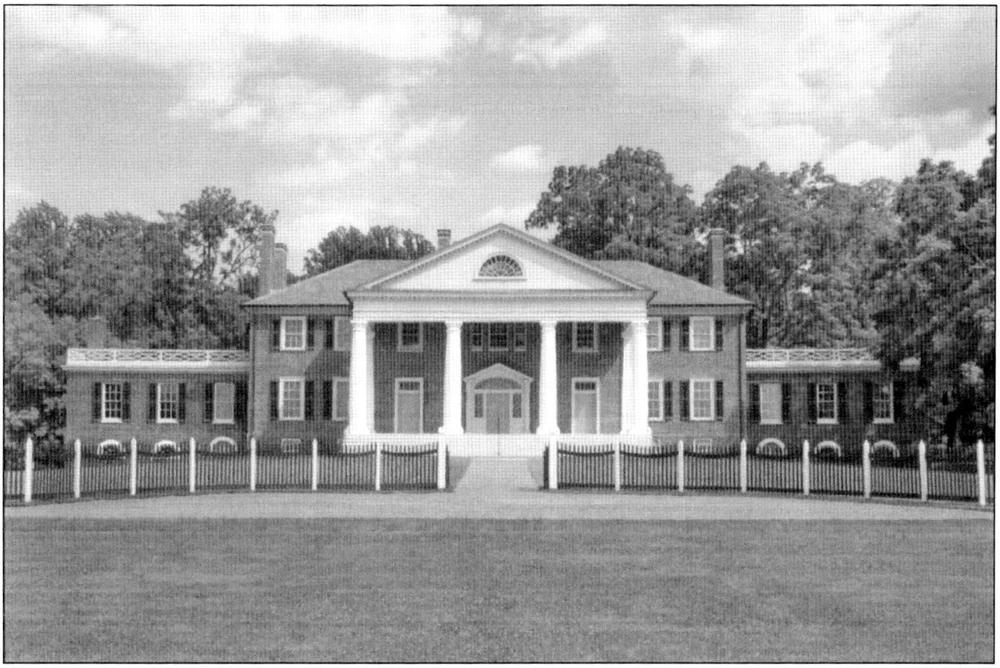

The ancestral home of Pres. James Madison, Montpelier, is located in Orange County and was patented in 1623. The president and his wife, Dolley, occupied the home through her death in 1844. Rough estimates based on known populations of slaves at the estate indicate that between 1732 and 1865, more than 200 enslaved men, women, and children died and were possibly buried on the property. (Montpelier Foundation.)

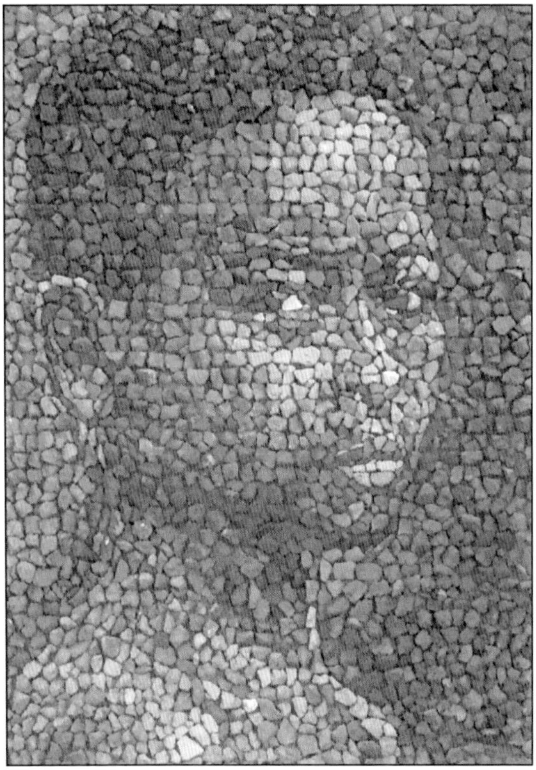

This detail of a poster designed by Barbara Shenefield is the face of a permanent exhibit at Montpelier. Titled The Mere Distinction of Colour, the exhibit focuses on slavery and its far-reaching impact. It tells the story of life on the Montpelier plantation from the perspective of its enslaved men, women, and children. The title of the exhibit comes from something written by James Madison, who served as president of the United States from 1809 to 1917: "We have seen the mere distinction of colour made in the most enlightened period of time a ground of the most oppressive dominion ever exercised by man over man." (Montpelier Foundation.)

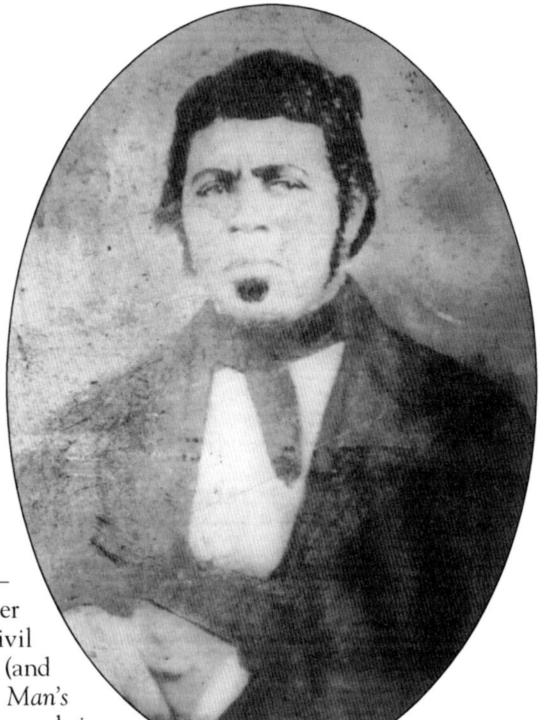

Paul Jennings (1799–1874) was an enslaved man who accompanied James and Dolley Madison to the White House. Married to Fannie Gordon Jennings (who remained at Montpelier with their children), he was the body servant to President Madison and thus an eyewitness to the War of 1812 and all historical events through the early 1840s, when his freedom was purchased by the revered Daniel Webster. Jennings' sons—Benjamin Franklin, John, and William—later served on the side of the Union in the Civil War. In 1865, he published his autobiography (and the first White House memoir), *A Colored Man's Reminiscences of James Madison*; this photograph is featured on the cover of the book. (Terry Miller.)

Sometimes individuals fought against the government for a cause they considered just. Dangerfield Newby was born around 1815 in Culpeper to a Scottish man named Henry Newby and his African American partner, Elsey. They moved to the free state of Ohio. In the meantime, Dangerfield married an enslaved woman in Prince William County and grew increasingly angry when he could not earn enough money to buy her freedom. He sought out the abolitionist John Brown, joined his crew of 18, and attacked the armory in Harper's Ferry, West Virginia, in 1859, where he was the first to lose his life. (Library of Congress.)

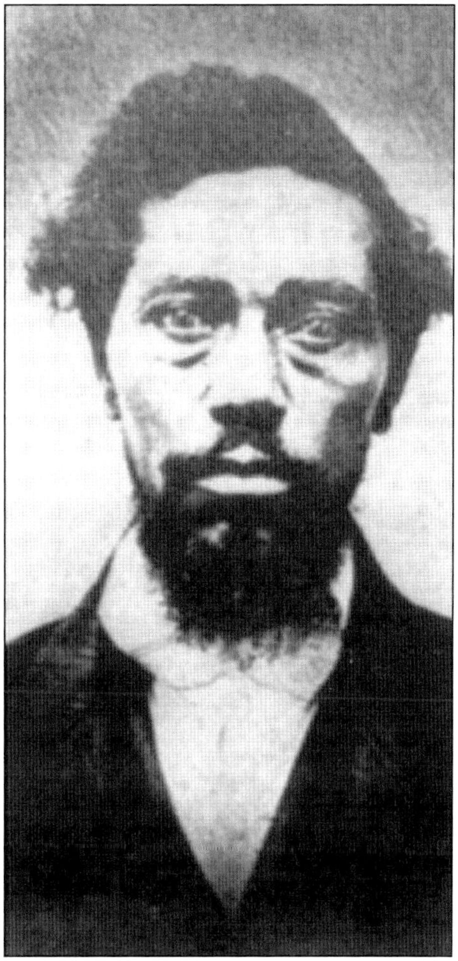

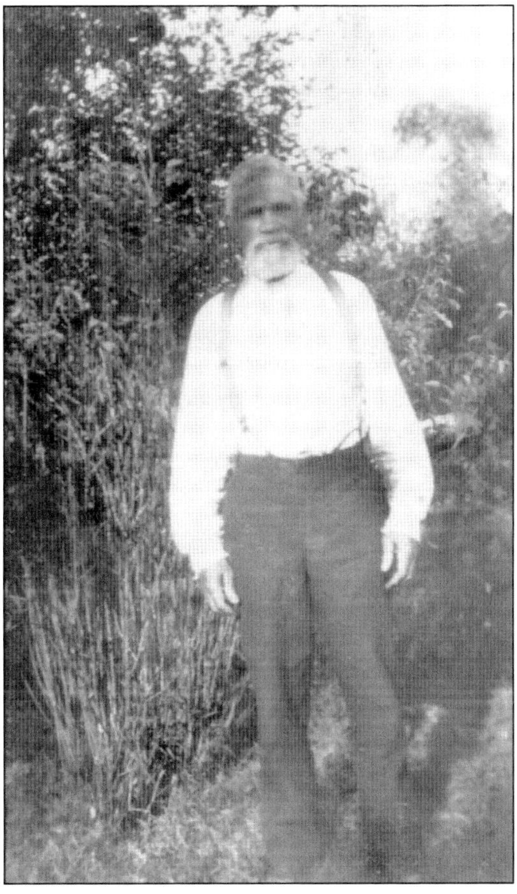

Madison native George Washington Davis was around 15 years old when he was drafted into the Civil War for the Confederacy as the body servant for the son of his owner, Robert Davis Twyman, in 1863. His mother, Harriett, was a slave of Twyman. When he was discharged in 1864, he married Cornelia, daughter of William Blankenbaker and Emma Arrington. They lived in the Uno neighborhood their entire adult lives and raised 13 known children. He applied for a pension at age 86, and he lived another 19 years, passing away in 1951 at the age of 105. He is buried in the Main Uno Baptist Church cemetery. (Kimberly Milai.)

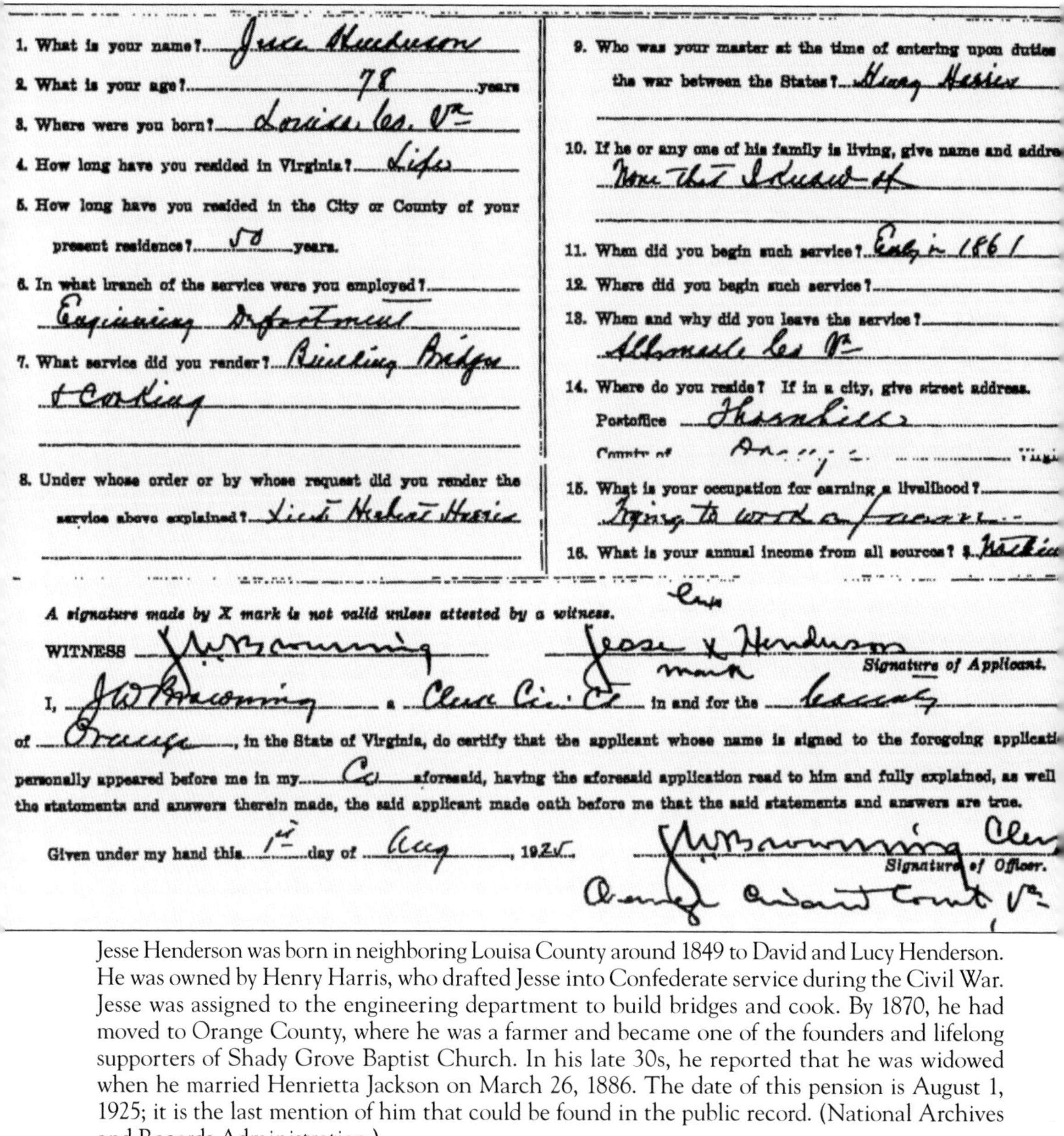

1. What is your name? Jesse Henderson
2. What is your age? 78 years
3. Where were you born? Louisa Co. Va
4. How long have you resided in Virginia? Life
5. How long have you resided in the City or County of your present residence? 50 years.
6. In what branch of the service were you employed? Engineering Department
7. What service did you render? Building Bridges & Cooking
8. Under whose order or by whose request did you render the service above explained? Lieut Herbert Harris
9. Who was your master at the time of entering upon duties the war between the States? Henry Harris
10. If he or any one of his family is living, give name and addre[ss] None that I know of
11. When did you begin such service? Early in 1861
12. Where did you begin such service?
13. When and why did you leave the service? Albemarle Co Va
14. Where do you reside? If in a city, give street address. Postoffice Thornhill County of Orange Virgi[nia]
15. What is your occupation for earning a livelihood? Trying to work on farm
16. What is your annual income from all sources? $ Nothing

A signature made by X mark is not valid unless attested by a witness.

WITNESS J W Browning — Jesse X Henderson his mark — *Signature of Applicant.*

I, J W Browning a Clerk Cir. Ct in and for the County of Orange, in the State of Virginia, do certify that the applicant whose name is signed to the foregoing applicati[on] personally appeared before me in my Co aforesaid, having the aforesaid application read to him and fully explained, as well the statements and answers therein made, the said applicant made oath before me that the said statements and answers are true.

Given under my hand this 1st day of Aug, 1925. J W Browning Cler[k] *Signature of Officer.* Orange Circuit Court, Va

Jesse Henderson was born in neighboring Louisa County around 1849 to David and Lucy Henderson. He was owned by Henry Harris, who drafted Jesse into Confederate service during the Civil War. Jesse was assigned to the engineering department to build bridges and cook. By 1870, he had moved to Orange County, where he was a farmer and became one of the founders and lifelong supporters of Shady Grove Baptist Church. In his late 30s, he reported that he was widowed when he married Henrietta Jackson on March 26, 1886. The date of this pension is August 1, 1925; it is the last mention of him that could be found in the public record. (National Archives and Records Administration.)

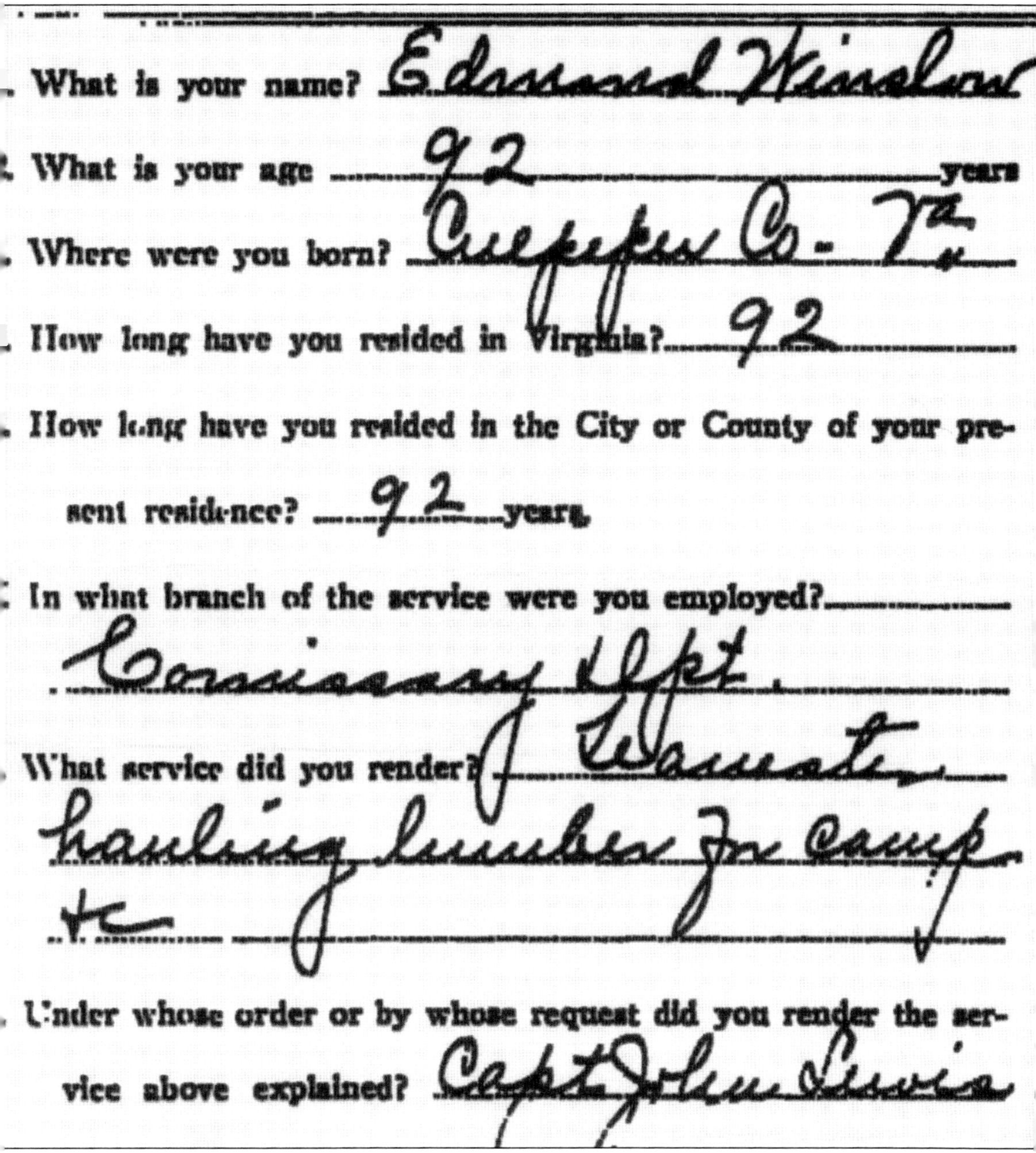
. What is your name? Edmond Winslow

. What is your age 92 years

. Where were you born? Culpeper Co. Va.

. How long have you resided in Virginia? 92

. How long have you resided in the City or County of your present residence? 92 years

. In what branch of the service were you employed? Commissary Dept.

. What service did you render? Wagoner hauling lumber for camp &c

. Under whose order or by whose request did you render the service above explained? Capt. John Lewis

While a slave of Confederate captain James Lewis of Culpeper, Edmond Winslow was drafted into the Civil War as a teamster in the commissary department. Available evidence shows that he was born on May 10, 1838, to Solomon Winslow and Clara Brown. He married Mary Rice, and the two raised 12 children until Mary's death. In his later years, he remarried to Elizabeth West. When he was 92, he applied for a pension for his Confederate service, although it is not known whether he received it. He died on March 2, 1934, at his home in Catalpa. (National Archives and Records Administration.)

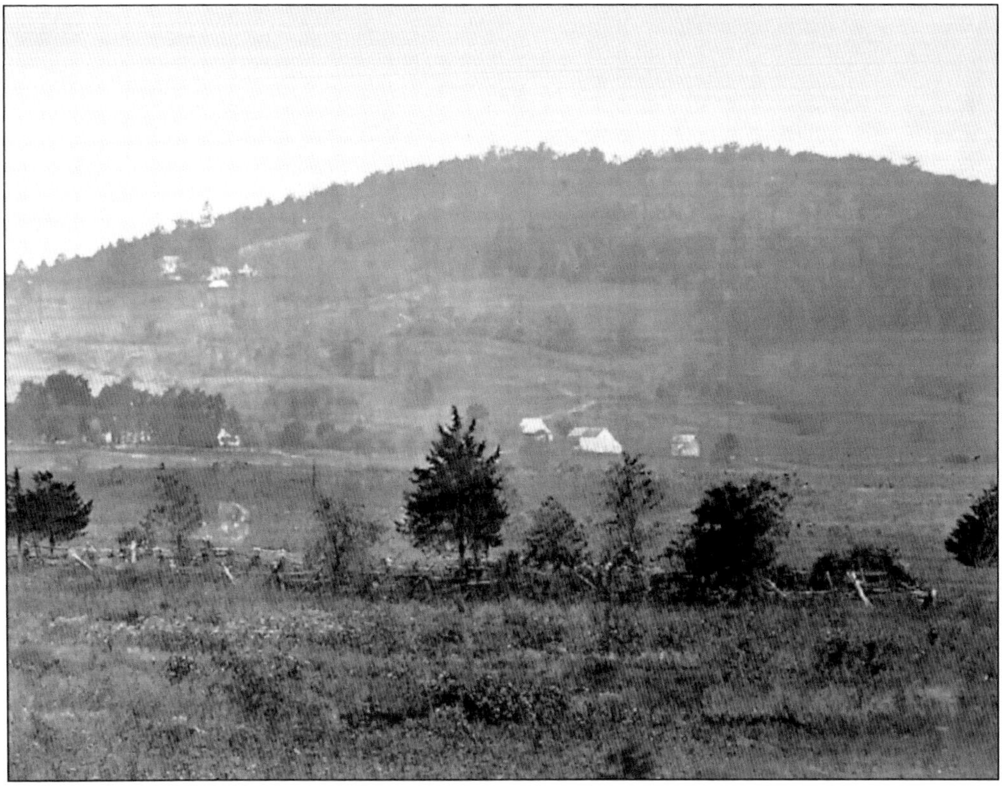

Six weeks after the Battle of Cedar Mountain (pictured above and below) was fought in Culpeper—during which more than 3,000 men were wounded or killed on August 9, 1862—Pres. Abraham Lincoln issued the Emancipation Proclamation, which was to take effect on January 1, 1863. On May 22, 1863, the War Department issued General Order No. 143, which created the US Colored Troops. Some eligible men had already fled to other areas such as Alexandria, the District of Columbia, Philadelphia, and Ohio, and they were readily recruited. Two of these recruits were Culpeper's Levi King and Orange County–born Qualls Tibbs, featured on the following page. (Both, Library of Congress.)

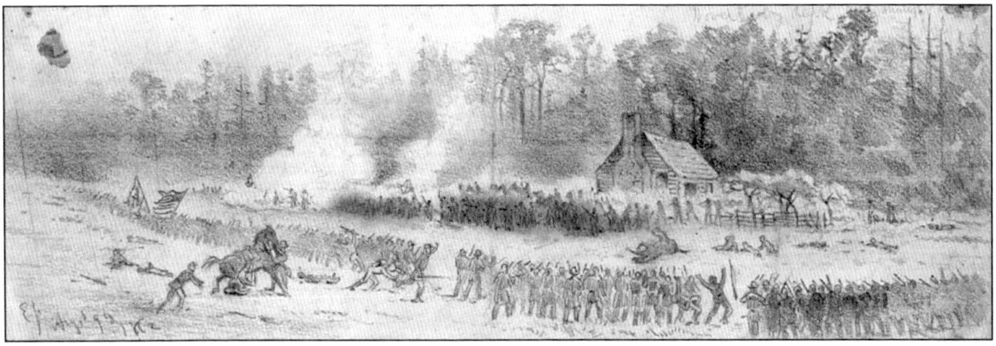

A blacksmith and farm laborer, Levi King was born in Culpeper in 1838. He was bought by Charles King (hence Levi's surname) and taken to Tennessee. He mustered into Company F, 1st Regiment, US Colored Heavy Artillery as a duty sergeant in Knoxville on April 17, 1864, and was quickly promoted. He fell victim to smallpox; was unable to carry out his regimental duties; was demoted; mustered out on March 31, 1866; and returned to the same farm on which he was enslaved. He sought help, applying for a pension on May 7, 1880, and the recorder inaccurately filled out the form. When investigating the claim, his former owner stated in an affidavit that he thought he was getting a healthy man rather than an asthmatic one. He produced a bill of sale stating he bought Levi in 1863 (Levi was probably a free man) for $3,250, and Levi's pension was denied. Levi died five years later. His wife and children received a widow's pension. (State Library and Archives of Florida.)

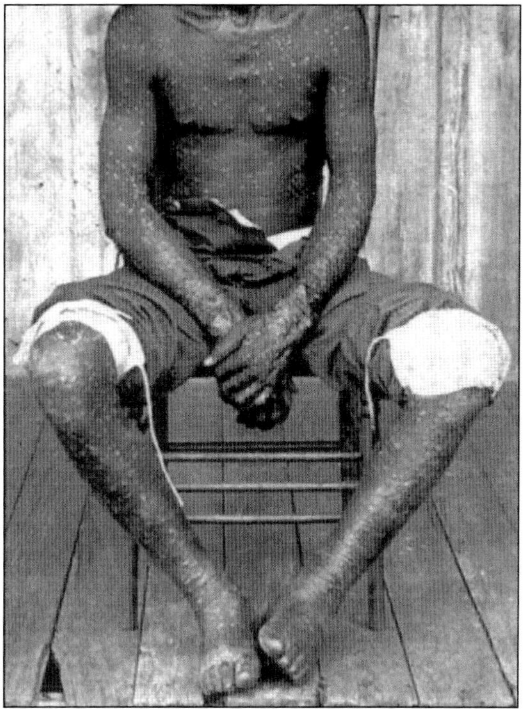

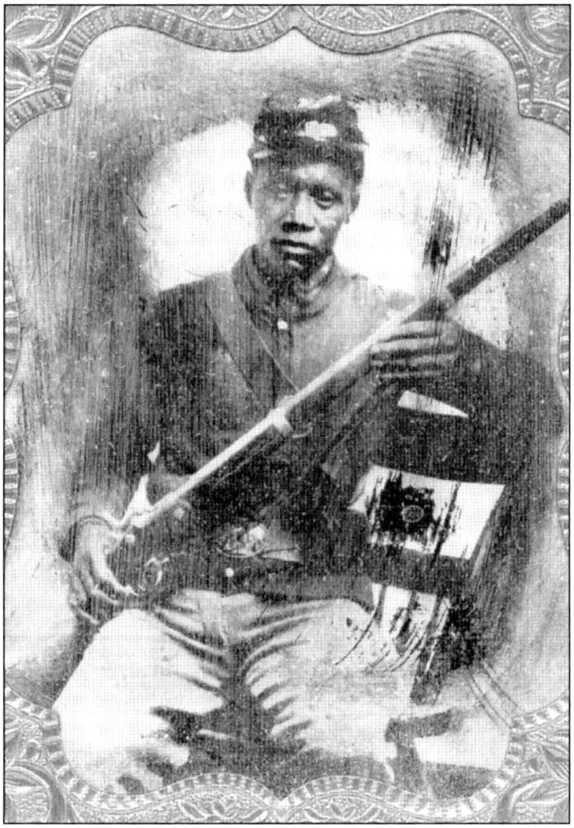

Qualls Tibbs was born March 3, 1836, in Orange County to freed slave Matilda Tibbs. She relocated her family to Ohio. In 1858, Qualls married Josephine Holmes, another Orange County native who had relocated to Ohio. He was 27 years old when he enlisted in Company E, 27th Regiment, US Colored Infantry in 1863. He was later wounded and received a medical discharge. He died at his home on October 25, 1922, and is buried in Elmwood Cemetery in Fairfield County, Ohio, next to his wife, who died in late 1900. (Tibbs family.)

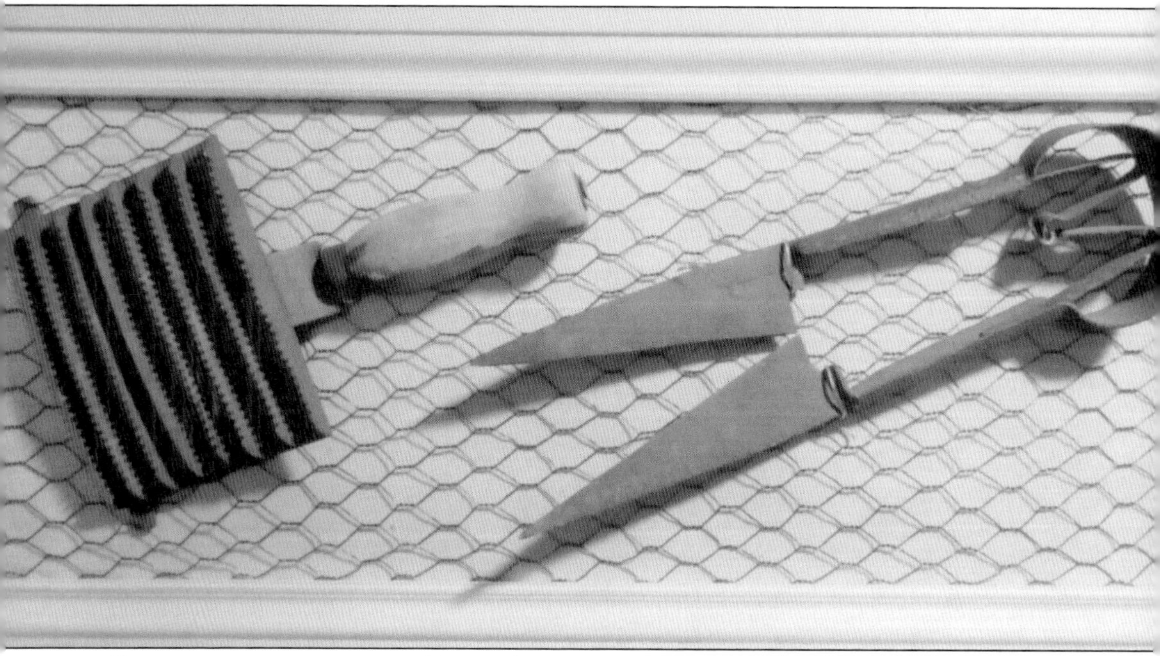

Shown are two instruments used by cavalrymen: a curry brush and horse hair clippers. Cavalrymen were viewed as elite soldiers because of the difficulty of learning how to fight while riding a horse. They also had skills such as self-reliance, alertness, and individuality, which rendered them effective as scouts. It cost three times more to equip a cavalryman than an infantryman. In addition to weaponry expertise, each soldier was required to take care of his horse (mount) and keep it in perfect shape, with responsibilities that included grooming, nutrition, and veterinary care. To date, 18 men have been identified from the counties of Culpeper, Madison, Orange, and Rappahannock as serving in four different regiments of both the US Colored Cavalry and the Massachusetts Colored Cavalry, with the latter having 11 soldiers. Two of these cavalrymen were Tom Williamson and James Whipp, featured on the following page. (Terry Miller.)

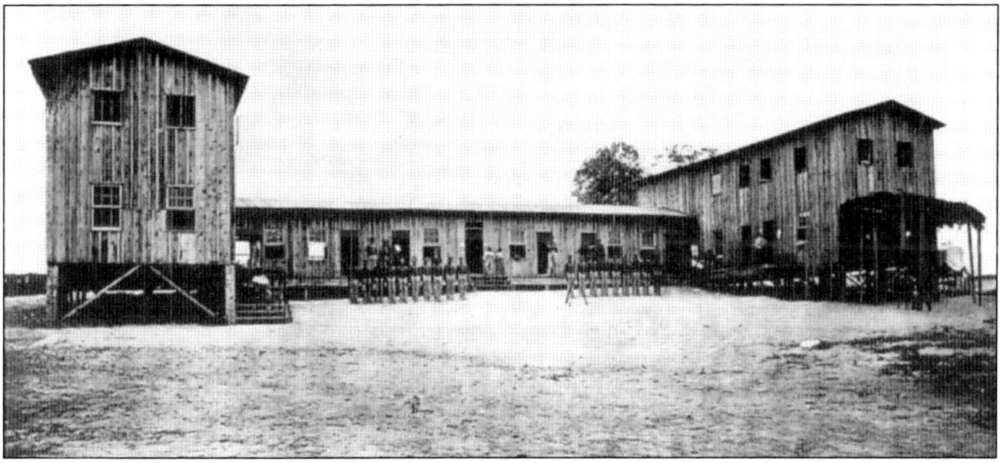

Madison County native Tom Williamson was a free man and only 22 years old when he enlisted in Lexington, Kentucky. He mustered into the 6th US Colored Cavalry at Camp Nelson in Kentucky (shown). His regiment first operated in southwestern Virginia from December 10 through December 29, 1864, capturing and destroying lead mines. His regiment then worked throughout Kentucky, Tennessee, and Arkansas until April 15, 1866, when he mustered out. He survived the war, but there is no evidence that he lived to 1870. (Library of Congress.)

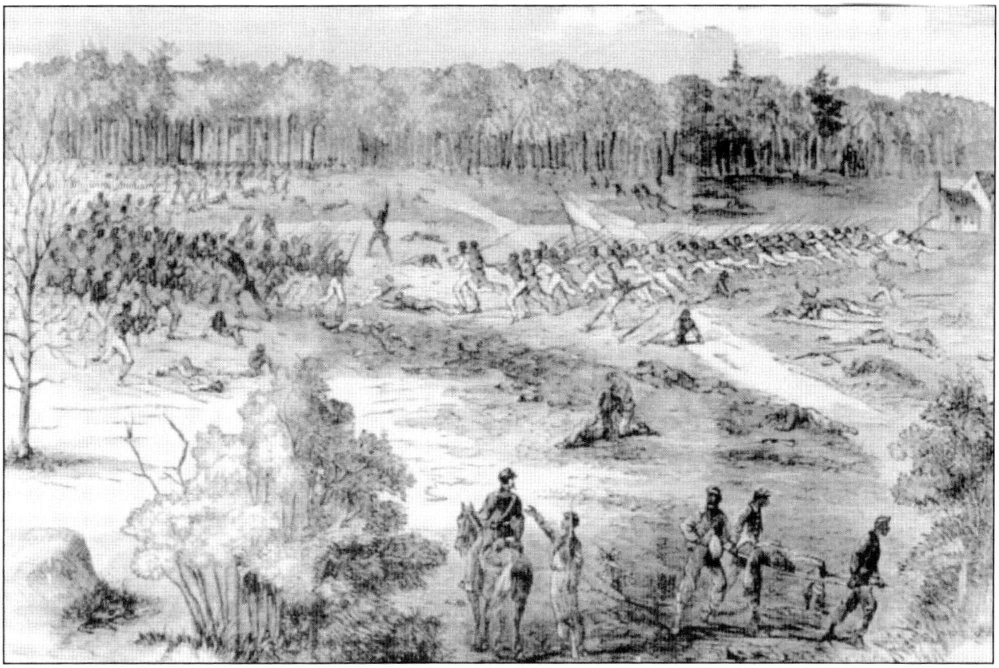

Recruited by Frederick Douglas Jr., 40-year-old farmer James Whipp mustered into the 5th Massachusetts Cavalry on April 12, 1864. He was the son of Harrison and Mary Lawler Whipp. His regiment fought at Baylor's Farm and later in the siege of Petersburg. They were also the first cavalry unit to enter Richmond after its fall. While assigned to Texas to help the Freedman's Bureau to resettle citizens, he took ill; mustered out on October 31, 1865; and returned to Jackson township. On March 18, 1871, he married Virginia Jordan, and by 1889, he had applied for and received a pension. He died in Dinwiddie County on February 17, 1896. (*Frank Leslie's Illustrated Newspaper* Archive.)

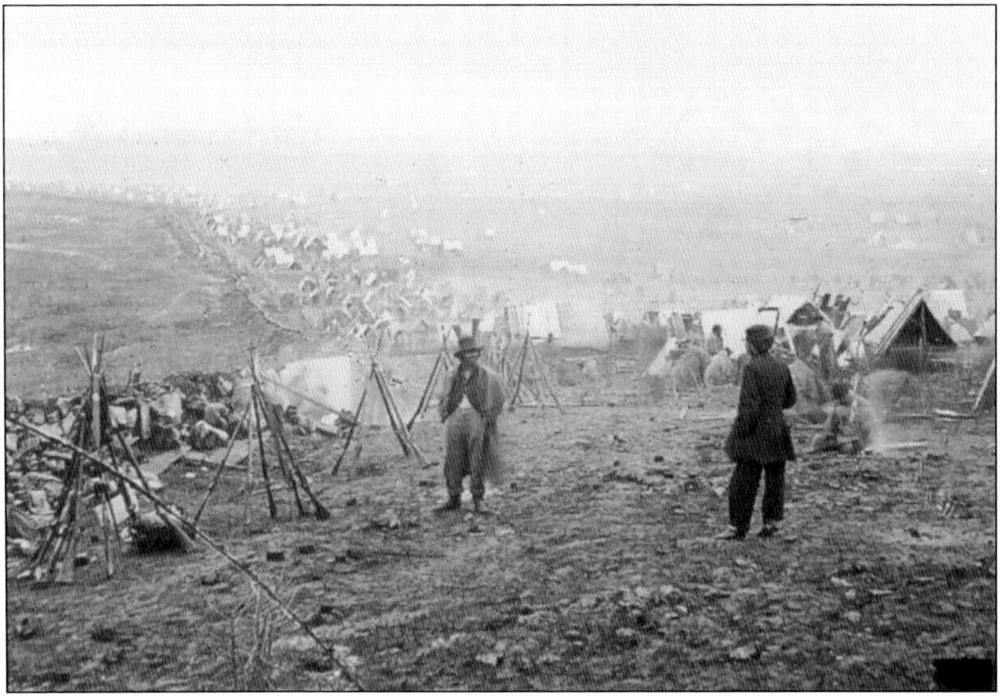

Frank Lipscomb was born around 1846 in the Salem area of Culpeper, sold south as a slave, and eventually ended up in Alabama. At 18, he enlisted into Company D, 12th Colored Infantry on February 18, 1864. He was assigned as a bugler and later officially mustered in at Kingston Springs, Tennessee, where his regiment fought Confederate general John B. Hood's attack on Johnsonville (pictured above) and pursued the general to the Tennessee River. Lipscomb died on June 22, 1880, from complications of wounds he received in the war. After several attempts over many years, his widow, Adaline Fowlkes Lipscomb, was awarded a pension (pictured below) in January 1897. (Above, Library of Congress; below, National Archives and Records Administration.)

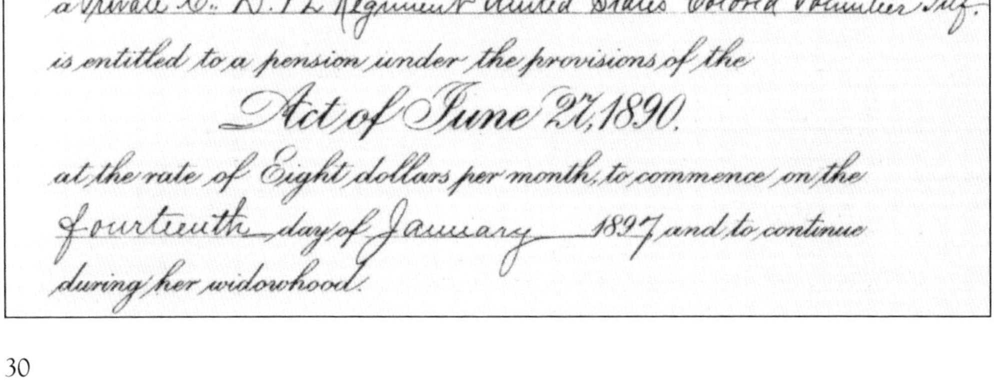

It is hereby certified That in conformity with the laws of the United States Adaline Lipscomb Widow of Frank Lipscomb who was a Private Co. D. 12 Regiment United States Colored Volunteer Inf. is entitled to a pension under the provisions of the

Act of June 27, 1890.

at the rate of Eight dollars per month, to commence on the fourteenth day of January 1897 and to continue during her widowhood.

Some men enlisted in poor health, requiring treatment by hot water canteen and/or a bloodletting tool (pictured). Two examples are Madison-born William H. Fields and Benjamin James, both 25 years old, Company G, 2nd Infantry Regiment, stationed at Fort Zachary Taylor in Key West. The doctor found that both had severe rheumatism, and Fields had an enlarged heart. They were discharged and deemed ineligible for pensions. (Terry Miller.)

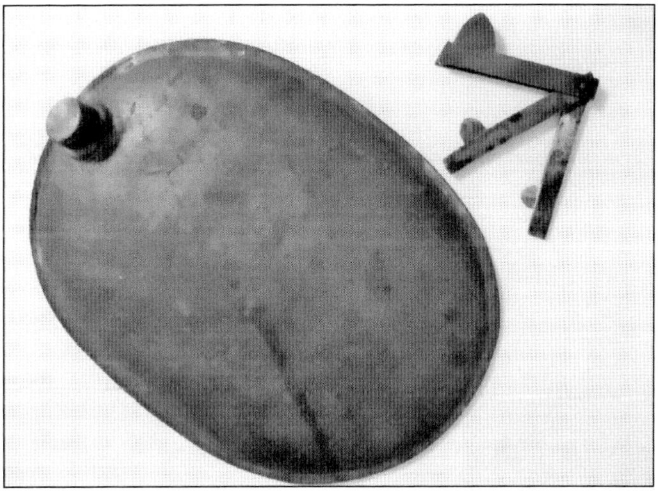

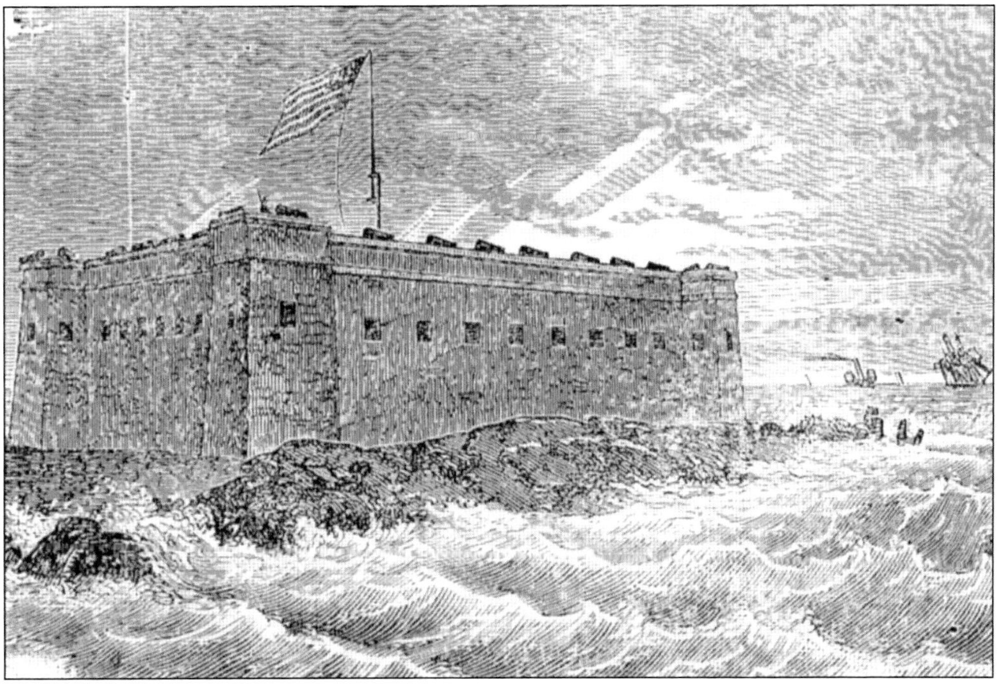

During the Civil War, Fort Zachary Taylor (constructed in 1845) was the headquarters for the US Navy East Gulf Coast Blockading Squadron. Twelve men from the four-county region featured in this book were enlisted into the US Colored Infantry, 2nd Regiment, and assigned to this fort. Of those, five were from Madison, four from Culpeper, two from Rappahannock, and one from Orange. (Library of Congress.)

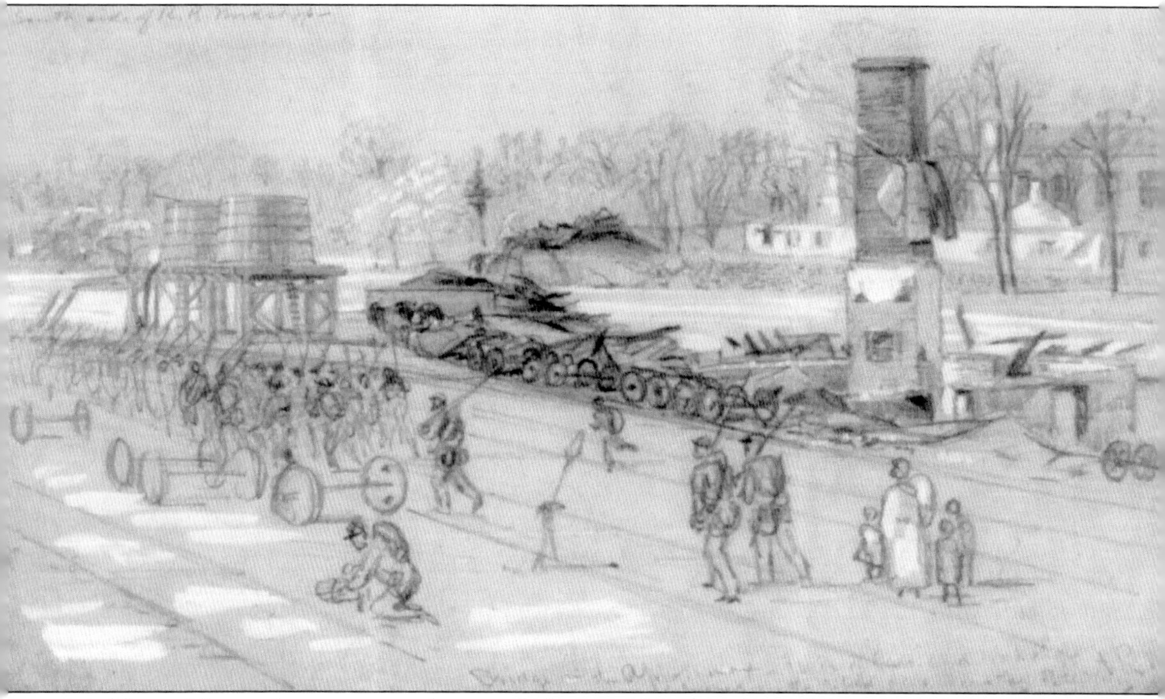

Three African American men born in Culpeper enlisted in the 29th USC Infantry: 23-year-old Samuel Brogden was free when he enlisted as a substitute on August 3, 1864, at Ellicott's Mill, Maryland; 22-year-old John Campbell, who enlisted August 3, 1864, at Camp Casey, Virginia; and 49-year-old Alexander Hamilton Howard, the oldest from Culpeper to enlist—he served as a nurse. The unit saw action in the sieges of Petersburg and Richmond, where it was involved in the Battle of the Crater, the Battle of Globe Tavern, the Battle of Poplar Grove Church, and the Battle of Boydton Plank Road. Afterward, the regiment served on the Bermuda Hundred front and at Richmond until participating in the Appomattox Campaign. The regiment served in the Rio Grande Valley until November 1865, when the soldiers mustered out. (Library of Congress.)

James Grayson reported on his pension application, "I was born [c. 1844] and partly raised at Washington, Rappahannock Co., Va, the property of Edward T. Jones. I was sold by my said first owner at Richmond, Va., prior to the Civil War when I was only a boy and was bought by John Atkinson who took me to Kentucky and placed me on his farm in Union County, Kentucky." Grayson enlisted from Paducah, Kentucky, into the 8th Regiment, US Colored Heavy Artillery on May 28, 1864, as a snare drummer. He mustered out on February 10, 1866, with the rank and medal (at right) of principal musician at Victoria, Texas. His health failed quickly, and he was awarded a pension. He died on April 1, 1917, in the National Home for Disabled Volunteer Soldiers (below) in Milwaukee, Wisconsin. One of his brothers, Joseph, was still living in Rappahannock. (Both, National Archives and Records Administration.)

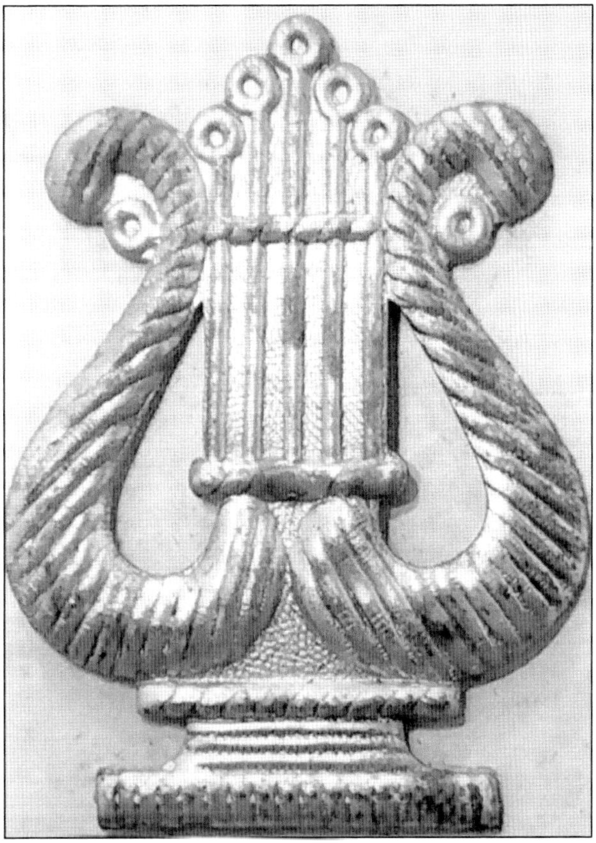

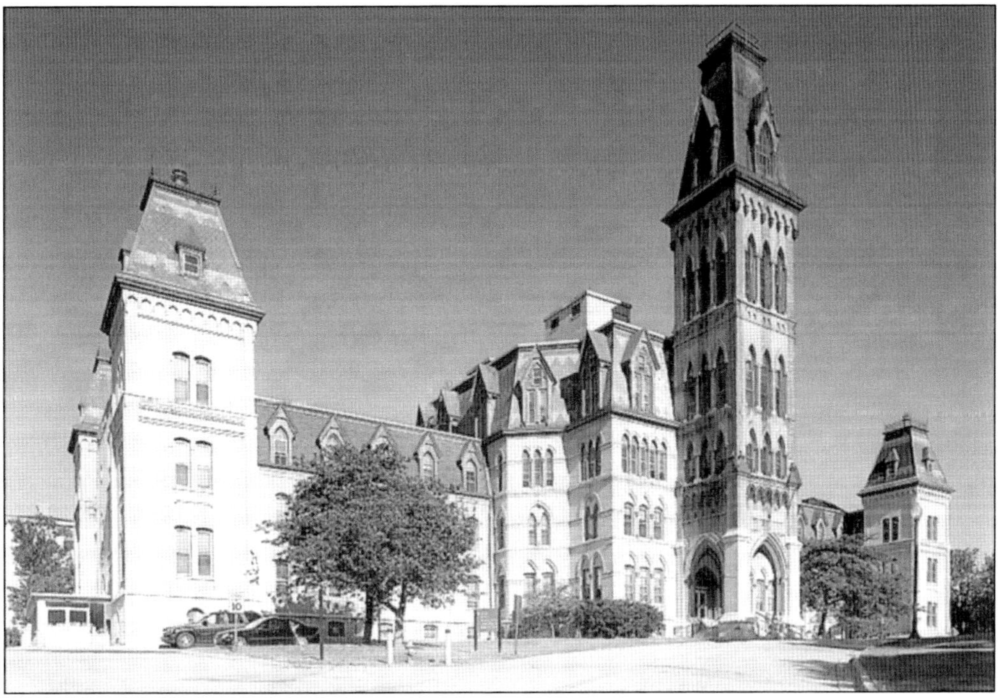

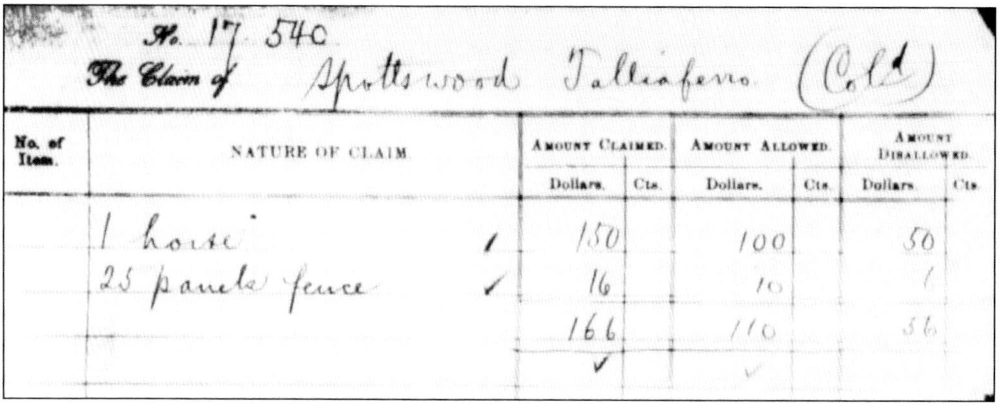

No. 17 540
The Claim of Spottswood Talliaferro (Col'd)

No. of Item.	NATURE OF CLAIM	Amount Claimed. Dollars.	Cts.	Amount Allowed. Dollars.	Cts.	Amount Disallowed. Dollars	Cts.
	1 horse ✓	150		100		50	
	25 panels fence ✓	16		10		6	
		166 ✓		110		56	

At the end of the Civil War, the Freedmen's Bureau settled disputes brought by both veterans and citizens. One example is Culpeper citizen Spottswood Talliaferro. According to the claim, Talliaferro's owner, Samuel Bradford, died near the start of the war without leaving provisions for his slaves. Talliaferro purchased a lot and house from relatives of his former owner. He fenced his land and also owned a horse. After a lengthy investigation, it was found that Union general John Pope's soldiers took his horse and fencing, and Talliaferro was reimbursed $110 on December 13, 1878. (National Archives and Records Administration.)

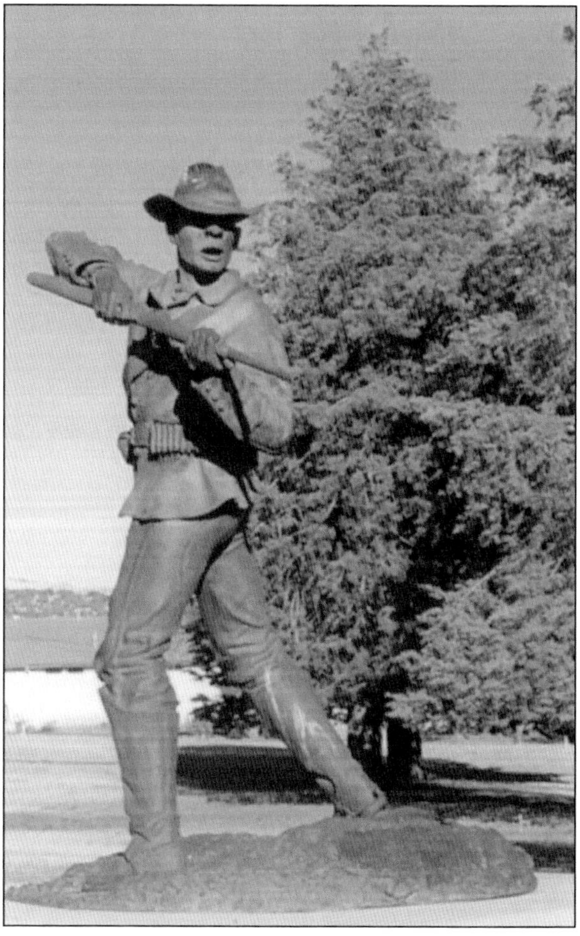

This statue of buffalo soldier Sgt. Clinton Greaves stands at Fort Bayard, New Mexico. He was born August 12, 1855, in Madison (his parents' names are not known). He first mustered into the 9th US Cavalry on November 21, 1872, stationed in New Mexico. In an attack by Apache Indians, he engaged valiantly in hand-to-hand combat, which allowed his fellow soldiers to break free. For his second enlistment, in 1877, he was stationed in Santa Fe. For his bravery during his first enlistment, he was awarded the Congressional Medal of Honor on June 26, 1879. He made the Army his career, retiring after 20 years. He made his home in Ohio, where he married Bertha Williams on November 26, 1890. He died on August 18, 1906, of heart disease and is buried in Green Lawn Cemetery in Columbus, Ohio. (R. Craig Bell.)

Culpeper native and World War I veteran John Simon Ford was the son of William Henry and Sarah Jackson Ford. He earned the rank of sergeant and was assigned to the 37th Construction Company for the Air Service, US Army. After his discharge, he married Ruth Regina Robinson. He worked as a carpenter in his youth and enjoyed building items both large and small, as evidenced by the model airplane in this photograph. To support his family of three sons, he took his carpentry skills to Colonial Beach and worked to build ships. Later, he commuted to Norfolk, Virginia, to do the same at the Norfolk Shipyard. John Simon Ford died of viral pneumonia on January 24, 1960. He was laid to rest in Culpeper National Cemetery. (Ruth Renee Lewis.)

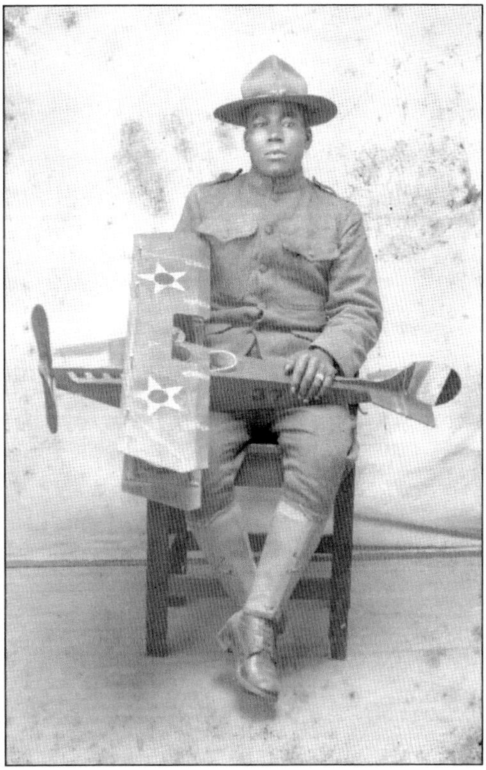

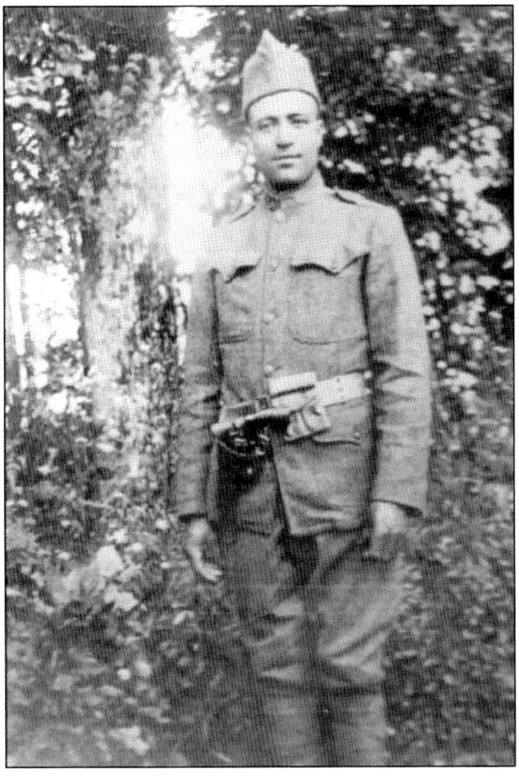

James Edward Carter was born in Madison to William and Lucy Jane Brown Carter on June 20, 1898. Drafted into the First World War in Company D, 511th Engineer Service Battalion, he was transported for duty on the ship *Mary Washington*. He was the husband of Nellie Arrington and father of two of the first Carver Regional High School graduates, Frances and Rebecca Carter. He died on Christmas Eve 1945. (Carter family.)

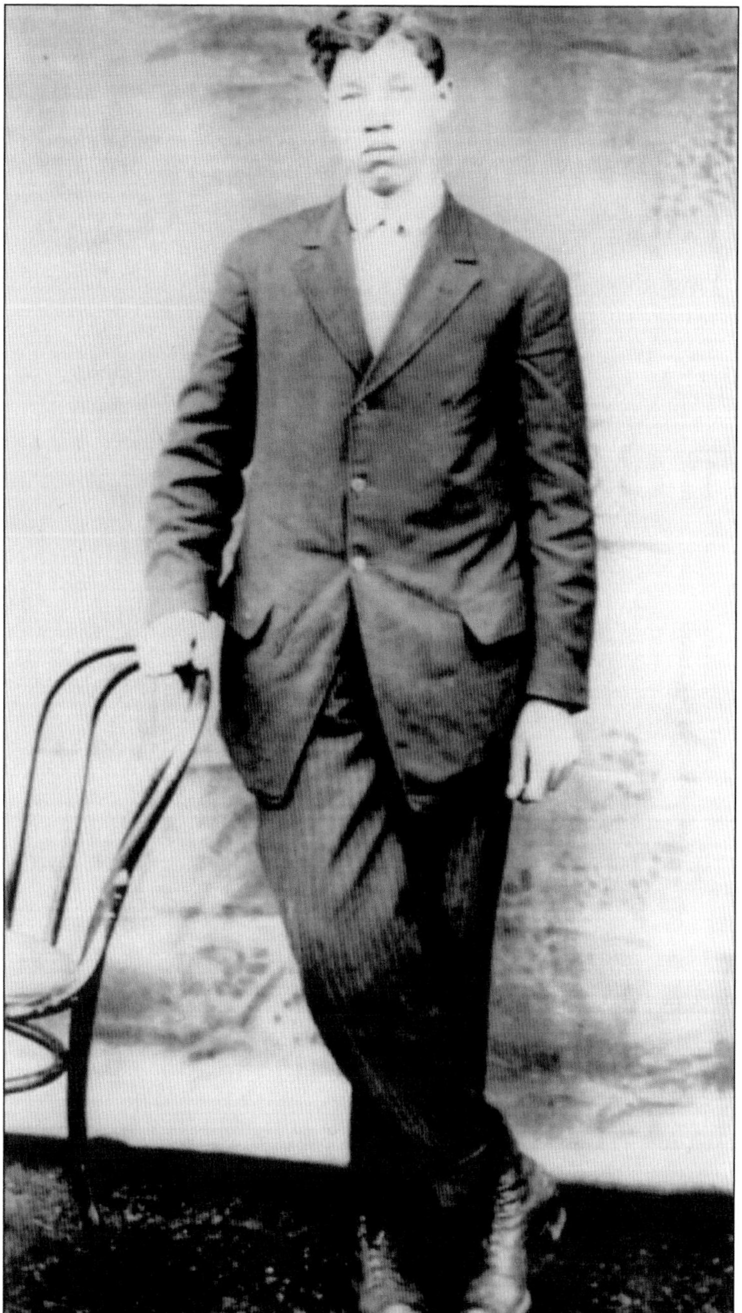

Newman Nighton Gibson was born in Peola Mills, Rappahannock, on May 10, 1897, to Lee Brown and Harriet Gibson. He began farming at age 12. In 1917, he was a member of Company K, 370th Infantry, in the First World War, where, when fighting alongside the French in trench warfare, he and his fellow soldiers were gassed. As a result, he only had one functioning lung. He married Fenton Frye on February 2, 1921, at age 25. The couple had six children, and Newman continued to farm. On March 10, 1937, at only 39 years old, he died of double pneumonia; he is buried in the Nazareth Baptist Church cemetery. (William H. Lewis.)

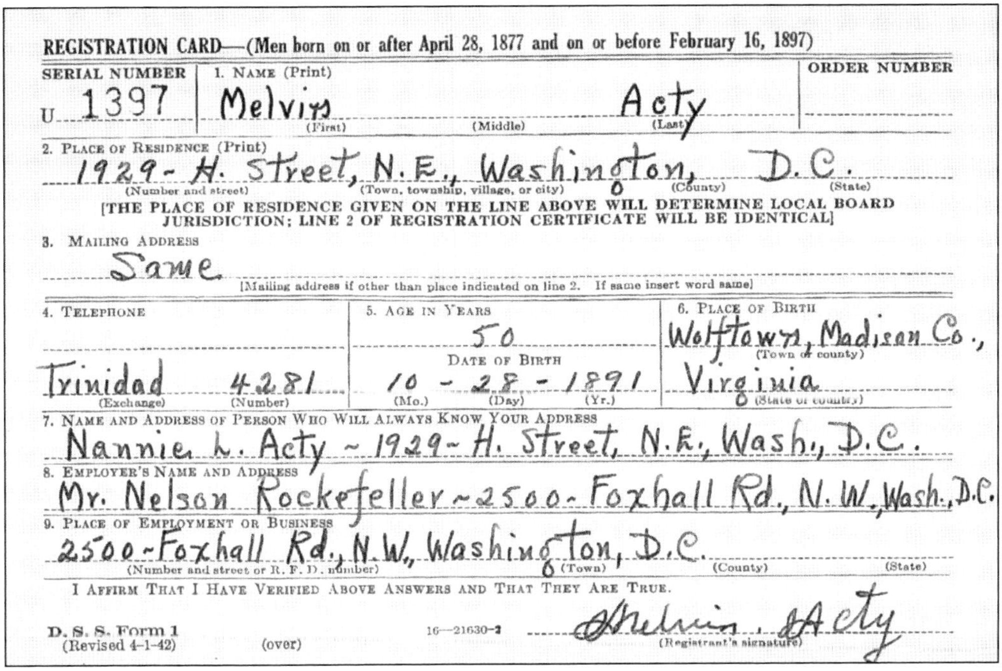

REGISTRATION CARD—(Men born on or after April 28, 1877 and on or before February 16, 1897)

SERIAL NUMBER U 1397 | 1. NAME (Print) Melvin (First) (Middle) Acty (Last) | ORDER NUMBER

2. PLACE OF RESIDENCE (Print) 1929- H. Street, N.E., (Number and street) Washington, (Town, township, village, or city) (County) D.C. (State)

[THE PLACE OF RESIDENCE GIVEN ON THE LINE ABOVE WILL DETERMINE LOCAL BOARD JURISDICTION; LINE 2 OF REGISTRATION CERTIFICATE WILL BE IDENTICAL]

3. MAILING ADDRESS Same [Mailing address if other than place indicated on line 2. If same insert word same]

4. TELEPHONE Trinidad (Exchange) 4281 (Number) | 5. AGE IN YEARS 50 DATE OF BIRTH 10 (Mo.) - 28 (Day) - 1891 (Yr.) | 6. PLACE OF BIRTH Wolftown, Madison Co., (Town or county) Virginia (State or country)

7. NAME AND ADDRESS OF PERSON WHO WILL ALWAYS KNOW YOUR ADDRESS Nannie L. Acty ~ 1929- H. Street, N.E., Wash., D.C.

8. EMPLOYER'S NAME AND ADDRESS Mr. Nelson Rockefeller ~ 2500- Foxhall Rd., N.W., Wash., D.C.

9. PLACE OF EMPLOYMENT OR BUSINESS 2500-Foxhall Rd., N.W., (Number and street or R. F. D. number) Washington, (Town) D.C. (County) (State)

I AFFIRM THAT I HAVE VERIFIED ABOVE ANSWERS AND THAT THEY ARE TRUE.

D. S. S. Form 1 (Revised 4-1-42) (over) 16—21630-2 Melvin Acty (Registrant's signature)

Melvin Acty was born in 1891 to Robert and Alberta Holmes Acty in Madison County. He mustered into World War I in Pennsylvania on July 10, 1918, as a Private in Company C, 543 Engineering Service Battalion in the Engineering Corps. After his honorable discharge, he relocated to Washington, DC, where he married Nanna (aka Nannie) Strother and raised a family. In 1940, when he completed his required World War II registration card, he was literate and working as a butler for Nelson Rockefeller. He died on May 19, 1966, and is buried in Arlington National Cemetery. (National Archives and Records Administration.)

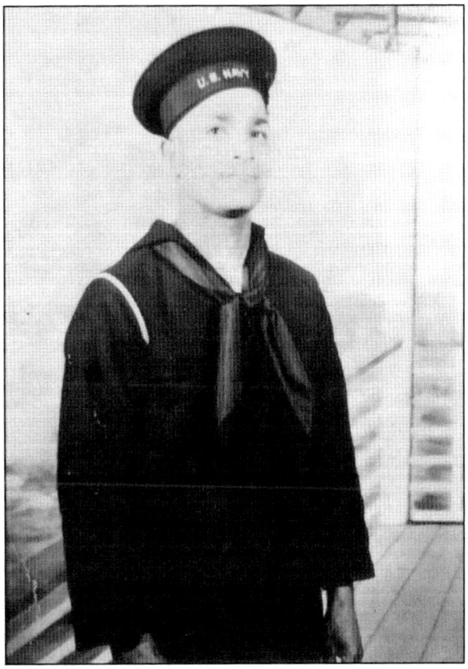

Rappahannock native Edward Homer Bailey Sr. was born on September 12, 1909, to Edward and Lovace Maggie Brown Bailey. On December 28, 1931, he married Ethel V. Timbers, daughter of Henry and Josie Fitzhugh Timbers. He served in the US Navy during World War II, from February 7, 1944, through November 2, 1945. After his discharge, he became a building contractor. He died on May 25, 1990, and is buried in the Mount Moriah Baptist Church cemetery in Amissville, Virginia. (Bailey family.)

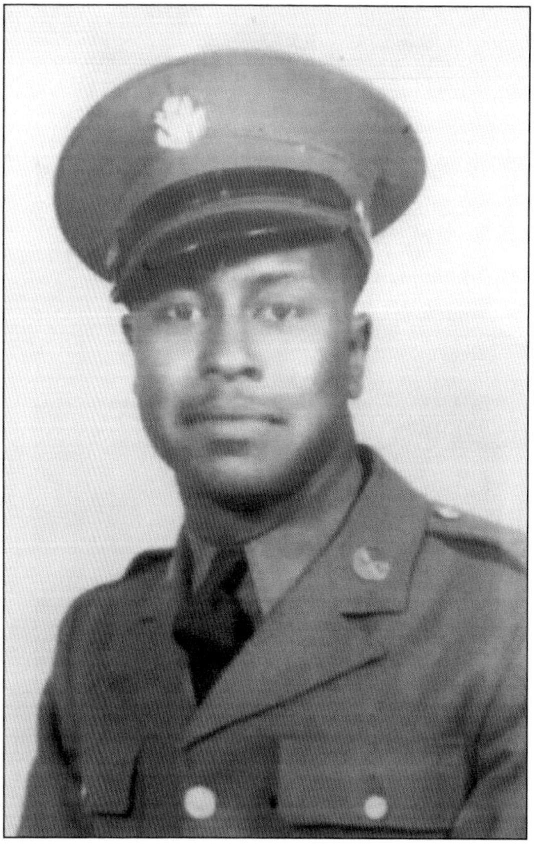

Charles Bruce Coleman III was the sixth child of Charles Jr. and Hattie Thompson Coleman. Born in Culpeper on June 17, 1917, he enlisted in the US Army and served from July 18, 1941, until his honorable discharge as a sergeant on January 12, 1946. A federal government civil servant, he died at 65 years of age on January 13, 1983, and was laid to rest in Culpeper National Cemetery. (Hortense-Hinton Jackson.)

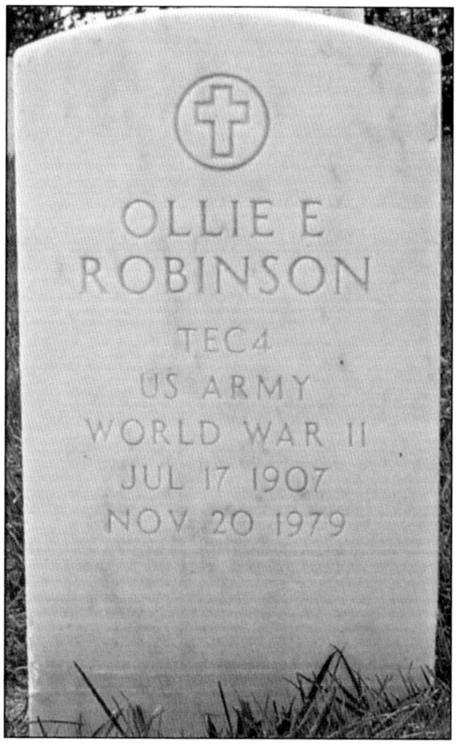

Ollie Earl Robinson was born in Culpeper on July 17, 1907, to John Quaintance and Sally Green Robinson. In his early 20s, he went to Pennsylvania and worked in a canning factory. Robinson enlisted in World War II on October 1943 and served until December 13, 1945. After his discharge, he worked as the custodian for Culpeper High School. He was the husband of Beatrice Fleshmon. Ollie Robinson died on November 20, 1979, and was laid to rest in Culpeper National Cemetery. (Terry Miller.)

George Everett Taylor was born in Culpeper on August 6, 1922, to George Washington and Ruth Etta Lewis Taylor. After his service in World War II, he returned home to a job doing brick masonry for the new high school for African American students that was under construction. That job was the foundation of a home construction business that supported George and his family throughout their lives. He was married to beautician Alice Eliza Washington, daughter of William Henry and Carrie Carter Washington, on September 24, 1952. (George Everett Taylor.)

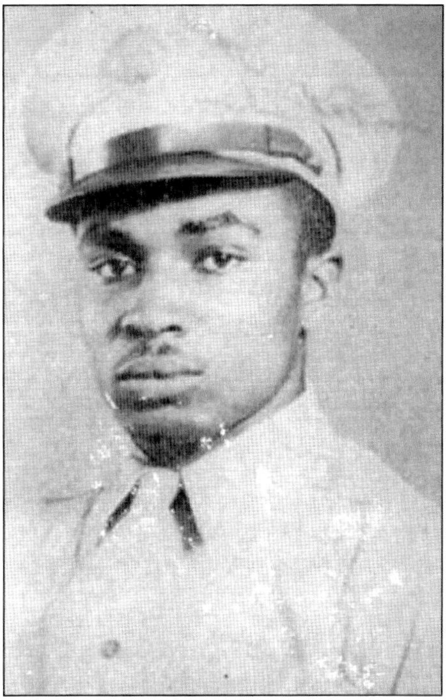

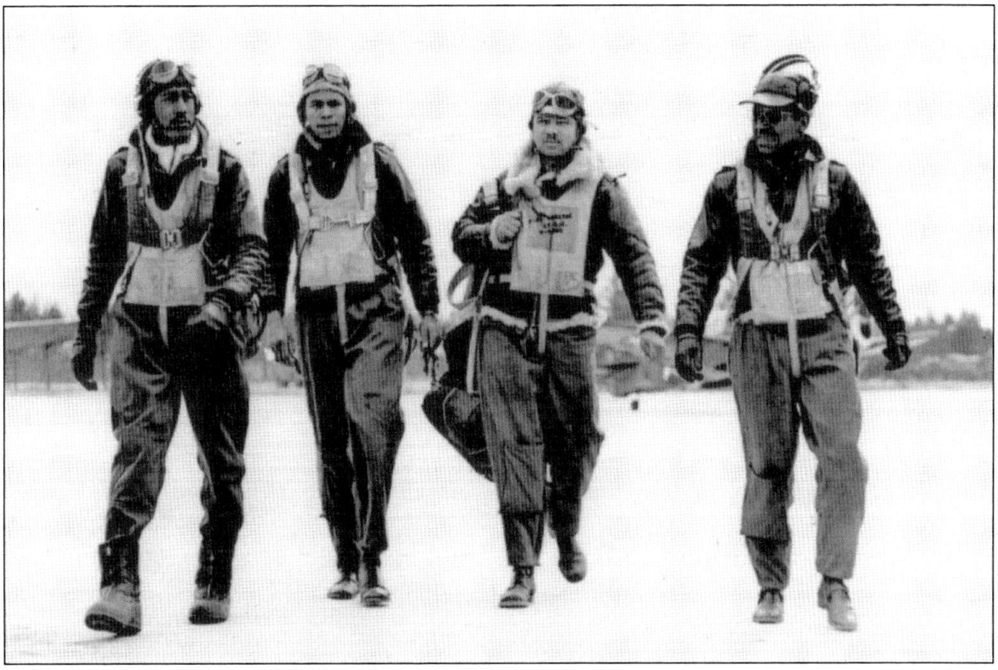

Andrew Maples Jr. (second from left) was born in New York, the oldest child of Andrew and Julia Michie Maples. His New York–born father was a World War I veteran and eventually relocated the family to Orange—his wife's home. Andrew Jr. was fortunate enough to be sent to Washington, DC, for high school, where he graduated from Armstrong High School in 1939 and then Hampton Institute in 1941. He enrolled in the Army Advanced Flying School in 1943, becoming an official US Air Force Tuskegee Airman. (US Department of Defense.)

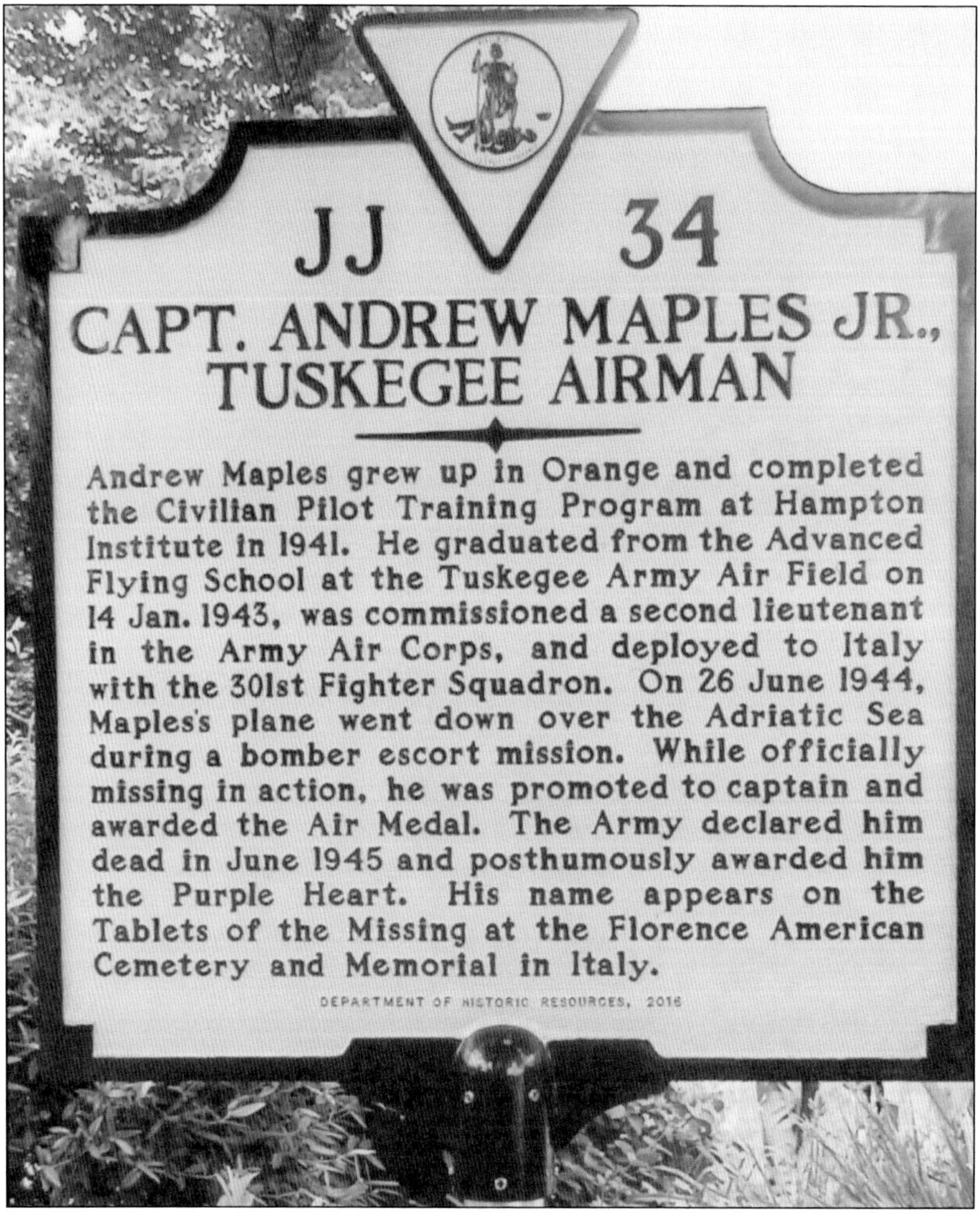

The family of Andrew Maples Jr. worked to erect a historical sign in Orange detailing his accomplishments and acknowledging the bravery of the valiant soldier. With support from the Orange American Legion Posts 156 and 74, the Tuskegee Airmen Association, and citizens of Orange, the sign was dedicated in July 2017. It is on Church Street near the home in which Maples was raised. (Terry Miller.)

John William Scott Jr. was the son of John and Ida Mae "Lummie" Williams Scott. Born in Culpeper on May 31, 1925, he enlisted in the US Navy and served aboard the USS *Strickland*. After his discharge, he married Lillie Mae Bannister. He worked as a truck driver until the age of 82, driving for Colonial Concrete for many years. In addition, he was a licensed private pilot like his father. He died on March 27, 2016. (George Everett Taylor.)

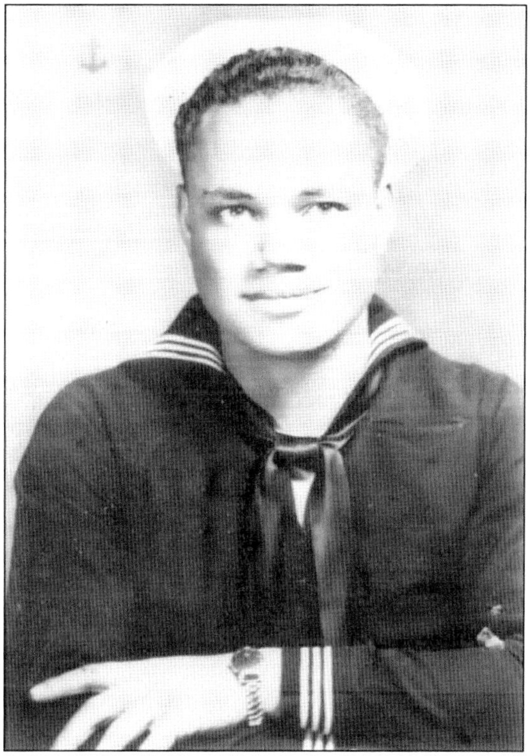

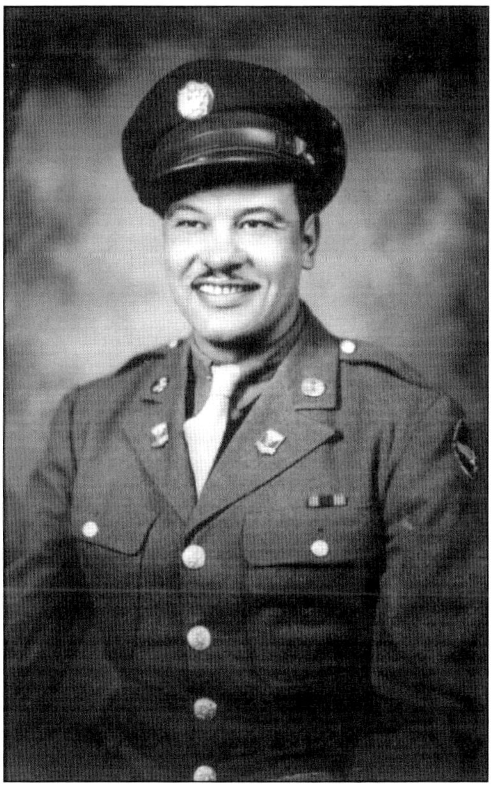

Charles Lewis Brown was born in Rappahannock in 1907 to Rev. Lewis and Irie Lee Williams Brown. He married Alice L. Grigsby, who died in 1933. With two sons to raise, he remarried—to Flossie Williams—on September 15, 1934. He died in 1988 and is buried in Hopewell Baptist Church cemetery in Sperryville, Rappahannock. (Brown family.)

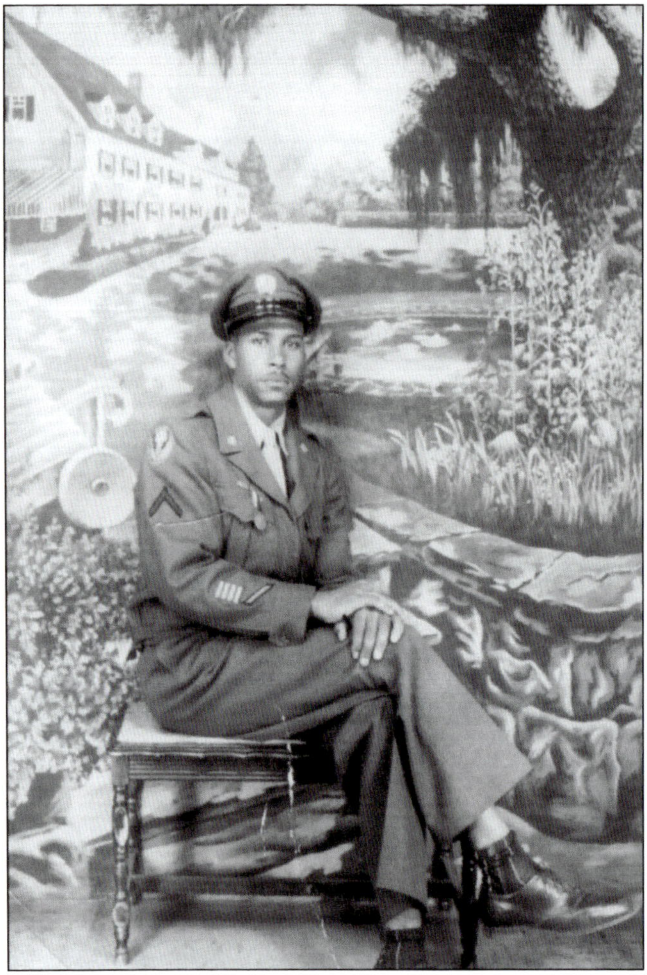

James Edmond Wood Sr. was born on April 13, 1923, in Orange to Fielding and Mary Banks Wood. His family members were members of Pilgrim Baptist Church. After a stint in the Army, he married Ruth Lewis of Spotsylvania on April 12, 1946, and the couple made a home there, having four children. He worked as a cement finisher. He contracted lung cancer and died of pneumonia on March 12, 1976, at only 52 years of age. (Wood family.)

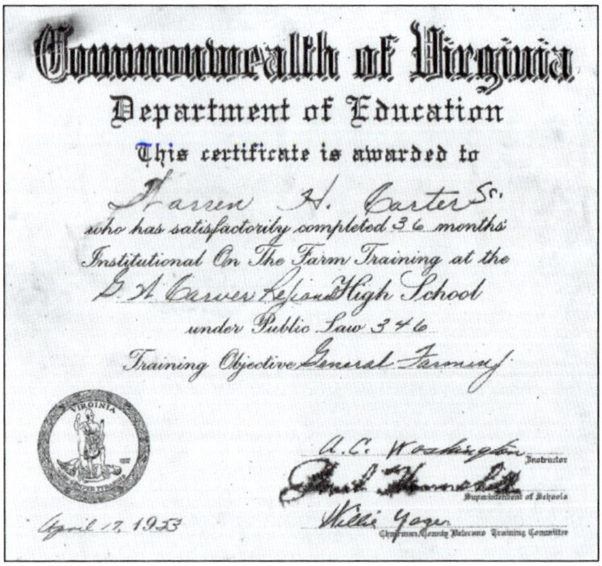

Commonwealth of Virginia

Department of Education

This certificate is awarded to

Warren H. Carter Sr.

who has satisfactorily completed 36 months

Institutional On The Farm Training at the

G. W. Carver Regional High School

under Public Law 346

Training Objective General Farming

A. C. Washington Instructor

Superintendent of Schools

Willie Yager Chairman, County Veterans Training Committee

April 17, 1953

One returning World War II veteran who successfully completed agricultural training at Carver Regional High School was Orange native Warren Harding Carter. Born on March 5, 1921, to John and Mattie Shirley Carter, he and his older brother, Lewis Adolphus, sent their pay home to their mother, who saved enough to purchase a 100-plus-acre farm. When the brothers returned, Warren earned his agricultural certificate, married Lucille White, raised a family, and was a much beloved member of his community and church, Orange Grove Baptist Church, until his death on January 20, 2000. (Michael Carter.)

Ananias Columbus Washington, born November 11, 1916, in Charles City, Virginia, was the oldest of three children of Luther Foster and Josephine Taylor Washington. He was a graduating agriculture major at Virginia State College in 1942 when he was mustered into World War II. Upon his return, he completed his degree and moved to Orange to teach. In 1948, he taught agriculture techniques to returning veterans and others from the community at the new Carver Regional High School. On February 24, 1971, he died after a long illness; he is buried in City Point National Cemetery in Hopewell. (Terry Miller.)

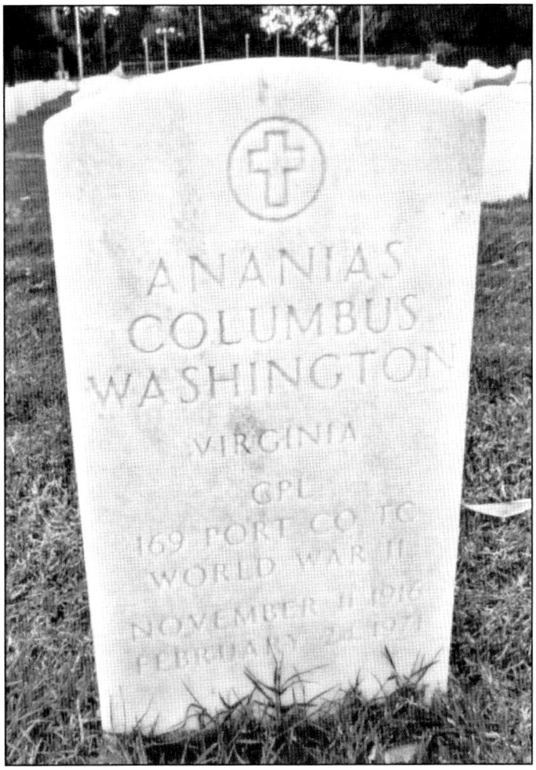

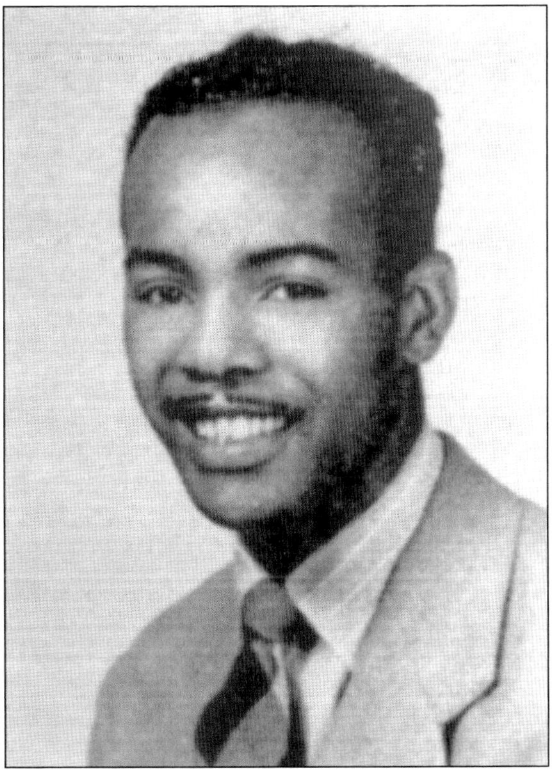

Overton Rexford Johnson was born in Dinwiddie on January 27, 1923, to Grover C. and Ruth Evelyn Wyatt Johnson. He served in the US Army from 1945 to 1947. After his honorable discharge, he married, earned a bachelor of science degree in agricultural education at Virginia State University, and joined the inaugural faculty at George Washington Carver Regional High School in Culpeper. He was so influential that his students named their chapter of the New Farmers of America in his honor. He left Culpeper after two years and continued his education at Virginia State, where he earned a doctorate and joined the faculty. (Terry Miller.)

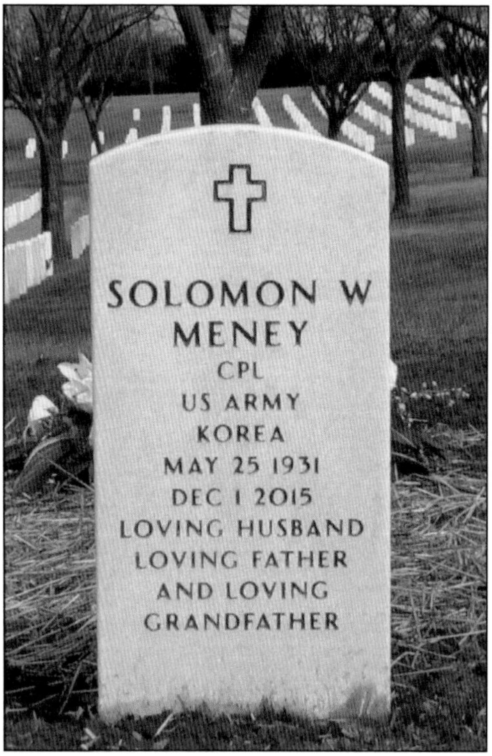

Solomon Wise Meney was born in the Brandy area of Culpeper to Nelson and Maggie Tibbs Meney on May 25, 1931. He was already a 21-year-old US Army soldier when he married Ruth Carolyn Brent. He served from March 1952 until his honorable discharge in February 1954. For more than 50 years, Meney owned and operated Culpeper Taxi Company. In addition, he was employed by Rochester Rope Corporation for 22 years. After his death at 84 years of age, he was laid to rest in Culpeper National Cemetery. (Terry Miller.)

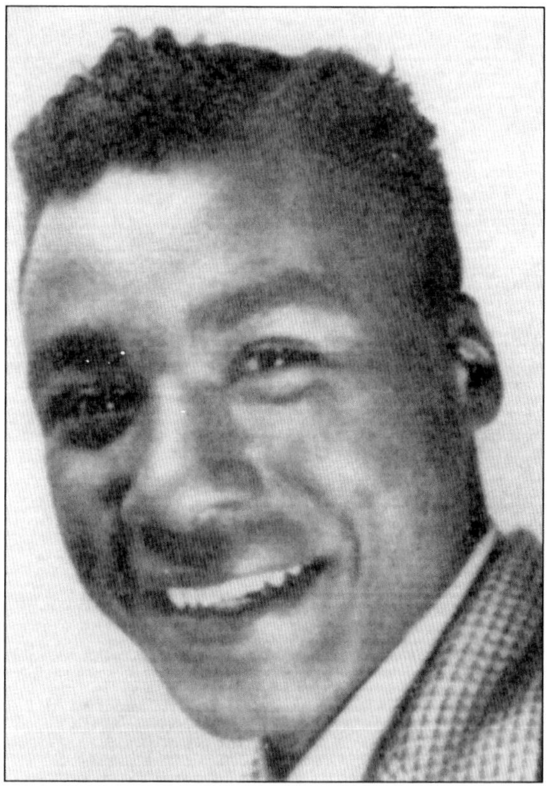

Born in Orange on August 21, 1931, to Augustus and Anna Taliaferro Ellis, Forrester Ellis graduated from Carver Regional High School in 1949 (his 1949 Carver *Hawks* yearbook photograph is shown here), nearly one year after his father's death. He enlisted in the US Air Force and served in the Korean War. He returned and made his home in Maryland with his wife, the former Geraldine Moore, and two children. He died in March 2011 and is buried in Arlington National Cemetery. (GWCRHSAA History Committee.)

Edward Homer Bailey Jr. was the son of Edward Sr. and Ethel Virginia Timbers Bailey. Born on December 23, 1933, in Washington, Rappahannock, he was working as a stone mason when, in 1952, he married fellow Rappahannock native Joan Armentra Barbour. From January 12, 1954, to December 29, 1955, he served in the US Army during the Korean War. He worked in construction as a bricklayer. At only 46 years old, he died from injuries sustained in a motorcycle accident on October 2, 1980. (Bailey family.)

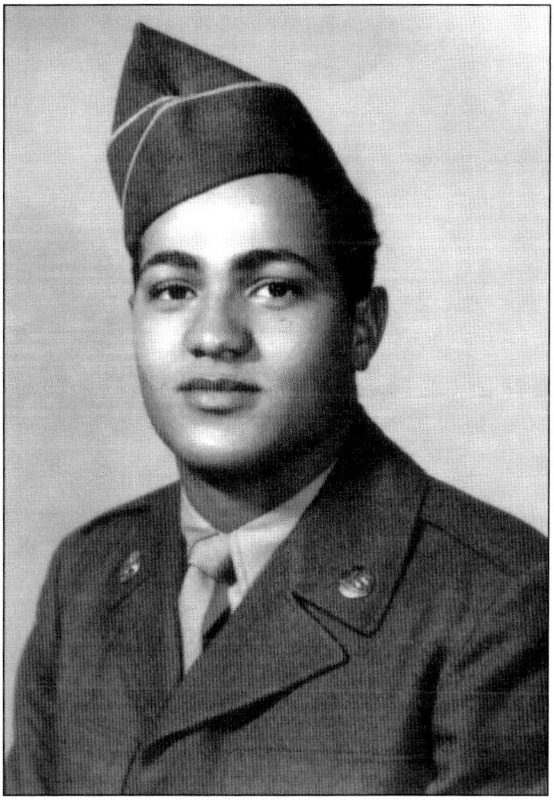

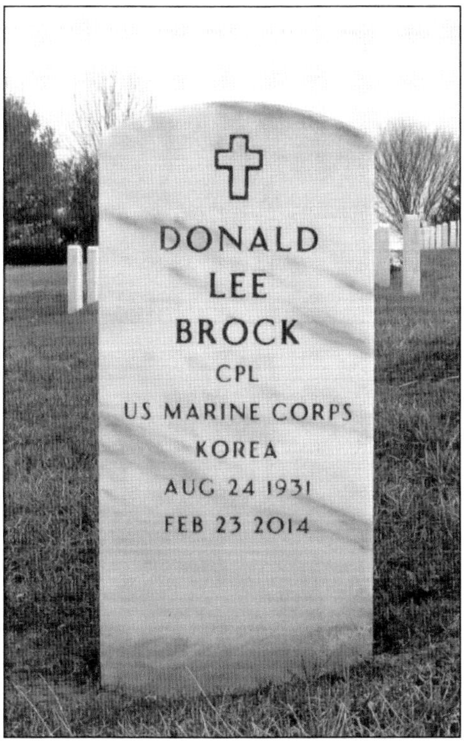

Donald Lee Brock, a 1949 graduate of Carver Regional High School, was born in Culpeper on August 24, 1931, to Robert and Henrietta Smith Brock. He was working as a clerk for Leggett's Department Store when he married fellow Culpeper native Louise E. Orange, daughter of Roy Gilbert and Sallie Orange, on February 15, 1960. He was a corporal in the US Marines in the Korean War. He died on February 23, 2014. (Terry Miller.)

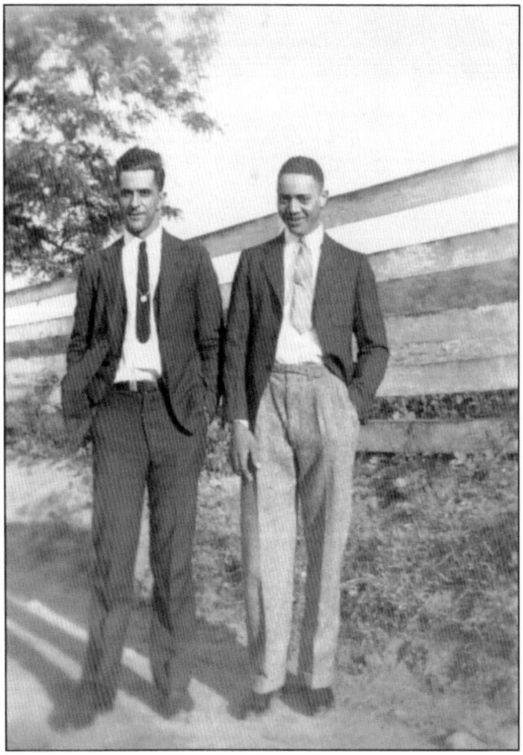

Brothers George (left) and Carl Washington (right) were two sons of Daniel and Bessie Blakey Washington. Their family had deep roots in Madison. Their paternal grandfather was a blacksmith long before the end of the Civil War. George was born on February 21, 1931, and was a US Army soldier in the Korean War. He died on January 8, 2003, in Fort Washington, Maryland, and was brought home and laid to rest in Madison Memorial Gardens in the Pratts township of Madison County. (Left, Florence Washington; below, Terry Miller.)

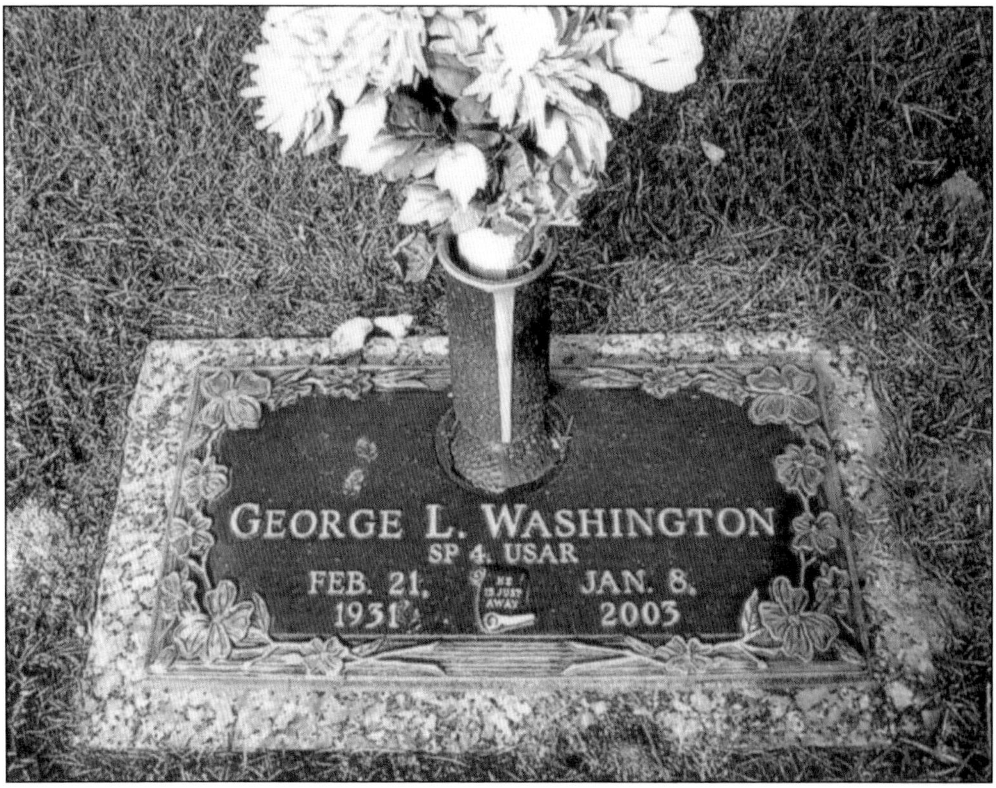

Otis Taylor Williams, born in Orange on November 11, 1931, was the older son of Jesse and Hilda White Williams. He and his brother, Herbert Roosevelt, had the benefit of growing up around their grandparents, Haywood and Mary White. After his 1949 graduation from Carver Regional High School, he trained for the US Air Force, where he made a career from August 30, 1951, to August 31, 1971, earning the rank of technical sergeant—the second–most difficult promotion to acquire next to senior master sergeant. After his death in September 2000, he was laid to rest in Culpeper National Cemetery. (Terry Miller.)

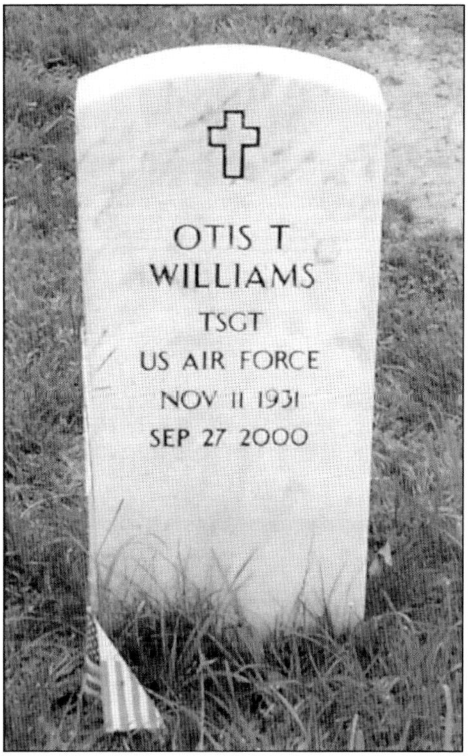

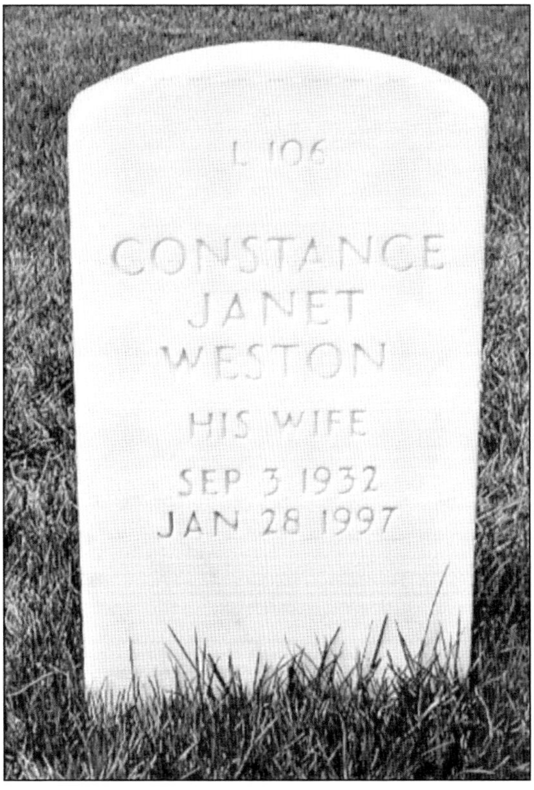

Women were supportive spouses to their military mates in many ways. Constance Weston, wife of James Hembrey Sr., was born in Pennsylvania, the daughter of Virginia natives John and Alice Weston. Her father worked in construction and, thus, had an opportunity to earn a better living for his family. As a young wife, she sailed from New York on May 8, 1956, on the USNS *Gen. Alexander M. Patch*, bound for the port of Bremerhaven, Germany. The couple later made their home in Orange. She died in 1997 and is buried in the Culpeper National Cemetery. (Terry Miller.)

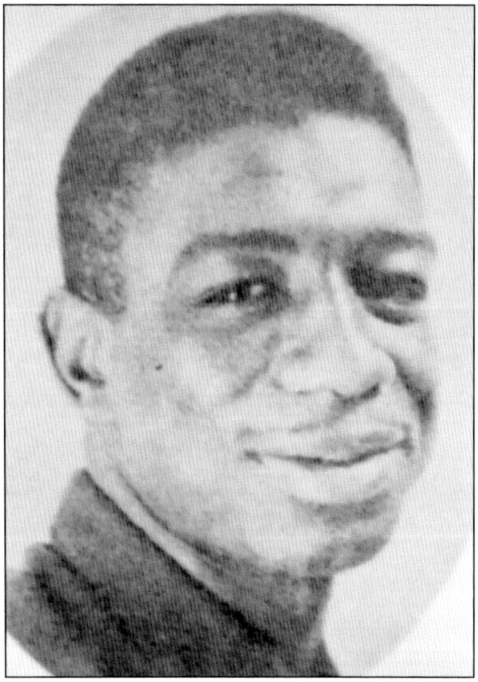

William Hamilton Alexander was born on January 19, 1931, in Orange County to Henry and Mary Smith Alexander. After graduating from high school, he attended Virginia State University, where he participated in the Reserve Officer Training Corps (ROTC). Upon completion, he entered the US Army as an officer at the rank of first lieutenant. After serving six years of active duty, he was honorably discharged as a captain. He taught briefly at Prospect Heights Middle School in his hometown of Orange, Virginia, and founded the first Boy Scout troop there. He then pursued a career as a computer analyst, working for many years for Unisys. He taught computer programming both nationally and internationally. This husband and father died on April 15, 2015, in Washington, DC. This is his graduation picture from the 1949 Carver Regional High School *Hawks* yearbook. (GWCRHSAA History Committee.)

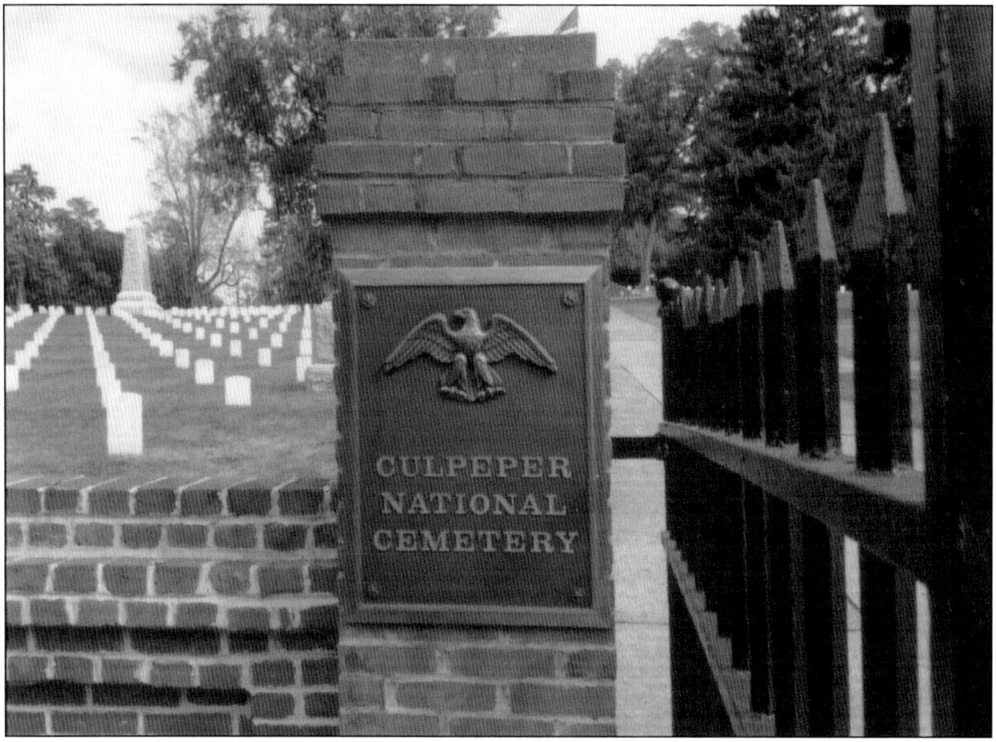

Culpeper National Cemetery is a part of The Journey Through Hallowed Ground National Heritage Area. It is also featured in the National Park Service's Discover Our Shared Heritage Travel Itinerary Series. The cemetery contains more than 7,500 graves and is still growing. It is the resting place for many veterans discussed herein. (Terry Miller.)

Three

When They Plowed

In 1782, Thomas Jefferson wrote in his *Notes on the State of Virginia* that "[t]hose who labour in the earth are the chosen people of God, if ever he had a chosen people, whose breasts he has made his peculiar deposit for substantial and genuine virtue." It is unknown whether those who farmed in Culpeper, Orange, Madison, and Rappahannock felt virtuous; they worked to feed their families the best way they knew.

Before and after the Civil War, farming was the primary source of employment. After the Civil War, of course, agriculture cultivation occurred within the new system of tenant farming. In addition, agriculture was not reliant on exports, thus, modern machinery did not have much of an impact until the late 1940s.

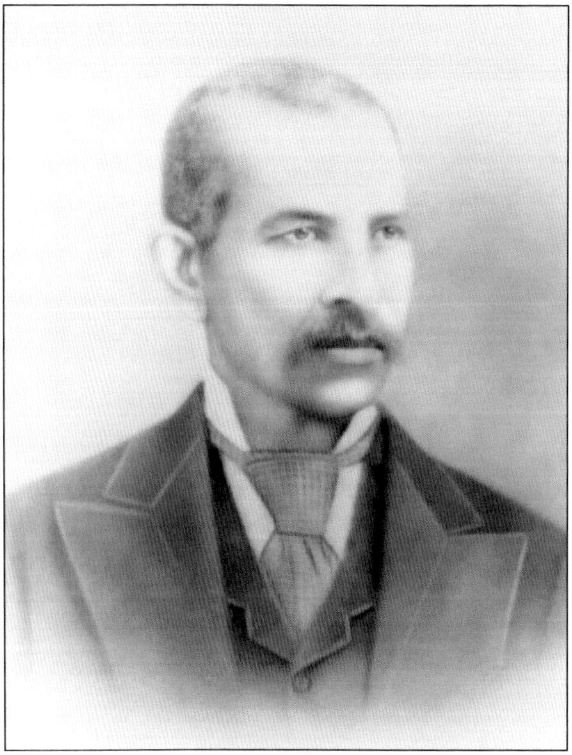

Twenty-five years before the end of slavery, Wilson Comfort was born on June 2, 1840, to Emily Comfort on the border of Spotsylvania and Orange Counties. Over time, his address was indeed designated within the boundaries of Orange. He married Sarah Ann Brown in 1866 and was the father of 11 children: 4 boys and 7 girls. He died on September 19, 1935, of heart disease and was buried on his farm. (Comfort family.)

Hired by the US Farm Security Administration to document conditions during the Great Depression, Dorothea Lange visited Rappahannock and photographed these mounds of wheat on Rappahannock farmlands. Lange became one of the premier photojournalists in the United States. Her photographs are often described as humanizing the consequences of poverty or other harsh conditions. (Library of Congress.)

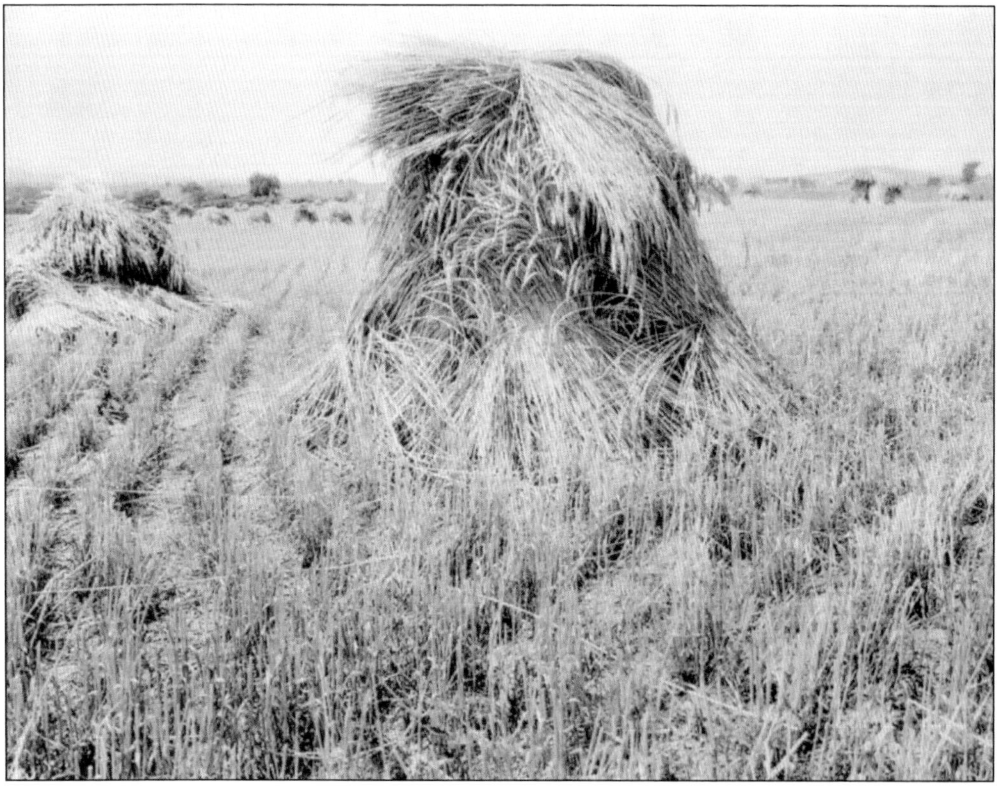

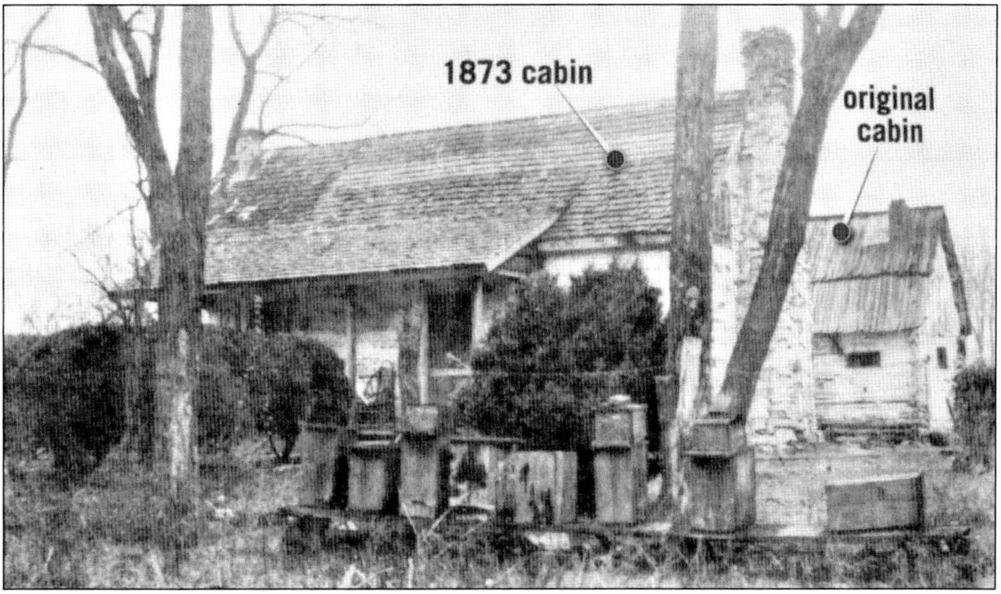

The Gilmore family constructed their home using scraps of wood from cabins previously used by Confederates. The Gilmores were formerly enslaved by the Madison family. This cabin was on the grounds of the Montpelier estate and serves as an important landmark in the African American history of the region. (National Park Service.)

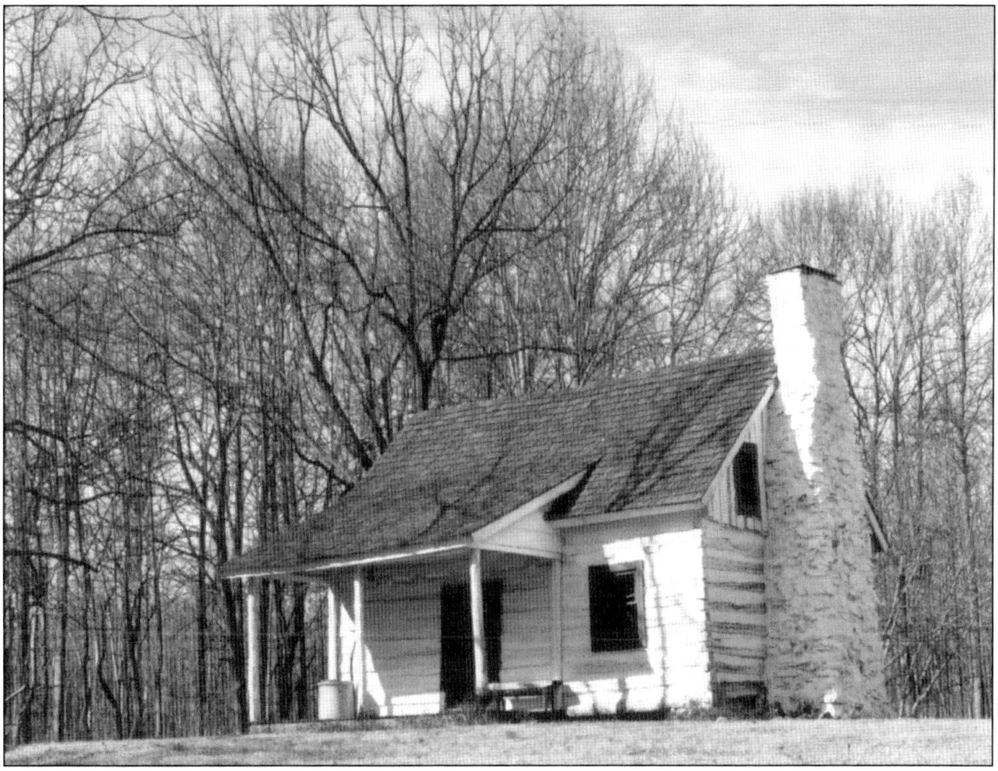

The Gilmore cabin and grounds were restored in 2004 and are included on the tour of Pres. James Madison's Montpelier estate. (Terry Miller.)

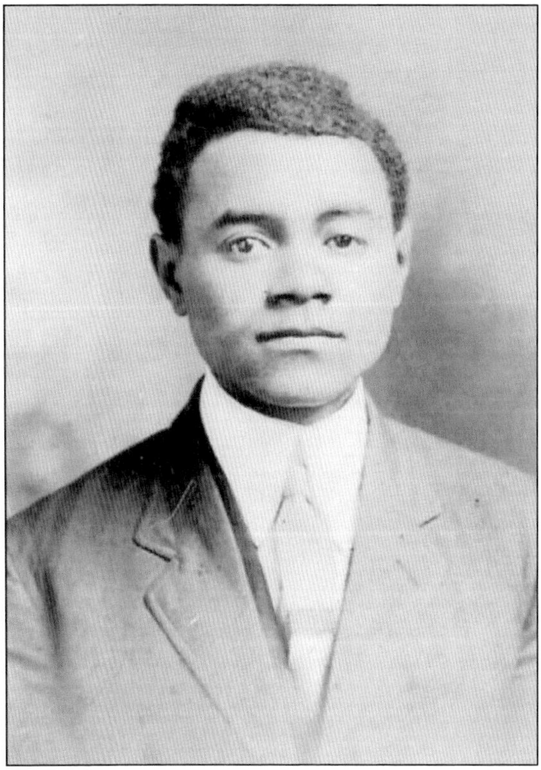

Harry Redcross Williams was born in 1891 to Augustus Williams (1855–1937) and Rose Redcross Scott (1870–?). He married Beatrice Lena Brown (1899–1988), Rappahannock native and daughter of George R. Brown and Annie Eliza Gordon. On March 7, 1959, a fatal accident in his barn resulted in him being incinerated almost immediately. He is buried in Hollywood Cemetery in Remington in Fauquier County. (Williams family.)

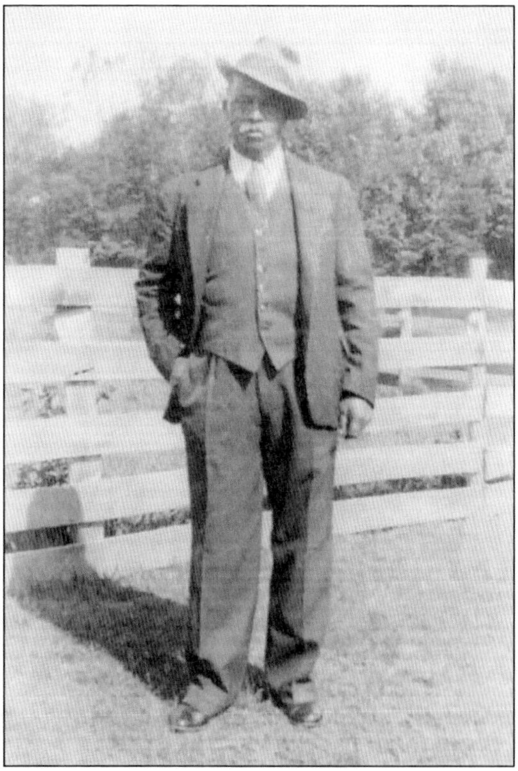

George Richard Brown was born on September 17, 1872, to Lewis Alexander Brown and Mary Brooks Titus. A lifelong Rappahannock native, he was the husband of Annie Eliza Gordon, who died in 1923 of tuberculosis. The couple had 10 known children. George Brown remarried to Laura Smith, and the couple had one child. Brown died on December 3, 1949, of heart disease and was laid to rest in the family cemetery in Amissville, Virginia. (Brown family.)

Red-haired with blue eyes, Matthew Lewis's (c. 1850–January 1922) parents, as recorded on his marriage license, were Leland Lewis and Delphia Terrill. A native of Orange, he married Jane Turner on January 17, 1875, and they settled in their community of farm owners, raising their nine surviving children (out of fourteen). They were founding members of Bethel Baptist Church and formed one of the cornerstones of a vibrant Freetown neighborhood. (Lewis family.)

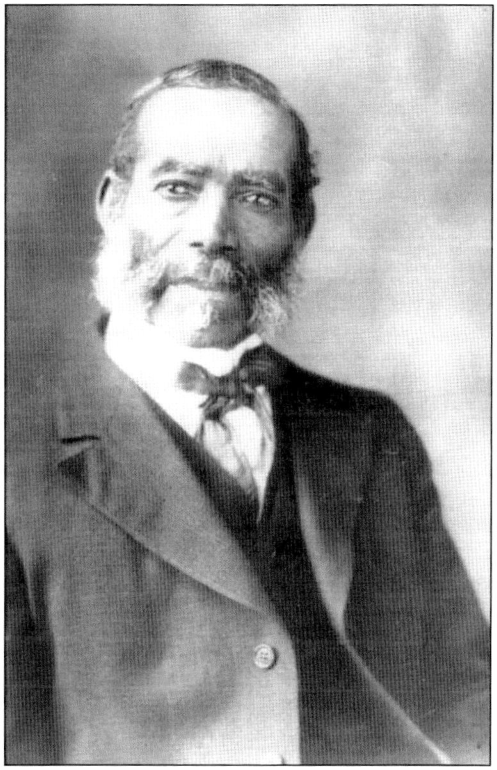

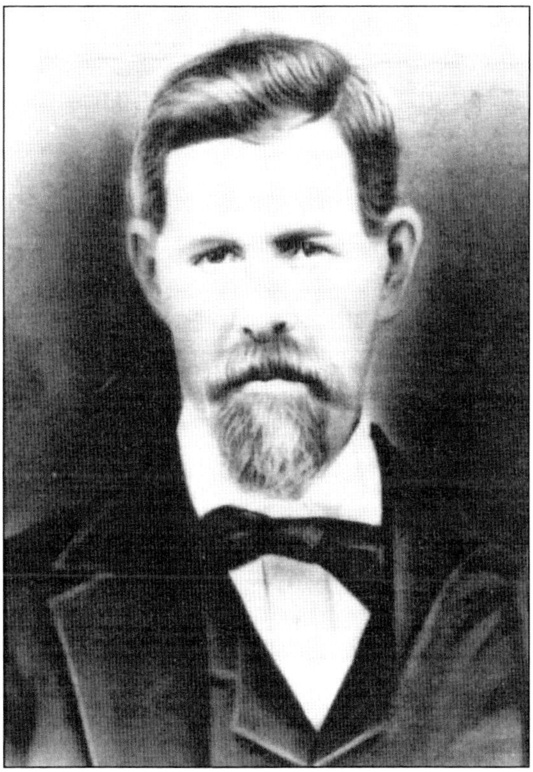

Laurence Wilhoite was born in 1842 to Samuel and Dicie Murray Wilhoite. He worked as a farmhand until he was able to purchase his own land in the Cedar Mountain district of Culpeper. He married Malinda Gardner around 1868, and through the years, the couple had 11 children. A few years after Malinda's death in 1902, Laurence remarried to Madison County native Addie Carter Brown. Their life together ended seven years later when he died on July 25, 1915. He is buried in the cemetery of his family church, Cedar Grove Baptist Church. (Wilhoite family.)

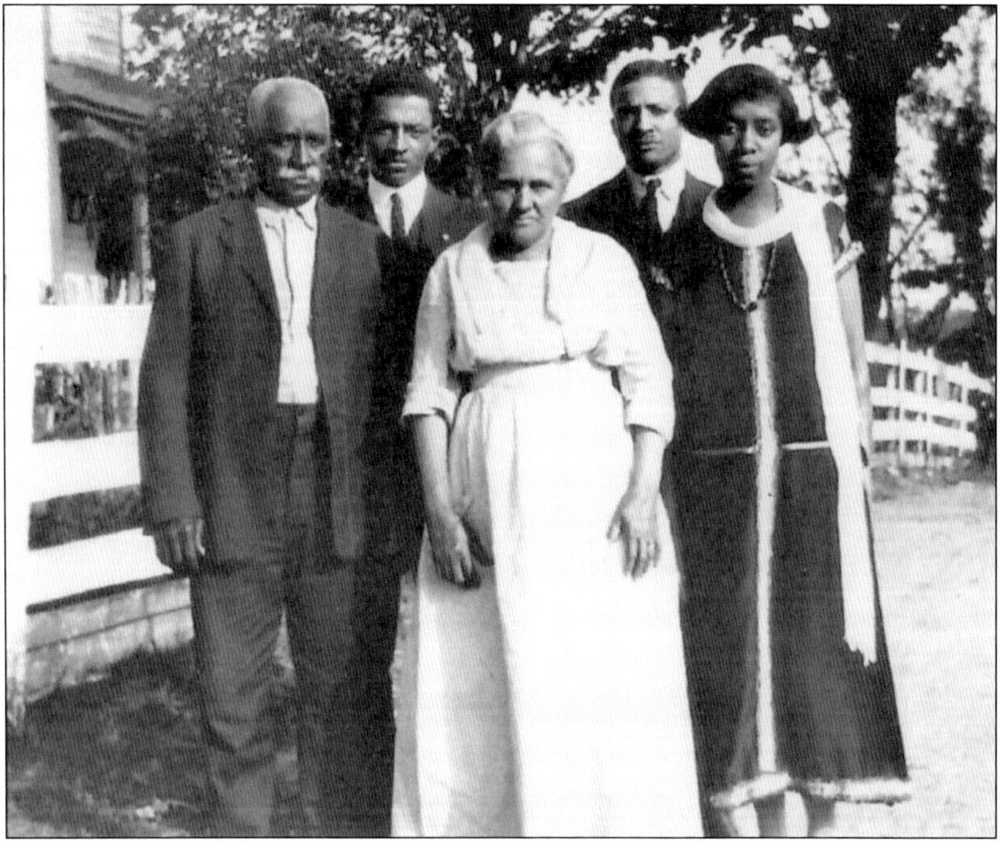

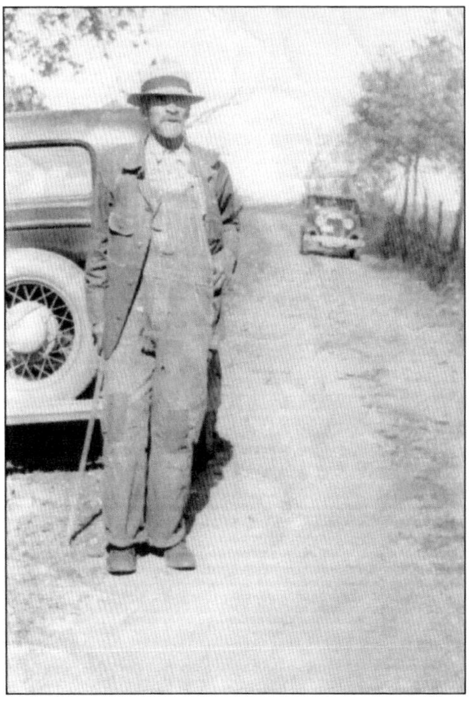

William Henry Davis (b. 1857, far left) and Olivia Ann Grasty (b. 1860, front center) married in Olivia's home county of Orange on November 17, 1878, and made a home together. Over the years, they had 10 known children and raised their family on a farm in the Stevensburg neighborhood of Culpeper. They were devout members of Ebenezer Baptist Church in Lignum, where many of the family members are buried. (Davis family.)

James R. Frye was born in Rappahannock on March 16, 1872, to Belle Frye. On August 5, 1894, he married Ida Jane Ralls. By 1900, they were living in the Hawthorne section of Rappahannock and raising three daughters: Lottie, Marie, and Fenton; their only son, Otis, was born later. Frye worked as a farm laborer until he earned enough to purchase his own farm in Madison. He died on September 15, 1947, of a brain hemorrhage. (William H. Lewis.)

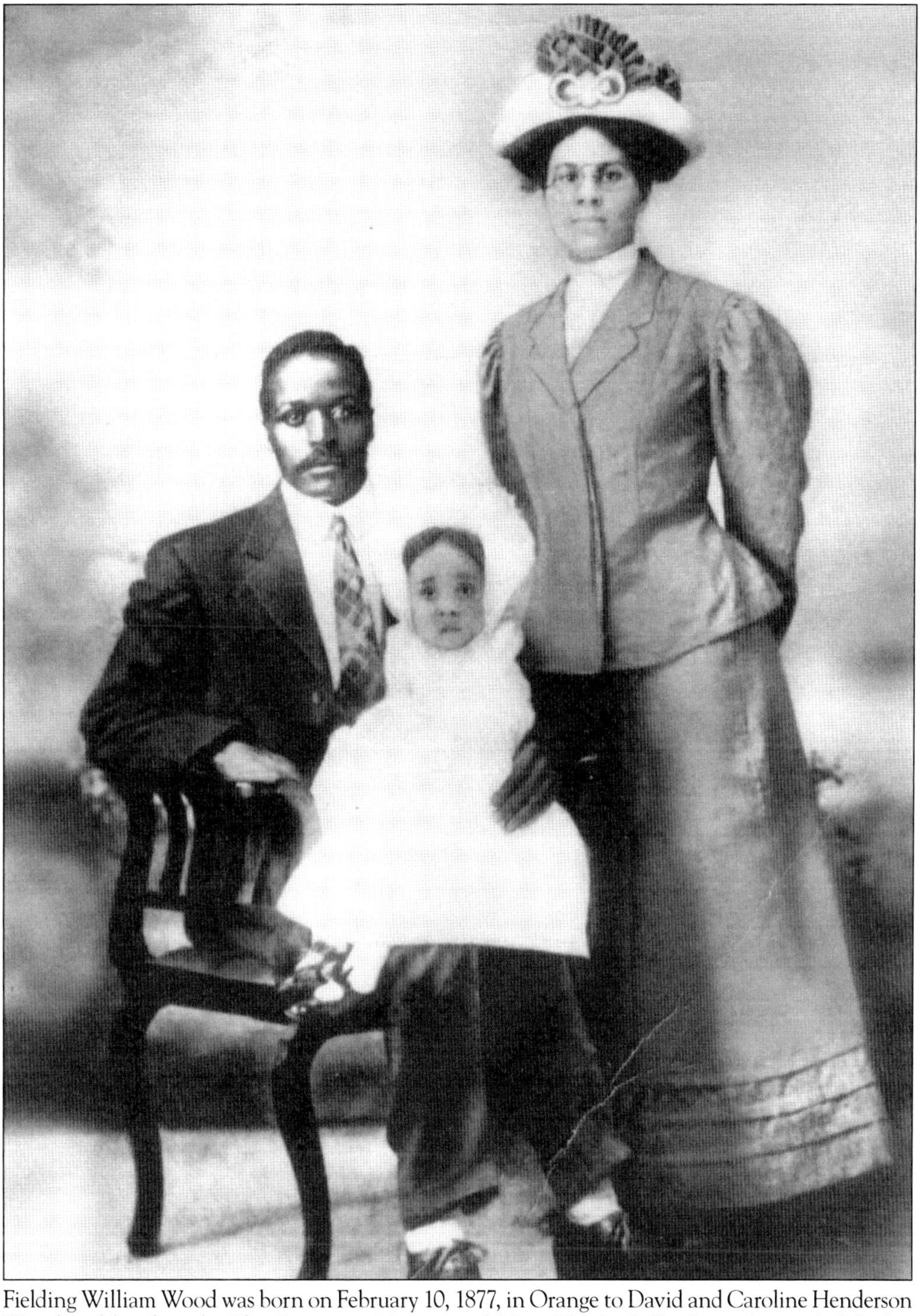

Fielding William Wood was born on February 10, 1877, in Orange to David and Caroline Henderson Wood and lived in the Flat Run area. He married Mary Elizabeth Banks and provided for his family as a farmer. The couple had eight known children, most of whom moved to urban cities north of Virginia. This photograph shows Fielding, Mary, and their daughter Josephine in 1910. (Wood family.)

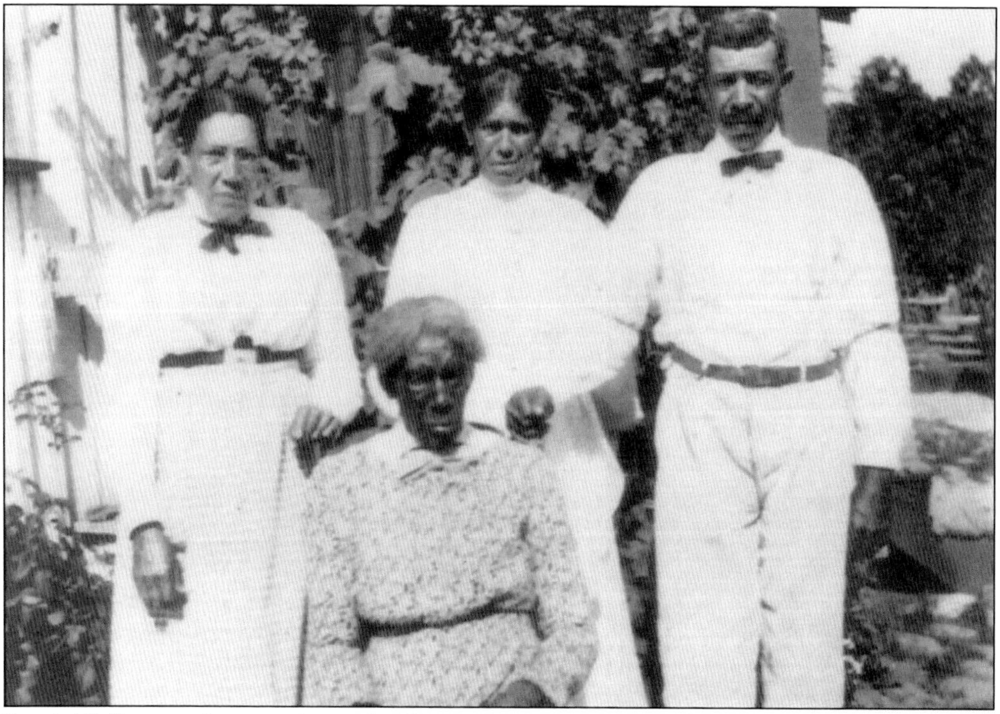

Frank Walker was born in the mid-1850s in Greene County and soon thereafter relocated to Madison County. In 1896, at the age of 40, he married Ella Carpenter, daughter of Tom and Mary Clore Carpenter. They had a blended family and were together for a little more than 15 years. Walker, who considered himself a small farmer, died of tuberculosis on October 13, 1914. (Davis family.)

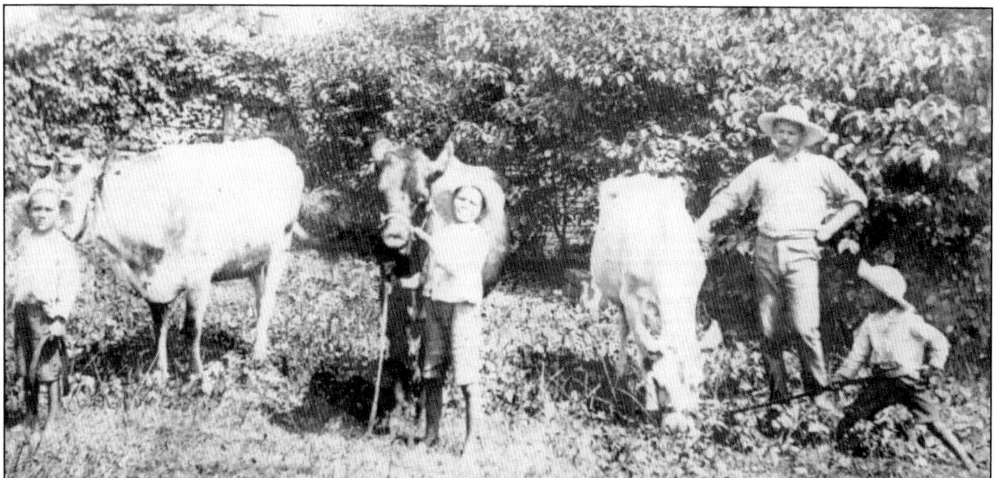

Solomon Winslow was born in Culpeper on September 11, 1872, to former Confederate teamster Edmond and Mary Wise Winslow. He worked as a laborer throughout the area until his marriage to Emma Carpenter in 1900. The couple had a daughter who died as an infant, and they soon relocated first to West Virginia and then established themselves in Wellsville, Ohio. Solomon is pictured here with his three sons (from left to right), Earl, Ralph, and Homer. He died on November 3, 1940. (Winslow family.)

Known as "Simon," Charles W. Kilby, born in Rappahannock in 1853, was the son of Nimrod Kilby and Juliett Ann Luby, a slave of Thomas and Mildred Kilby. When he was preparing to marry Lucy Frances Wallace (1857–1933), he was given written permission to do so by her mother, Martha P. Wallace. Since both of Simon Kilby's parents were deceased, his identity was attested to by merchant and community leader Paschal M. Finks. Over the years, the couple made a home on their own land and raised seven sons and four daughters. They maintained a lasting relationship with the Finks family, as evidenced by one of Simon's sons, John Henry Kilby Sr., who worked as a farm laborer for some Finks descendants. Simon Kilby died on October 4, 1924, and was laid to rest in the cemetery of Nazareth Baptist Church. (Kilby family.)

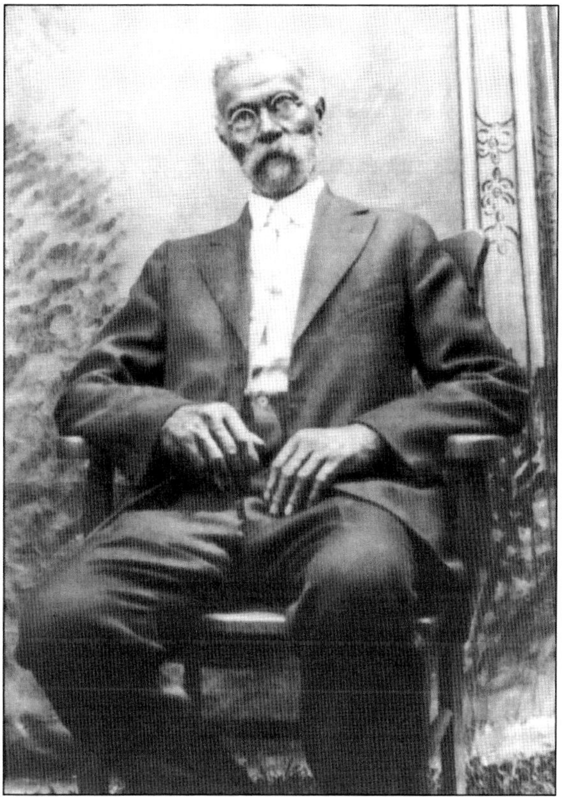

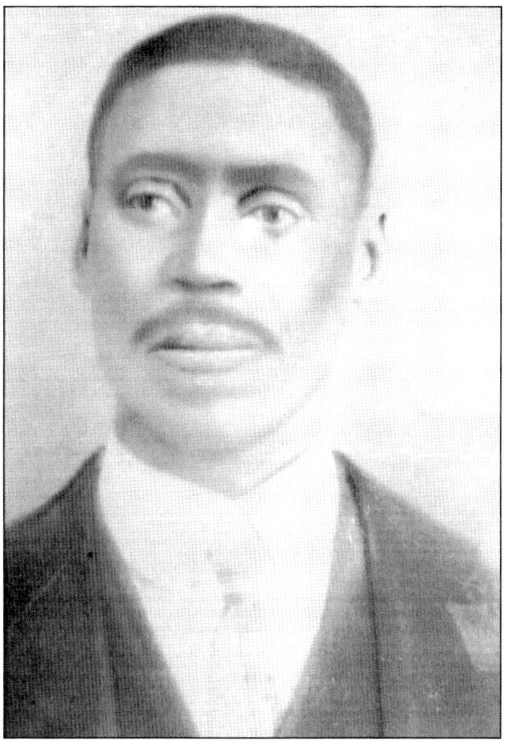

Arthur Bannister (1875–1957) was a Culpeper native and farmer. The son of Abraham and Emily Dawson Bannister, he visited and worked in urban areas during some summers. The December 1902 edition of the *Caledonia Era* newspaper wrote: "Arthur Bannister and . . . Molly Sutton . . . colored young people of Orange . . . returned home Monday after spending the summer hereabouts on farms and at various employment." He married Sutton and, by 1930, owned his farm free and clear while his wife kept house and cared for their 13 children. He died in January 1937 of tuberculosis. (Bannister family.)

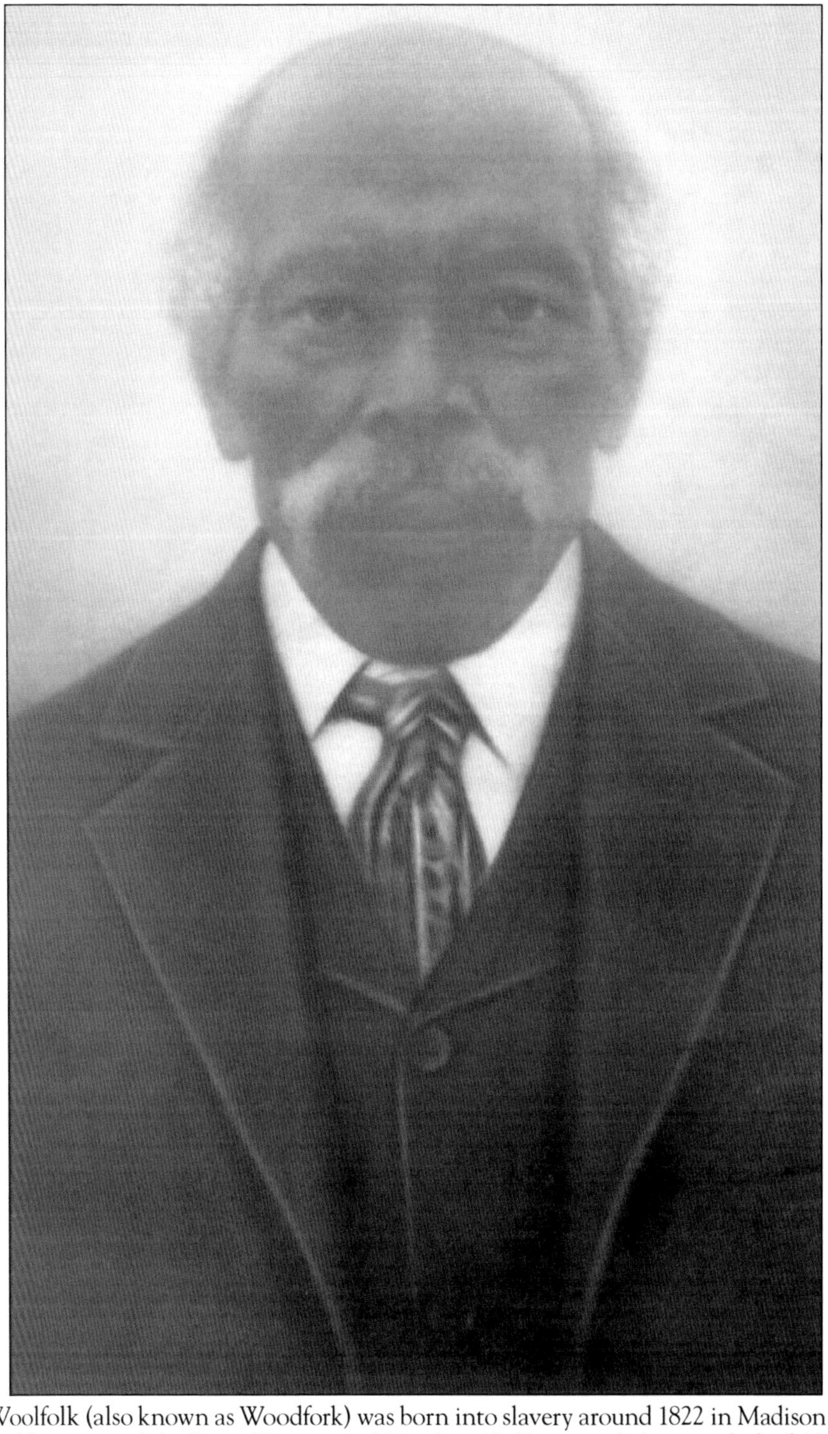

Lewis Woolfolk (also known as Woodfork) was born into slavery around 1822 in Madison County and lived his entire life there. He married Everline Tolliver, and the couple had 11 known children. By 1880, he owned the farm on which he supported his family. He reportedly died in 1907; the state of Virginia did not keep a statewide record of births or deaths between 1896 and 1912. (Patricia Kelley.)

Four

When They Made a Home

Four devastating events have marked the area of these four counties: destruction during the Civil War, tuberculosis and influenza outbreaks in the late 1920s and early 1930s, and the Great Depression. Women who made a home worked through all of these calamities.

While the men in their lives earned the majority of money for the household, wives and daughters ensured the home ran smoothly. This sometimes meant that females took in laundry to supplement the household income. It always meant, however, that women designed and sewed clothing; gathered, cooked and preserved food from the garden; bartered for services; assigned chores to their children; and taught the children how to pray. Those same children wanted their children to get an education. Moreover, they made sacrifices and shed tears.

Many of the women celebrated herein were born before the end of slavery in Virginia and birthed and/or raised children who were not the blood kin of the African American men they may have married after 1865. A well-known biography is that of Sister Caroline of Rappahannock. Her story is illustrative of the two required tasks that enslaved women were forced to undertake: be available for the sexual release of owners, overseers, and other designees, and perform farm/field work.

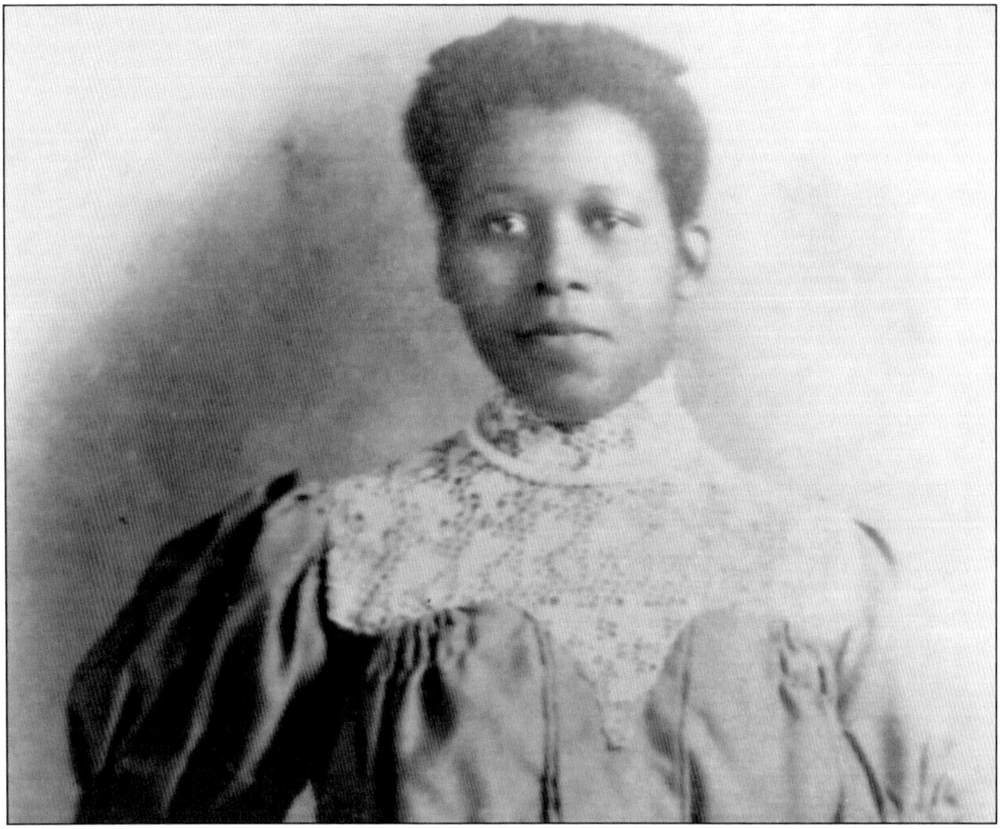

Olia Carpenter was the daughter of James and Sallie Thoms Carpenter. She was born in Madison on April 1, 1888, one of 10 known children. She married William Seldon "Sonny" Banks in 1909, and from the time of their marriage through 1928, they had nine children. Shortly after giving birth to her last child, she died of sepsis on May 18, 1928, at only 40 years old. (Leroy Hackley Jr.)

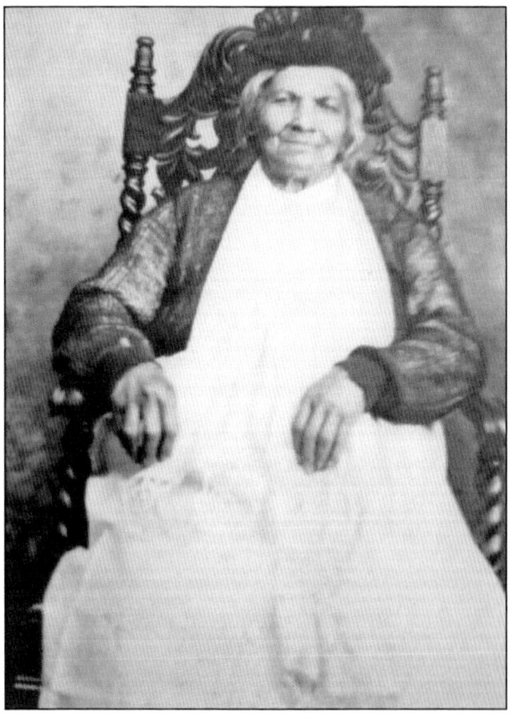

Rappahannock native Lucy Mildred Terrill (aka Terrell) Peyton was born around 1856 to Harriett Peyton. In 1879, she married farmer Edward Fletcher (1856–1927), and they had five children. Their home was full of encouragement, resulting in their children becoming professionals in their own right. Nephews and grandchildren also lived with them at times. After Lucy's husband died on October 31, 1927, following a long illness, her oldest daughter, Neter, moved back to the homeplace and cared for her mother, who died at 76 years old on September 30, 1932. (Randi Simon-Serey.)

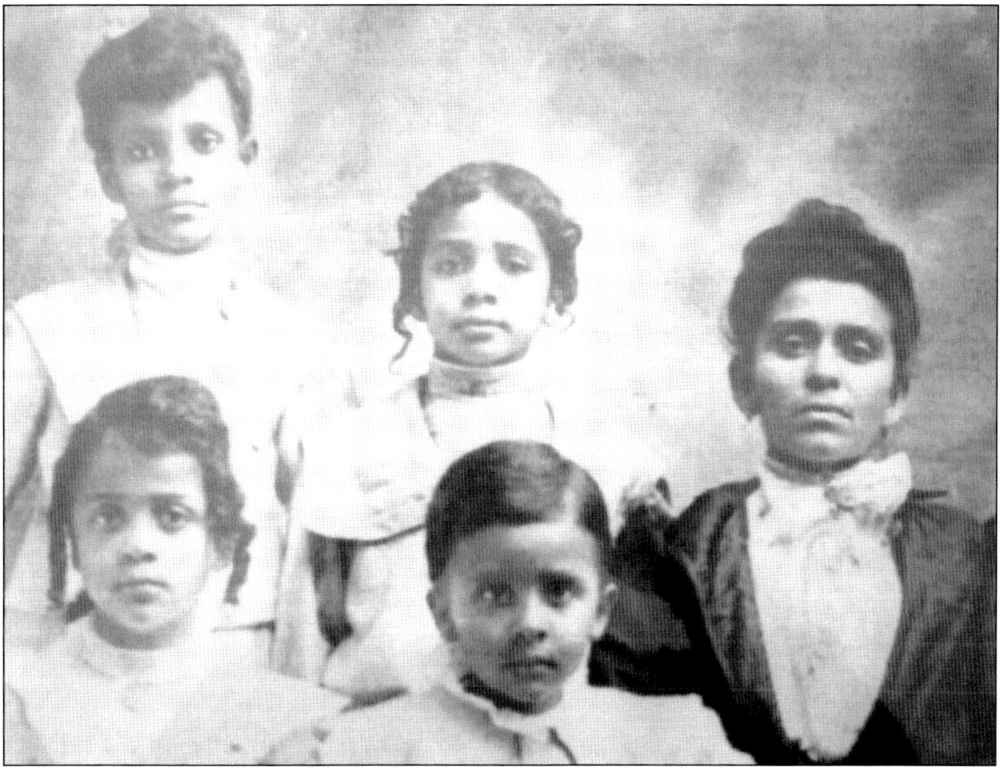

Ida Ralls Frye was born in Rappahannock around 1874 to Andrew "Cafie" and Jane Jenkins Ralls. She married James Frye on August 5, 1894; set up housekeeping; and raised their family of four children. Pictured in this c. 1905 photograph are, from left to right, (seated) Fenton, Otis, and Ida; (standing) Lottie and Marie. (William H. Lewis.)

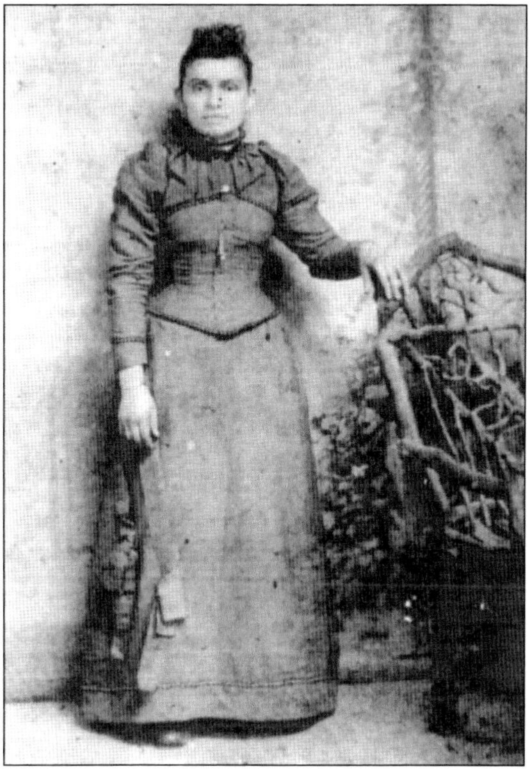

By 1940, Ida Ralls Frye and her husband, James, were living in Madison on their farm on scenic State Road 603 at the foot of Shenandoah National Park. They were not alone in their senior years, as their son Otis and his new wife, Georgia, were living with them. Ida died on June 18, 1948, nine months after her husband passed. Interestingly, they both died of a brain hemorrhage. (William H. Lewis.)

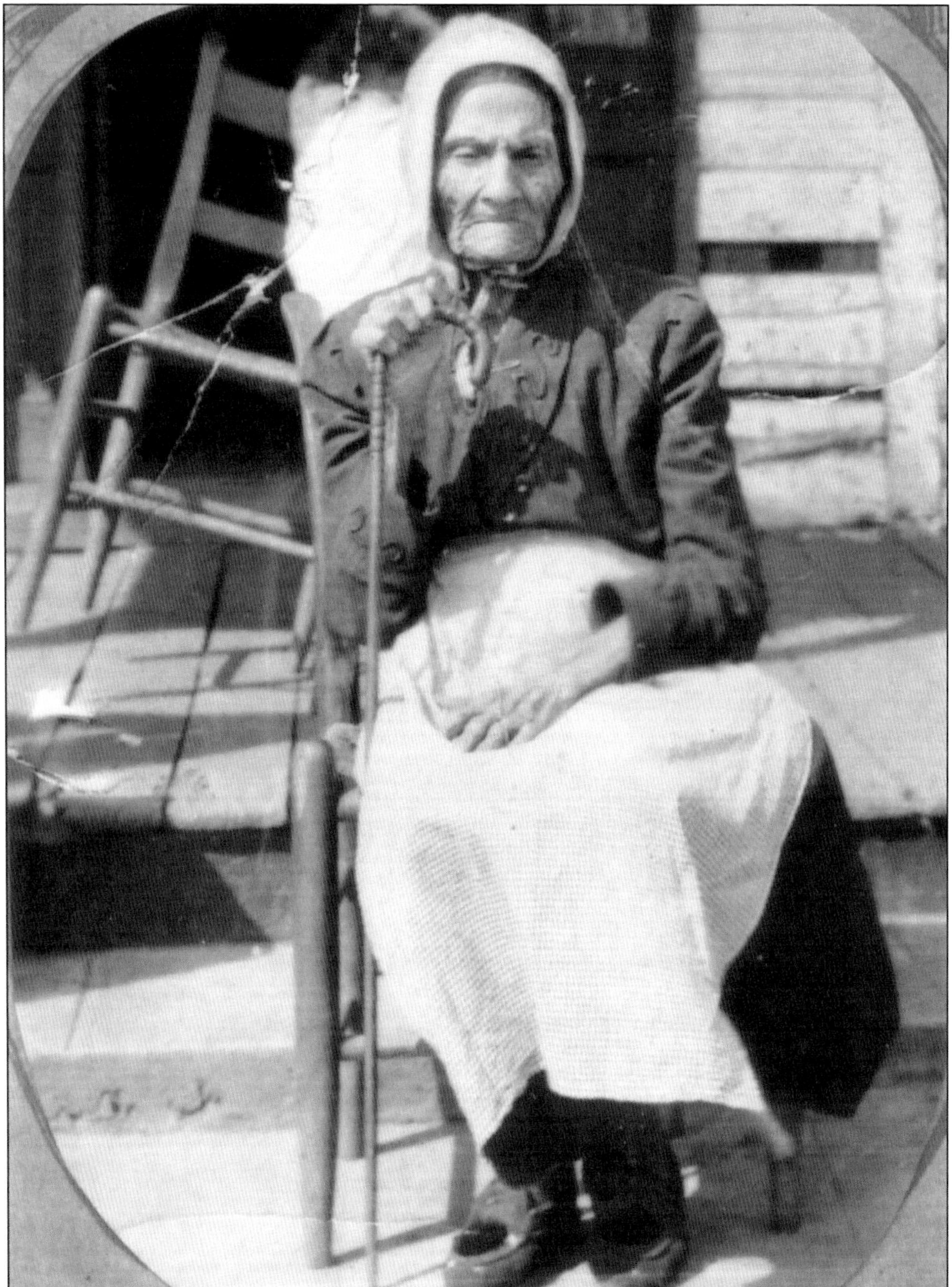

Members of Emily Arrington's family were listed as free people of color in Madison as early as the 1840 census. Emily's journey, however, is not a straight line from around 1815 to her death in 1923. The best evidence states that her parents were Mariah Cooper and a man whose surname was Arrington. She was married after the end of slavery to Harrison Proctor. It is unknown how many children the couple had, but it is clear that she lived to see them all grow up and be laid to rest. (Kimberly Milai.)

Lucinda Milton Tansimore was the daughter of Harper Milton and Fannie Beckham Green. Born in Orange on March 31, 1867, she married Lewis Tansimore, and the couple had 12 children; 11 survived. Her husband died unexpectedly in 1917, and she continued to farm the land along with her sons. She did not want them to be limited to the land, however. Her children grew up to become teachers, military men, and other professionals. She lived to be 84 years old, dying on December 9, 1951, of heart disease. She is buried in the cemetery of Mount Holy Baptist Church in Unionville. (Tansimore family.)

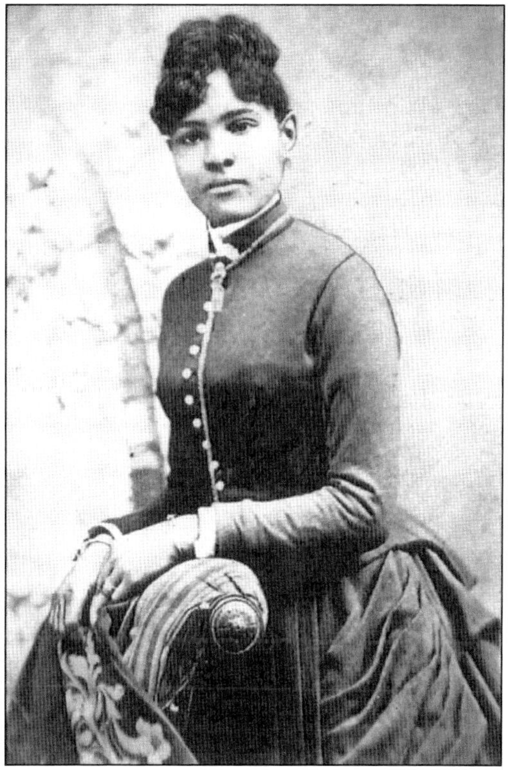

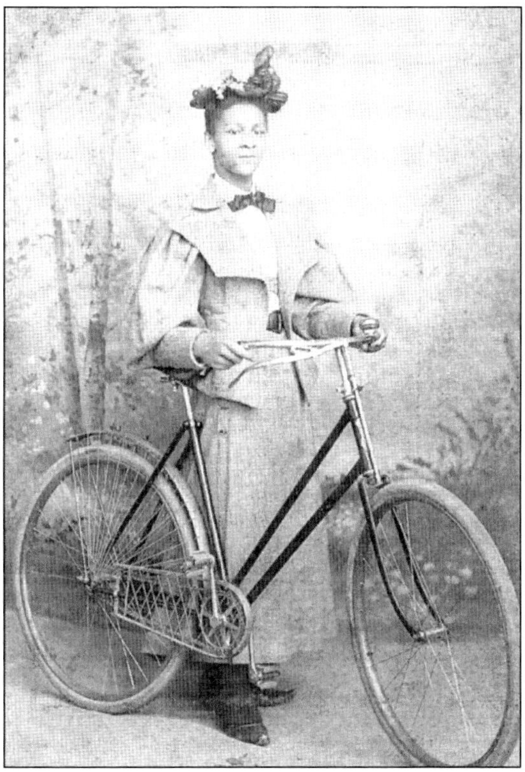

Emma Carpenter was born on May 1, 1872, in Culpeper to Mack and Irene Ralls Carpenter. She married Solomon Winslow (1872–1940), and the couple had four children. After the death of their infant son in 1900, they relocated first to West Virginia and then to Wellsville, Ohio. She died on June 21, 1962, of old age. (Winslow family.)

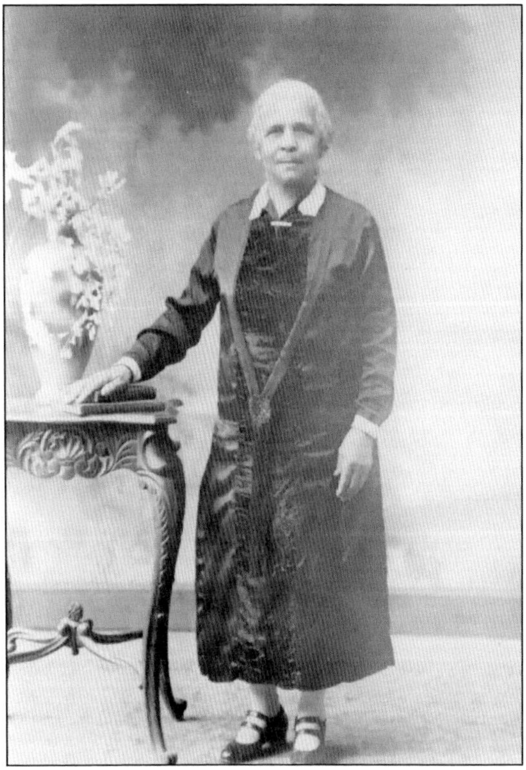

Madison County native Delilah Terry, daughter of Fountain and Mary Jackson Terry (aka Tyree), was 19 years old when she married farmer Allen Jackson on January 6, 1872. The couple had nine children—seven boys and two girls. After Allen's death in 1903, some of Delilah's older sons helped with the youngest—they taught him carpentry, and he earned money to attend college. Cared for by her children, she lived a fulfilled life until she died on March 19, 1941, at age 69. (Lindsay Jackson.)

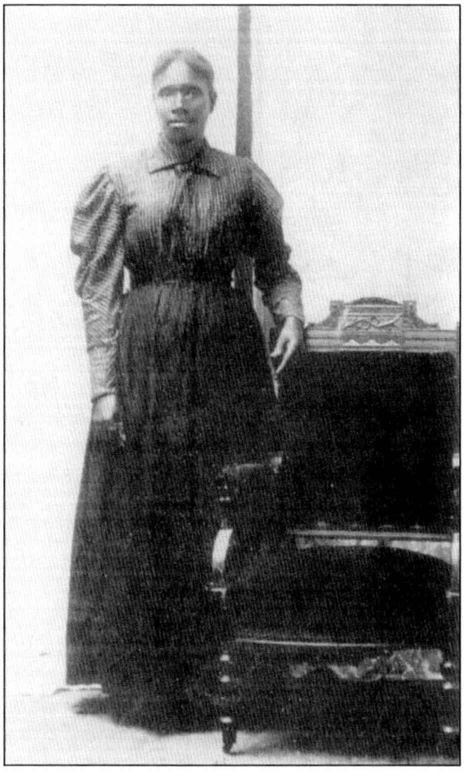

Called "Bertha," Tabitha Bannister was born in 1847 to Arthur Bannister and Abbie West. She married Osceola (often called "Oscar") Atkins, who had migrated northwest from Sussex to Culpeper on February 23, 1871. The couple had nine children, and most of them relocated to northern cities, especially to Rochester, New York. She died in 1921, and her husband followed in 1925. (Bannister family.)

Virginia "Jennie" Beck (aka Becks) was born in Culpeper in June 1855 to William and Catherine "Kittie" Carter Beck. She married Minor Morton May on November 20, 1878, and they began their family. By 1881, the couple and their one-year-old son William moved to Ohio, where she raised six more children. Her husband worked in the steel mill, earning enough money to educate their children. One of their daughters became a nurse. Virginia Beck May died on October 30, 1939. (Debra Lynn Ashburn.)

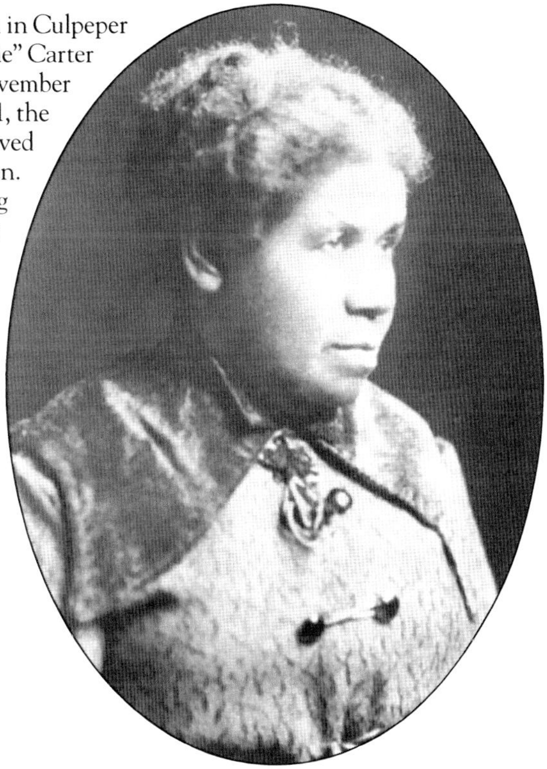

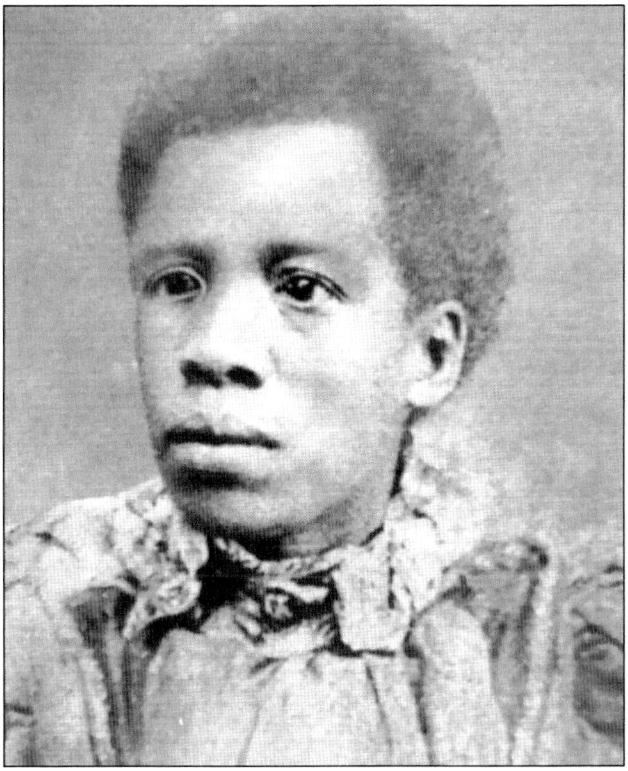

On September 1, 1881, at 18 years old, "Sallie Neal, daughter of Jno and Lise" married "Chs. Coleman, son of Clayton and Julia"—this is how Sallie Coleman was first noted in the public record. What is known is that she was the matriarch of a family of confident, striving, successful sons, several of whom relocated to New York and established careers and families. The oldest, Charles Jr. (born in 1883), formed one of the foundational families in Culpeper, helping to found Eckington school and supporting the growth and development of Free Union Baptist Church. (Hortense Hinton-Jackson.)

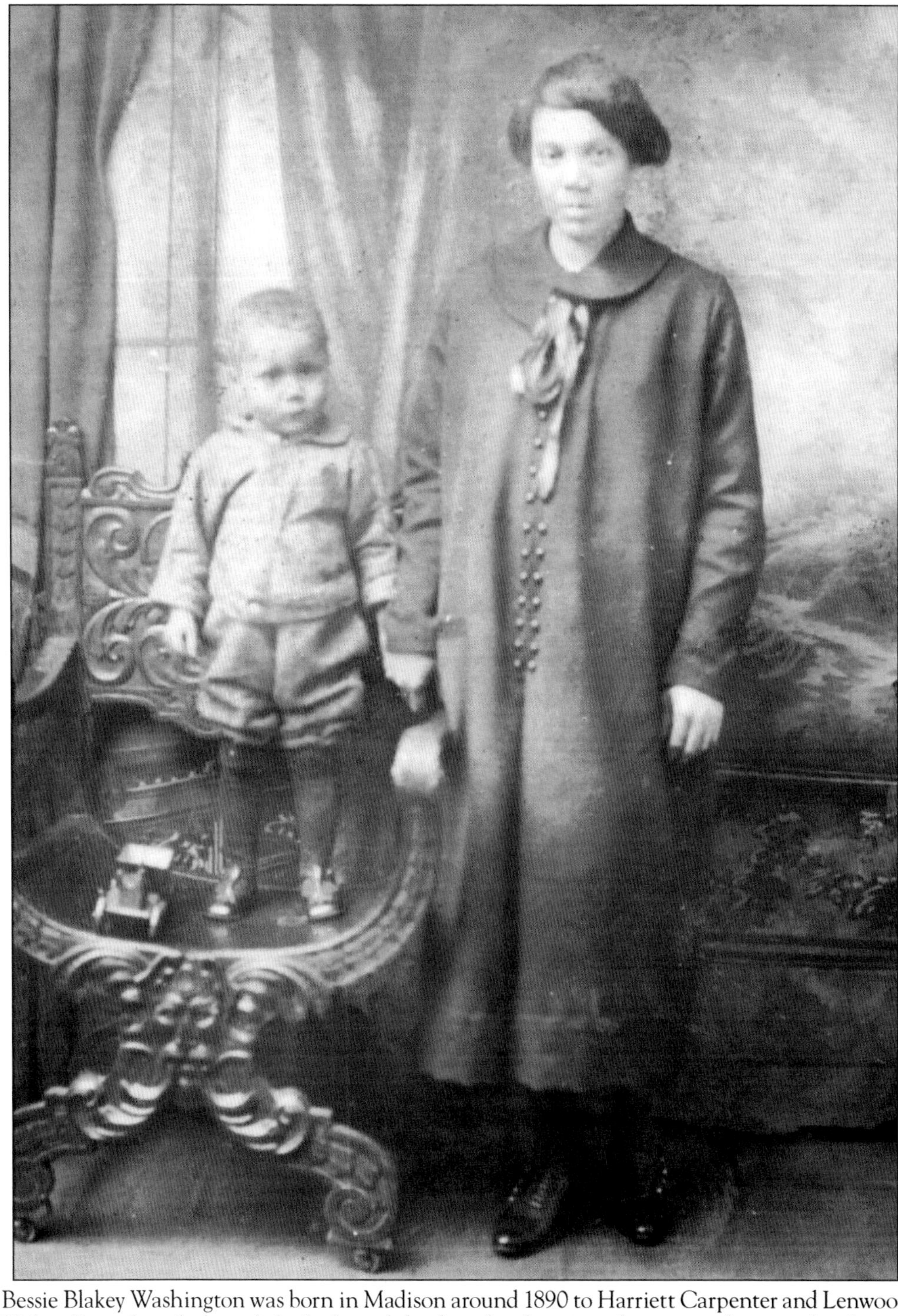

Bessie Blakey Washington was born in Madison around 1890 to Harriett Carpenter and Lenwood Blakey. Even though she only had a formal third-grade education, she was taught to read and write by her mother. Bessie is shown here with her son Carl. She was the wife of Daniel Washington and matriarch to a family of boys. She died in April 1983 and is buried at Second Robinson Baptist Church in Madison. (Florence Washington.)

Eva Blanche Wilhoite was born on January 11, 1890, to Samuel and Helen Snead Wilhoite in Culpeper. After her education, she met and married Illinois-born Herman Charles Beeler. He became a schoolteacher, and the couple moved to her ancestral home in the Cedar Mountain area of Culpeper, where they raised their four children. Herman died in 1946, and Eva supported herself and the family as a domestic worker. She died on October 17, 1964, of a heart attack and is buried in the family cemetery in Buena. (Lindsay Jackson.)

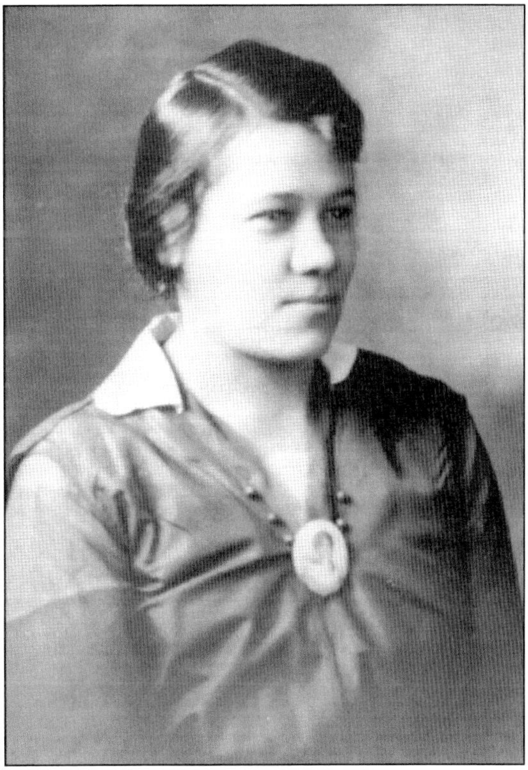

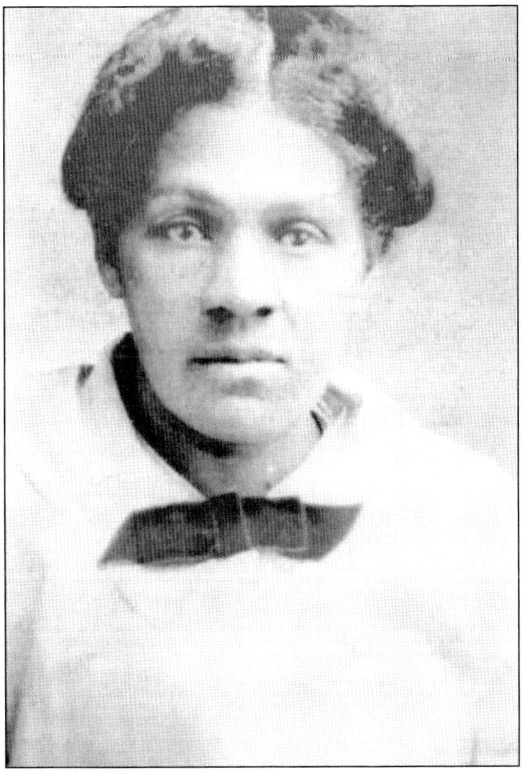

Florence Cordelia Johnson was born in Culpeper in July 1869 to Jacob and Annie F. Johnson. She married James Henry Washington on December 3, 1896. In her lifetime, she birthed 12 known children. When she was only 59 years old, her husband unexpectedly died of a stroke in 1927. Choosing not to remarry, she supported her family as a domestic worker while still tending the family farm. She died on April 10, 1961, and is buried in the family cemetery. (Johnson family.)

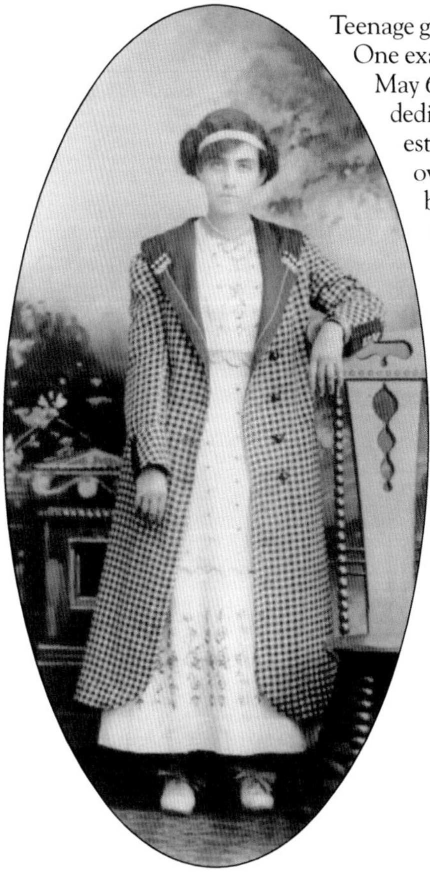

Teenage girls largely learned to be homemakers from their mothers. One example is Fenton Frye, daughter of Ida Ralls Frye. Born on May 6, 1898, Fenton married Newton Gibson, a wounded yet dedicated and determined World War I veteran, in 1921. They established their household near his ancestral home, and over eight years, the couple had six children. In 1937, she became a widow at only 37 years old when her husband died of pneumonia. With the help of family, she and her children thrived. After Fenton's health failed due to cancer complications, she died on January 15, 1967. (William H. Lewis.)

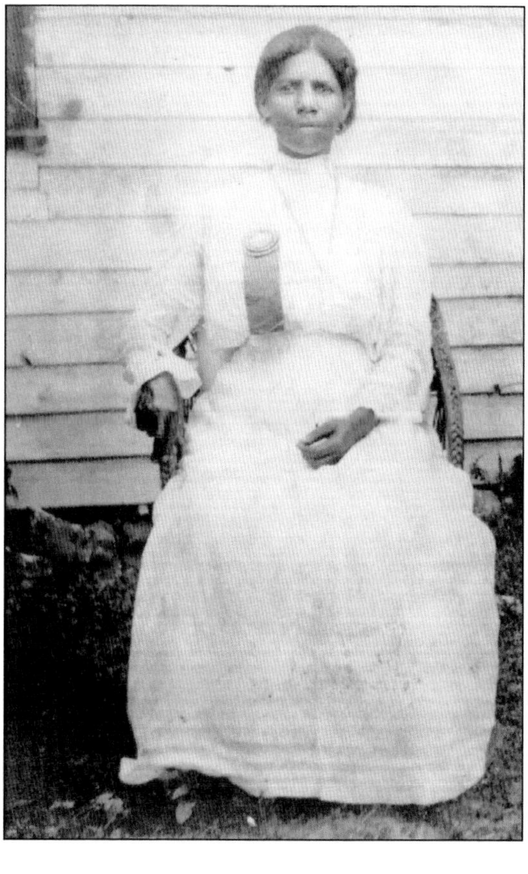

Susan Madison was born around 1864 in Orange to Nathaniel Madison and Eveline Williams. She married William Hills Ellis on January 8, 1889, and the couple had five children: Tump, Matt, Julia May, Jennie, and Fannie. By 1920, her youngest child was a teacher. To help support her household, Susan worked as a laundress while encouraging her children and grandchildren to understand the value of an education. At 97 years old, she died on March 22, 1958, of heart disease and was laid to rest on her own land in the family plot. (Ellis family.)

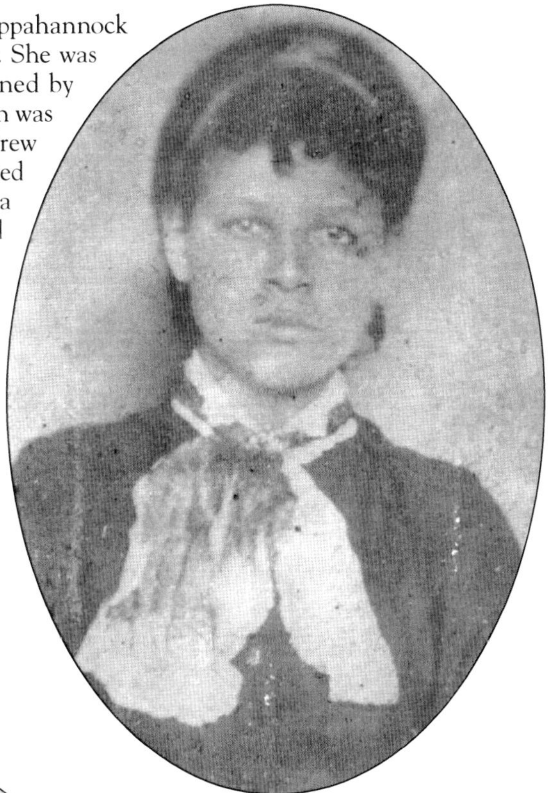

It is unknown how Amy Gordon got to Rappahannock after her enslavement in Caroline County. She was recorded as being born to Mary and owned by Bazil Gordon in 1859. By 1870, Amy Gordon was living in Rappahannock in the John Andrew Bowersett household; both are listed as married (assumedly to one another). Bowersett was a local merchant. In Amy's lifetime, she had three children. She does not appear in the public record after 1889. (Brown family.)

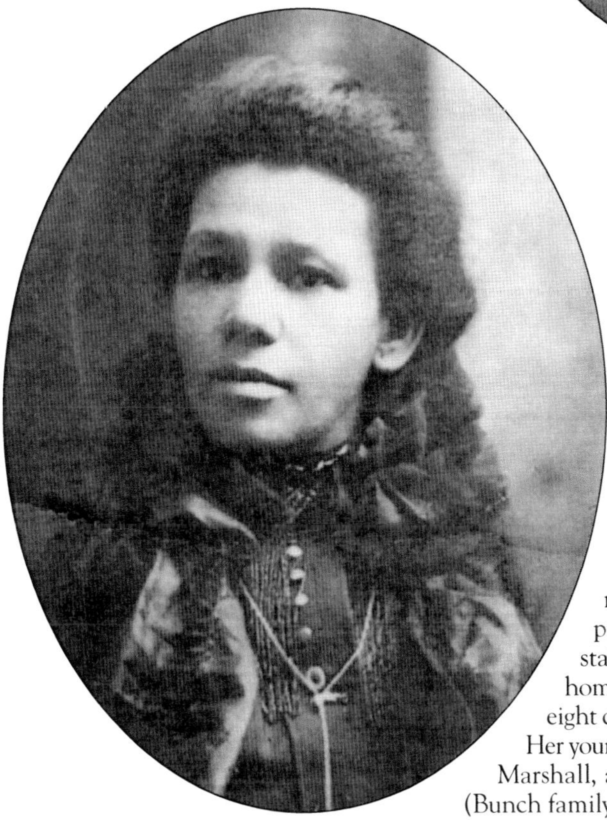

The woman known as Maria Clifton Tyler was born around 1858. The location of her birth and her parentage are unstated. She was married on January 3, 1878, to Walter Wellington West (1857–1937), who worked for the US Postal Service railway. Because of his profession, he provided a large measure of financial stability to the family. Maria opened their home to boarders. Over the years, she had eight children, and six survived to adulthood. Her youngest daughter, Ruth, married Mortimer Marshall, a prominent undertaker in Culpeper. (Bunch family.)

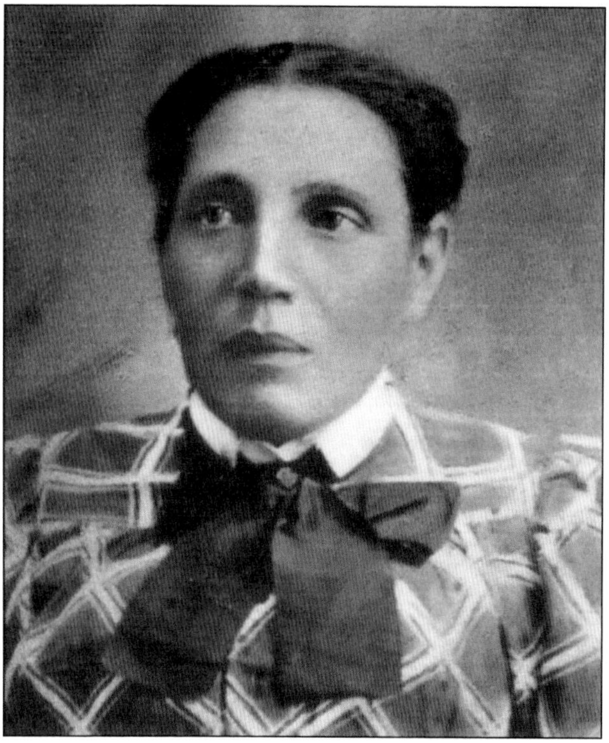

Ella Carpenter Walker was married to Frank Walker, and they lived in Madison. Born around 1859 to Charles and Mary Tutt Clore, she and her husband had 10 children. The couple and some of their neighbors were instrumental in organizing both Oak Park Baptist Church and the adjacent school. She died on September 16, 1934, and is buried in the church cemetery next to her husband. (Clore family.)

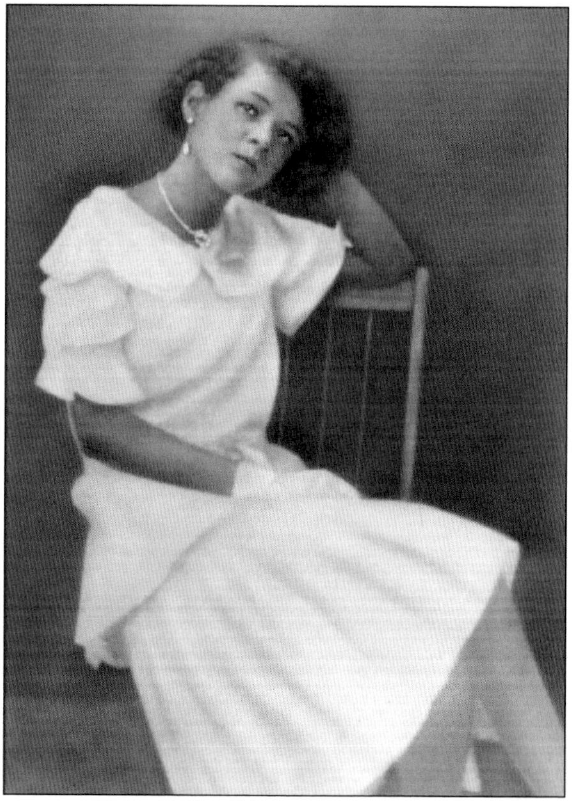

Alice L. Grigsby was born in 1914 to Albert Pendleton and Fannie Rebecca Williams Grigsby. She married Charles Lewis Brown (1913–1988) on August 3, 1930, and the couple had two children, Raymond, born in 1931, and Charles, born in 1933. Alice died shortly after giving birth to Charles. (Brown family.)

Rappahannock native Annie Phillips was married to Alexander Robinson Sr. Born in November 1870, she reportedly was the daughter of William Jonathan Huff and Lucy M. Phillips. She married Alexander on March 3, 1889, and the couple relocated to Harrisburg, Pennsylvania. They raised a family of four children. Their last child was Alexander Lancaster Robinson, born on February 12, 1903. Annie died six months later, on August 27, of pneumonia and is buried in the historic Lincoln Cemetery in Harrisburg. (Robinson family.)

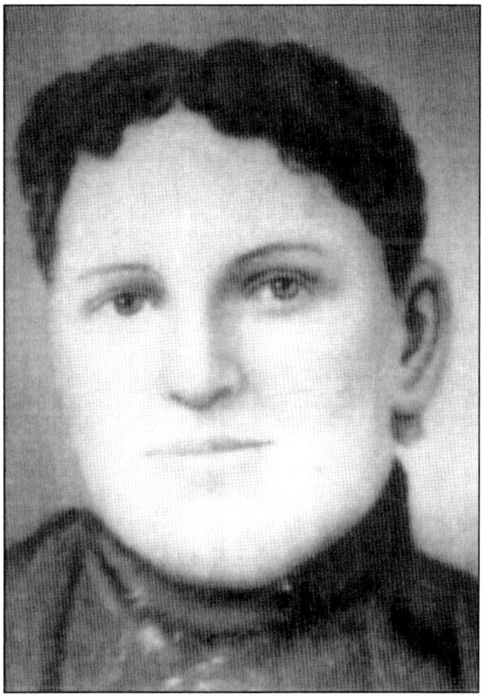

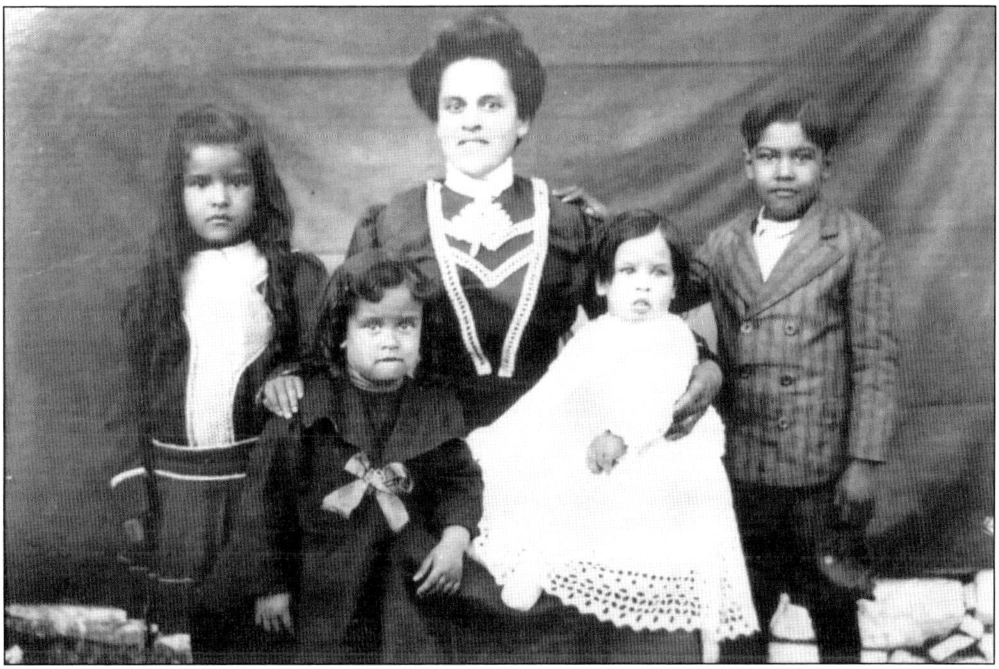

The oldest of five known children of Charles and Edmonia Williams, Irie Lee Williams Brown was born in neighboring Fauquier on February 7, 1883. Around 1906, she became the second wife of widower Rev. Lewis Brown and moved to Rappahannock. Twenty-five years her senior, Reverend Brown was both a farmer and minister and, by 1930, reported $7,000 in wealth. He died in 1932 of stomach cancer. They were the parents of eight known children. Many years after Brown's death, Irie was remarried for a brief time to Pendleton Wilson Williams Jr. (Brown family.)

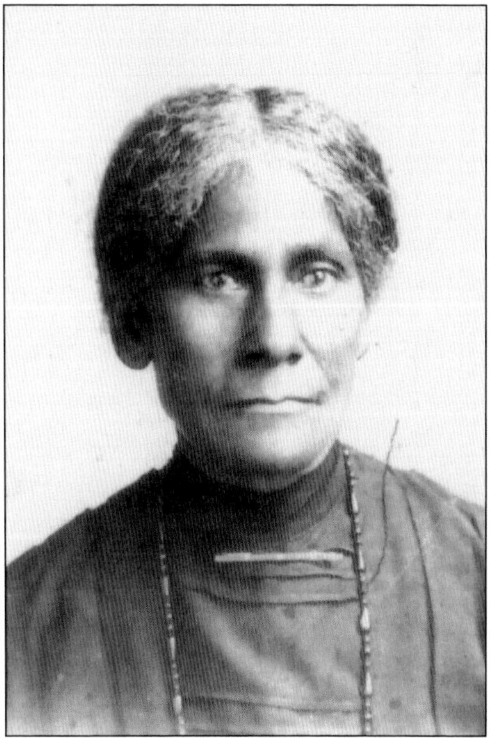

Dora Bundy was born on June 15, 1853, in Culpeper to Warner and Annie Bundy. She married Frank French Menefee Jr. on December 27, 1876. The couple had nine known children. Frank was a farmer who died in 1917. Dora continued to care for the farm and family until her elder years, when she relocated to Pennsylvania with one of her children, Daniel. She died on March 10, 1931, of a stroke. Her family brought her body home to Culpeper and buried her in Fairview Cemetery. (Bundy family.)

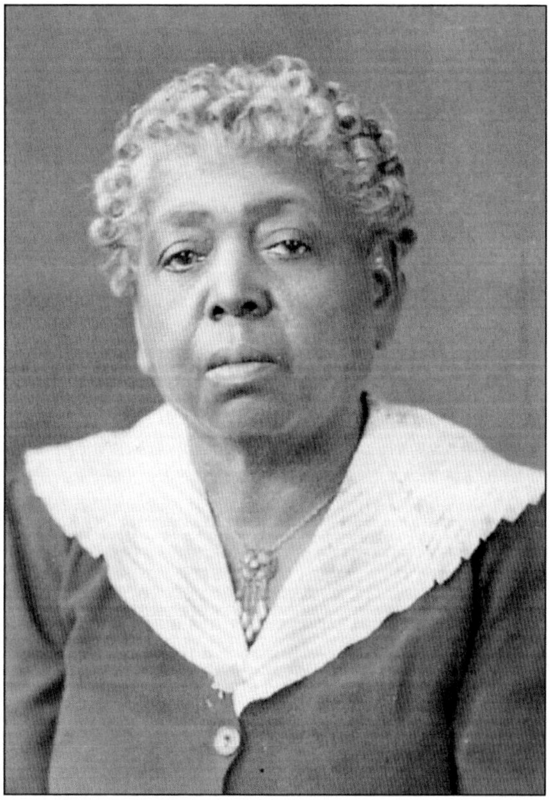

Kate Victoria Williams was born in Orange to James T. and Hannah Payne Williams on April 16, 1878. She married Moses Prophit Jackson in 1905, and the couple had seven known children. Her oldest, Cora, died of tuberculosis in 1933, and barely two years later, her husband died of kidney disease. She relocated to Pittsburgh to be near one of her other children, where she worked as a domestic. She died on March 26, 1955, and is buried in Pittsburgh. (Jackson family.)

Born in Orange in 1864, Mildred Williams Willis was the daughter of Anderson and Eveline Presley Williams, the younger sister of Baptist minister James Williams, and the wife of William Granville Willis, whom she married on February 7, 1889. She was known as a woman of strong and independent religious beliefs at a time when convention was better accepted. She and Williams had nine known children, and her home was often filled with her grandchildren, many of whom she raised after the deaths of her oldest son and his wife. She died on October 25, 1965, at age 101. (Katrina May.)

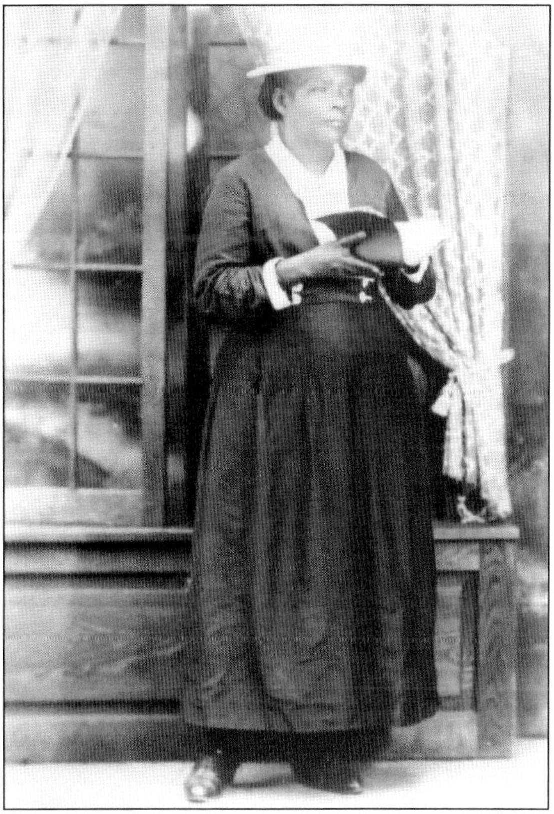

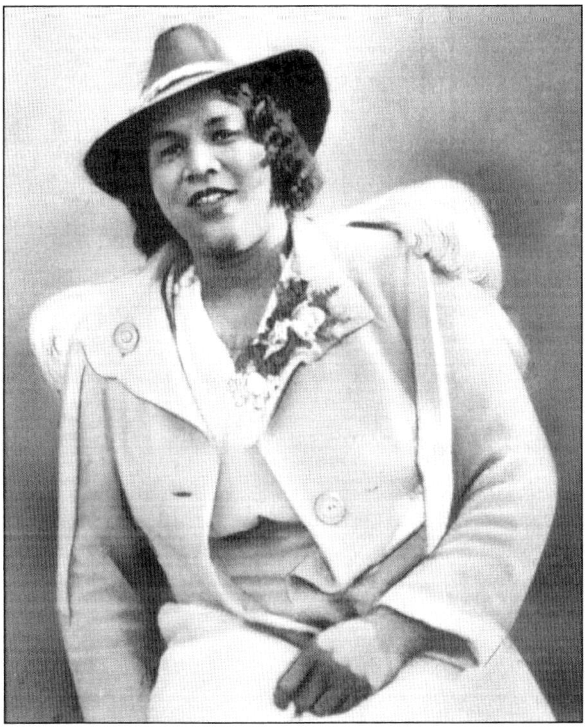

Daisy J. Green was born in Orange to Susan Minor on September 23, 1913. By 1916, Daisy's mother had relocated to Pittsburgh, Pennsylvania, and Daisy remained in Orange and was raised by her grandmother, Polly Minor. On April 14, 1923, her widowed grandmother remarried to John W. Carter, and after 10 years of marriage, Polly Minor passed away. A teenaged Daisy had already left Orange County for Pittsburgh and obtained employment as a live-in maid for a private family. She had begun a new life for herself in Pennsylvania, and in early 1941, she married Leroy Smith. Within a few months of her new marriage, she died on June 9, 1941, from a combination of complications of larynx surgery and heart disease. (Smith family.)

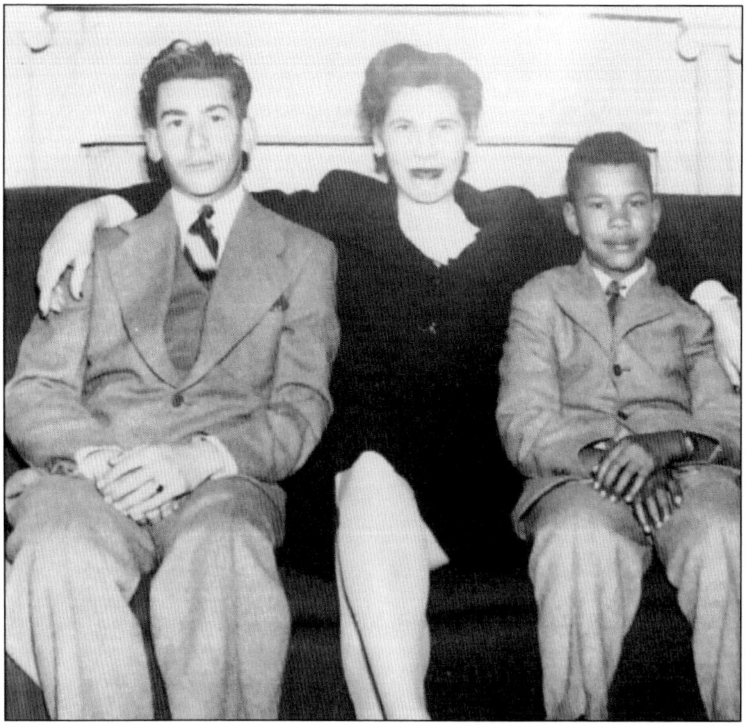

Madison-born Martha Wright (b. 1908) was the only known child of James and Dora Goffney Wright. Her parents were instrumental in the rearing of her older son Willie (left) so that she could relocate to earn a living. She later married Roy Rose Jackson and had another son, Robert (right). She lived most of her adult life in Washington, DC, and died there as Martha Wright Jackson Hatcher in March 1990. (D.K. Tinsley.)

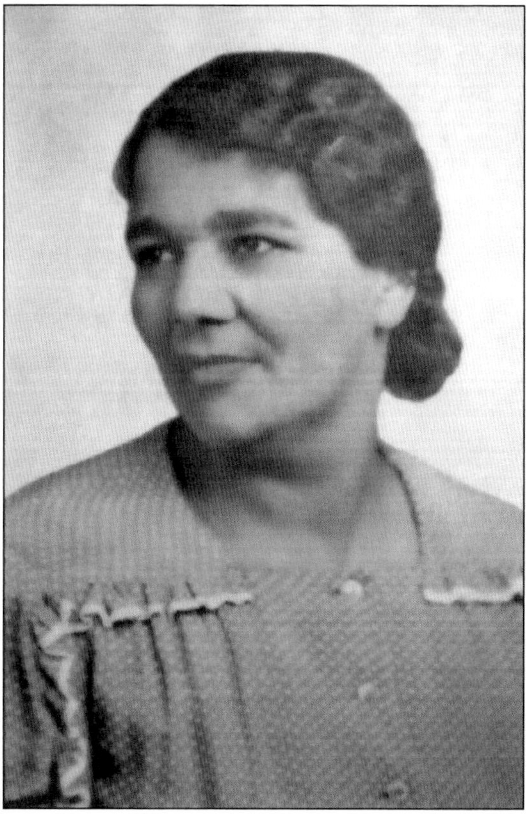

Born in Rappahannock in November 1899, Zephyr Jones Jackson was the third child of Catherine Jones. Zephyr was initially raised in the home of her grandmother, Ida Jones, and Zephyr's mother married Hugh Jackson in 1906. As a child, Zephyr and her family were tenants on the farm of William and Nannie Yancey. She married World War I veteran and widower Henry Glasker (1896–1973) on April 20, 1929. He came to the marriage with four children under the age of 10. The new couple had an additional five children. She died in January 1991 and was laid to rest in Shiloh Baptist Church cemetery in Rappahannock. (Samuel Glasker.)

Five

When They Chose Another Profession

Not everyone chose farming as an occupation, especially upon emancipation in the mid-1860s, when a large number of the labor force, especially males, left the region. Those who remained were skilled blacksmiths, stonemasons, and carpenters. Others began new careers as railroad men, sawmill workers, tailors, and medical doctors. Women used their homemaking skills, such as sewing and laundering, to increase their number of customers. Some professionalized their caretaking skills and became midwives. Men seeking professions that did not require walking behind a mule chose careers that required relocation to northern industrial states such as Maryland, Pennsylvania, New York, and New Jersey. Washington, DC, was an excellent source of government employment, and into the 1930s, many residents found the means to begin a new life there.

No matter how they chose to earn money, the generation that grew up after slavery ended worked diligently to provide better opportunities for their children and grandchildren than they were afforded.

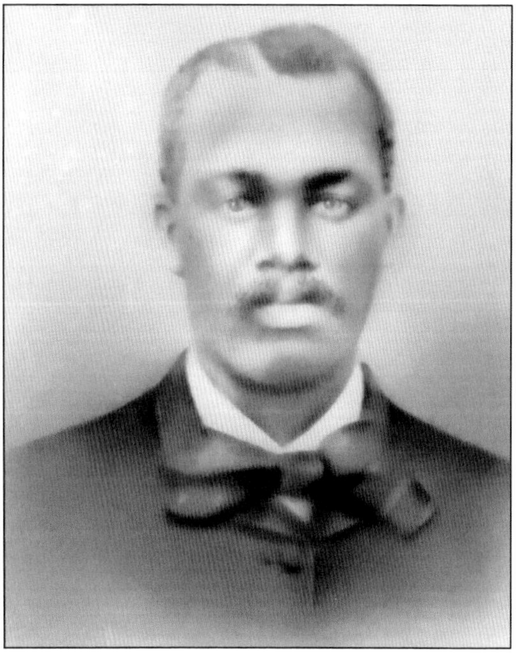

After slavery, Sawney Payne left Louisa County and settled in Culpeper. This son of Joseph and Gracie Bell Payne met and married schoolteacher Cora Lee Lewis in October 1885, earned his professional barber's license, and purchased a house in an integrated neighborhood of downtown Culpeper, where he opened his shop on Main Street and served a mostly white clientele. He raised his family of five boys and two girls, who grew to become professionals in their own right. Sawney Payne died on January 8, 1922. (Angela J. Chapman.)

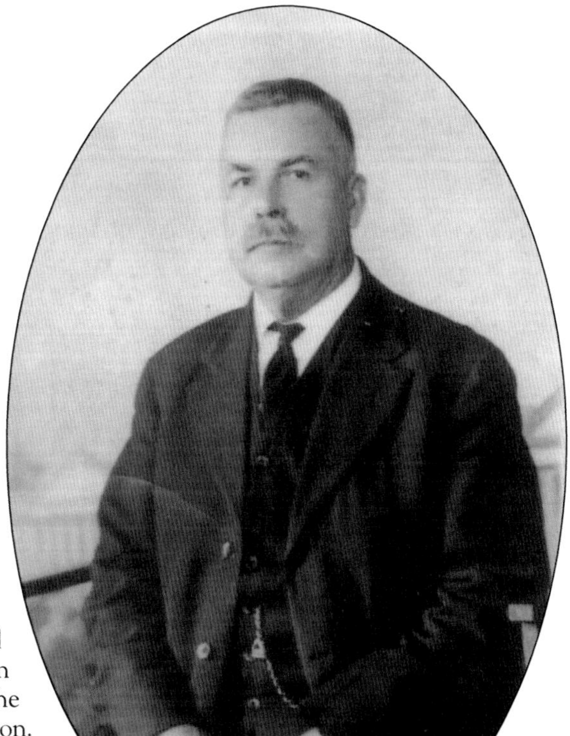

Walter Wellington West was born in Culpeper on May 6, 1857, to Betty Dean. He married Maria Clifton Tyler, and the couple had six surviving children. West was an active member in Virginia's 8th Congressional District of "colored Republicans," participating specifically in 1889 to draft a resolution supporting the presidential election of Benjamin Harrison. He was a 35-year US Postal Service railroad employee, affording his family opportunities for wider experiences than those available to many of their peers. He died on February 20, 1937. (West family.)

Culpeper-born Belle Morton supported herself as a cook for a private family. She was born around September 1877 to Henry and Lena Morton and lived in the Cedar Mountain area. By 1900, she was working as a nurse, caring for the newborn of the Daniel and Kate Slaughter family, who were white. (Morton family.)

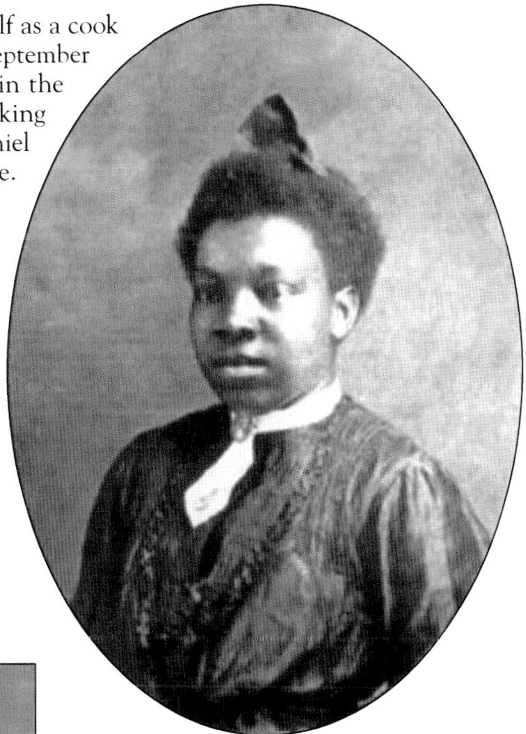

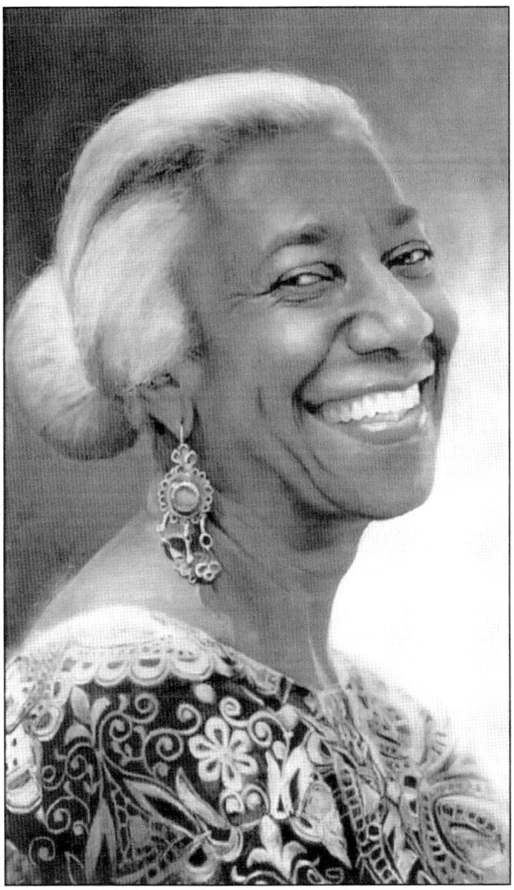

Entrepreneur, master chef, restauranteur, and author Edna Lewis was born in 1916 in the Freetown community of Orange County. She was the second of four children of Eugene and Daisy Belle Lewis. Her father died in the 1920s. After her mother died in 1941, she accepted an opportunity to become a chef at a New York restaurant where her clients were the literati and celebrities of the city. She died in 2006 at age 89. In 2014, the US Postal Service honored her with a Forever Stamp (the portrait featured on the stamp is shown here) celebrating her as one of the premier chefs of Southern cooking. (Lewis estate.)

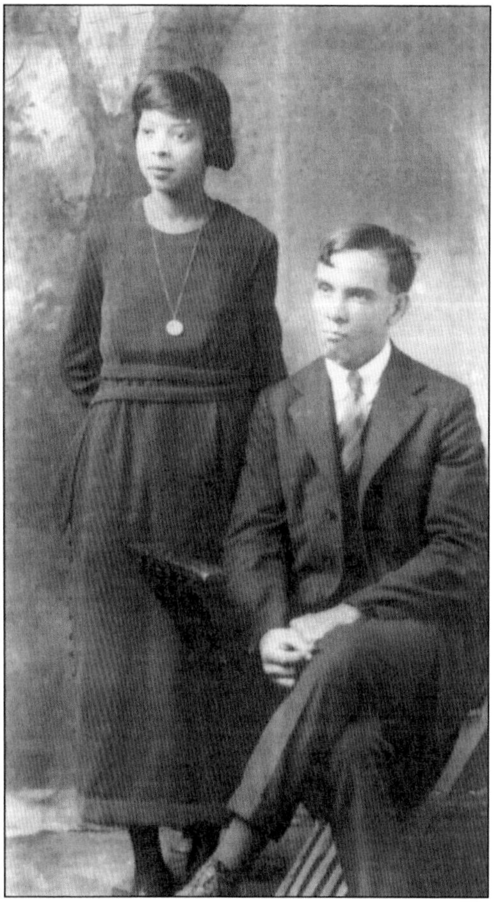

The daughter of Lee Becks and Dora Holmes, Sadie Nora (August 12, 1900–1992) was married to Linwood Frye (January 20, 1901–March 25, 1973). His parents were Elliott and Lena Frye. He first supported his family as a sawyer, and, in his later years, he farmed his land. (Beck family.)

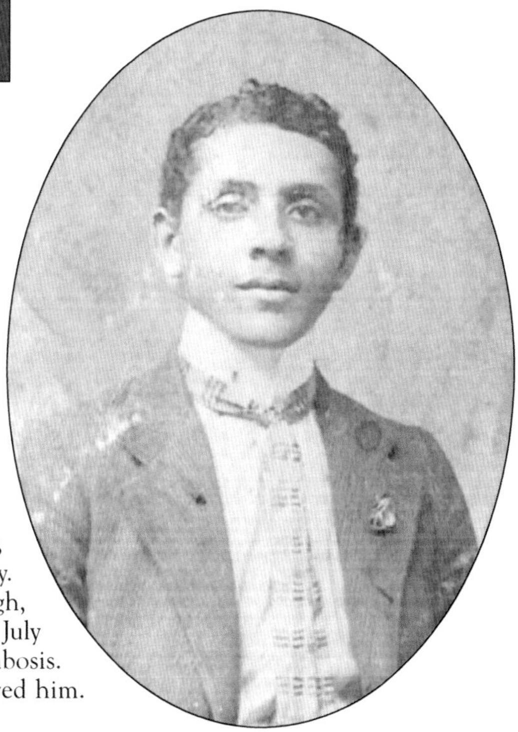

Henry Lee Jeffries Sr., son of John Jeffries Sr. and Ella Parker Brooks, was born October 1, 1877, in Amissville. In 1902, he married Rappahannock native Sarah Catherine Grigsby, daughter of Albert and Louise Toliver Grigsby. By 1904, the couple had moved to Pittsburgh, Pennsylvania, and started a family. He died on July 30, 1964, of pneumonia and cerebral thrombosis. He had worked as a janitor. His wife survived him. (Jeffries family.)

Herman Charles Beeler was born in Grand Tower, Illinois, to Curtis and Emma Jones Beeler. In 1917, he was working in Indiana as a bookkeeper. When he registered for the First World War, he reported that he suffered from heart trouble. He eventually relocated to Washington, DC, where he worked as a schoolteacher and married Eva Wilhoite. The couple had four children (daughter Emma is shown with her father) and moved to Eva's homeplace in Buena, Culpeper, where, in 1941, Herman was appointed US postmaster of the Buena station. He died on November 13, 1946, of heart disease. (Beeler family.)

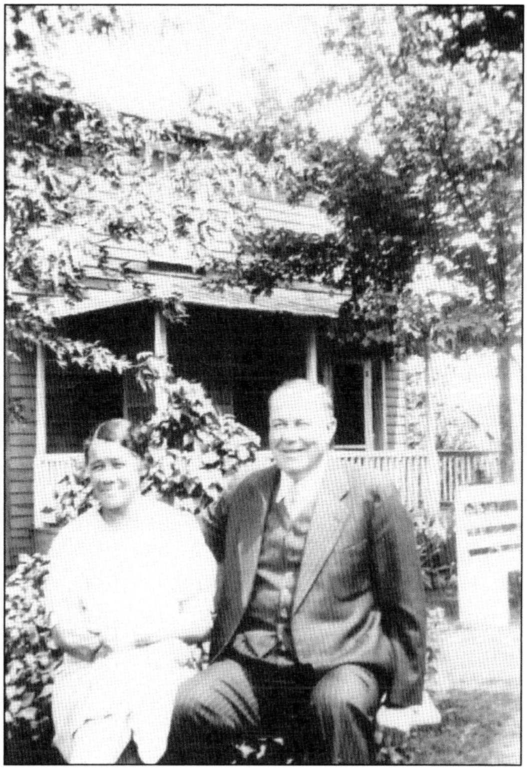

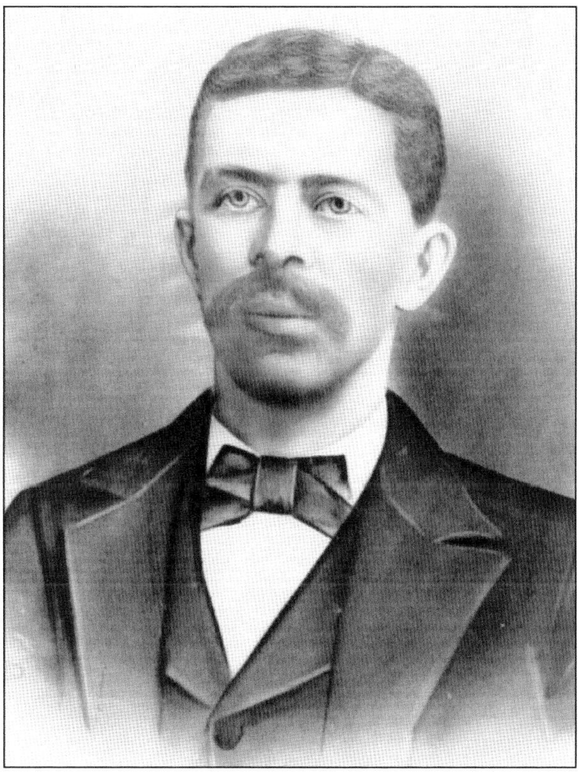

John Thomas Jackson was born in Culpeper on December 12, 1862, to Philip and Sarah Newby Jackson. By the time he married Lillie George Jameson, he was working as a farmer, merchant, and tanner. He was appointed postmaster in Alanthus on March 23, 1891. It is said that no one was more prominent in the Alanthus neighborhood than John, a father of six, and his family. He was 85 years old when he died on October 26, 1948. (Jackson family.)

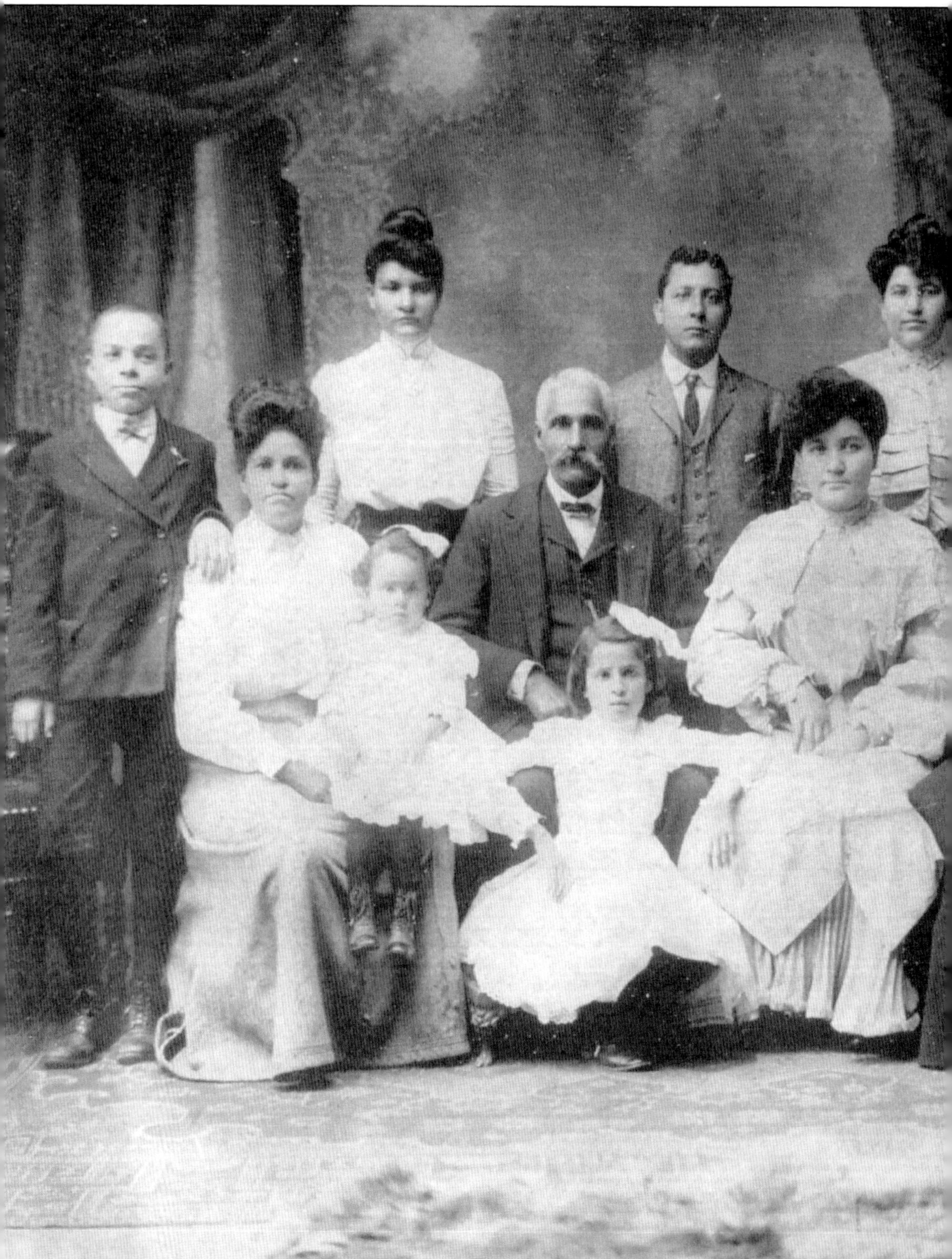

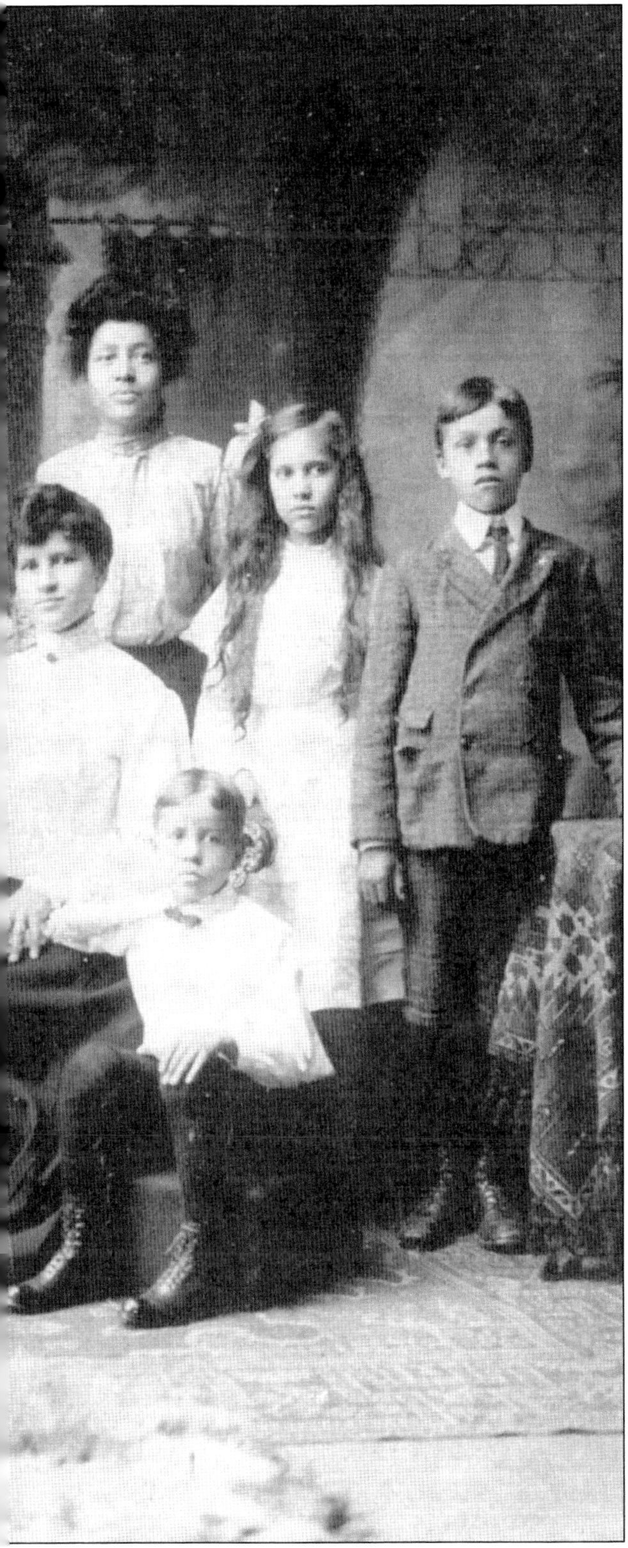

Champ Clore was born in Madison County around 1838 to Aaron and Eliza Clore. He thrived in his profession as a cooper. He first married Virginia "Jennie" Jackson, daughter of Pete Jackson. After her death in 1888, he remarried in 1894 to Agnes Lane. In his older years, he relocated to the Pittsburgh suburbs and was cared for by one of his daughters, Ella Maria (seated at far right). Others in this photograph who are positively identified are (left to right): Champ's daughter Crim Memoria (seated); Champ's daughter Sarah (standing next to Crim); the patriarch, Champ (seated); Champ's son-in-law Frank Amoreaux (standing behind Champ); and Champ's daughter Anna Blanche Clore Amoreaux (standing next to Frank). Champ Clore died at age 90 on December 22, 1928. (Kimberly Milai.)

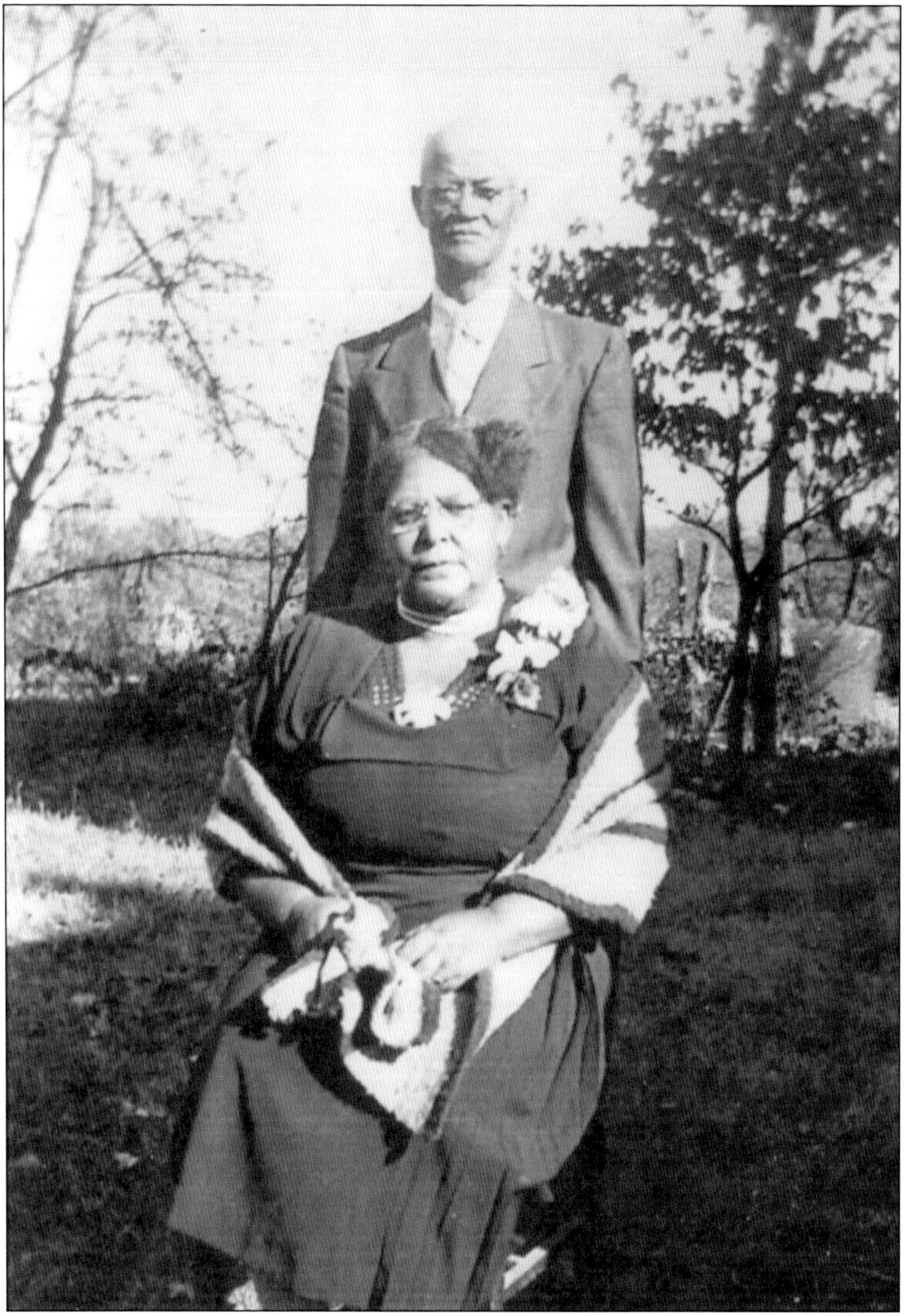

Madison County natives Isaiah and Rebecca Snyder James celebrated their 50th wedding anniversary in 1954. He was a twin born to Curtis and Lucy M. James on May 30, 1884. His wife was born to Edmund Snyder and Martha Winkie. They had four children, one of whom died from tuberculosis. The James family sent their children to schools outside of the region. Isaiah was a farmer with significant family ties to the Walker family, originators of the Woodberry Forest School, where he worked. (Davis family.)

At times, one's worth cannot be measured by regular payments received on a job. Circumstances can dictate choices. Being available to assist elderly parents was the choice of John William Willis, oldest son of William G. and Mildred Willis of Orange. He briefly worked in Pennsylvania, where he married Phoebe Rose Terrill on May 29, 1919. He and his wife returned to the homeplace, had children, and he helped his father with the farm as well as laboring in local industries. John's father died in 1940, his wife died in 1943, and he died in 1948. (Katrina May.)

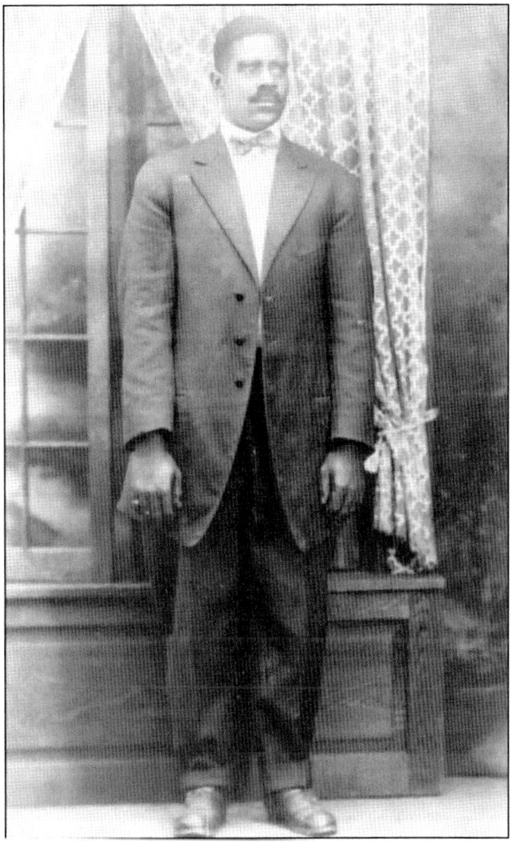

Born to Tobias and Sally White Goings on December 17, 1896, Frederick Alexander Goings was the general contractor for brick masonry work on the Carver Regional High School in Culpeper. He married Kathleen Chapman, and the couple worked together to create several successful businesses. Tobias continued contracting and also operated a garage. Sally cooked and sold lunches and dinners from their store, and they also had a service station for vehicles. Tobias died from injuries received in an automobile accident on November 23, 1963. (Angela J. Chapman.)

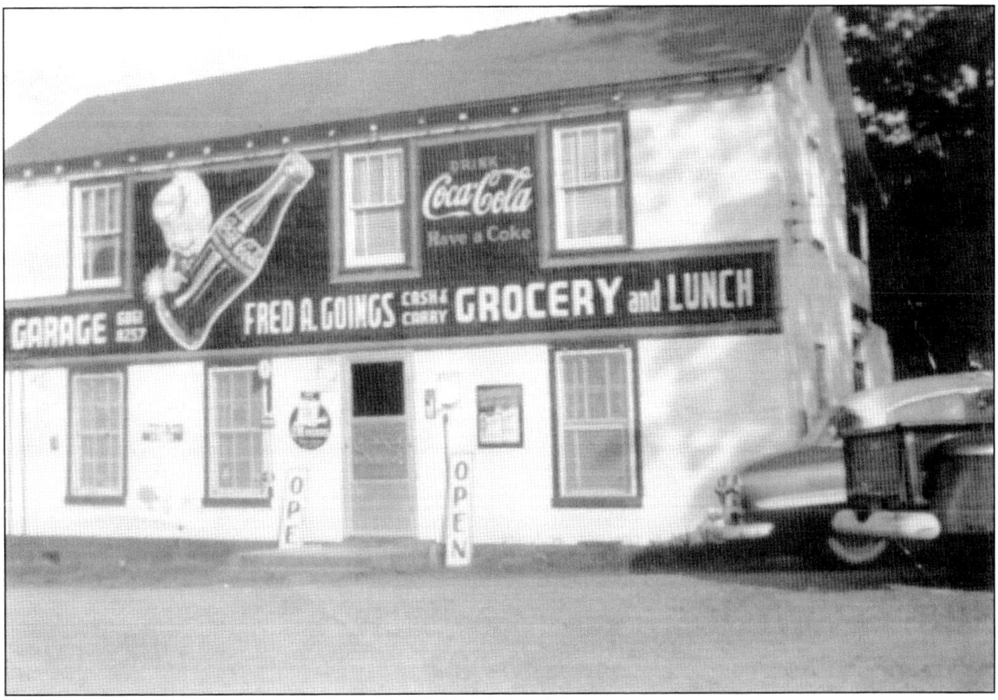

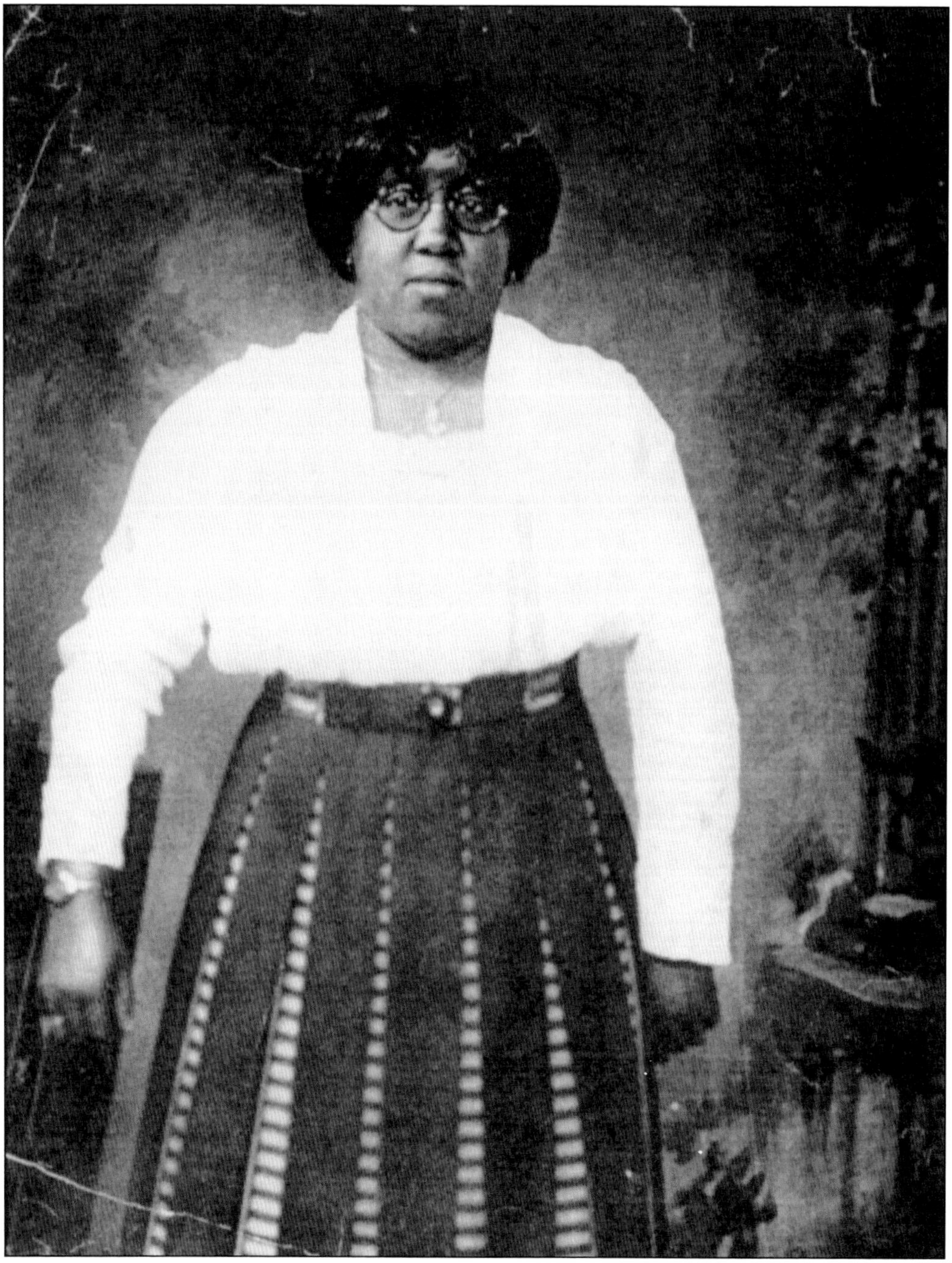

Bertha Gray, one of five children of Lewis and Ellen Martha Atkins Gray, was born in Culpeper around 1892. Her grandparents were Oseola Atkins and Tabitha Banister Atkins. By 1910, she and one of her younger brothers had moved to Rochester, New York, and lived with their aunt and uncle. She made New York her home, giving birth to one child, whom she named after her mom, Martha. By 1930, she had set up a business as a laundress. Her daughter, son-in-law, grandson, and her aunt, Martha Tibbs, also lived with her. In addition, she took in boarders. She died of unknown causes. (Atkins family.)

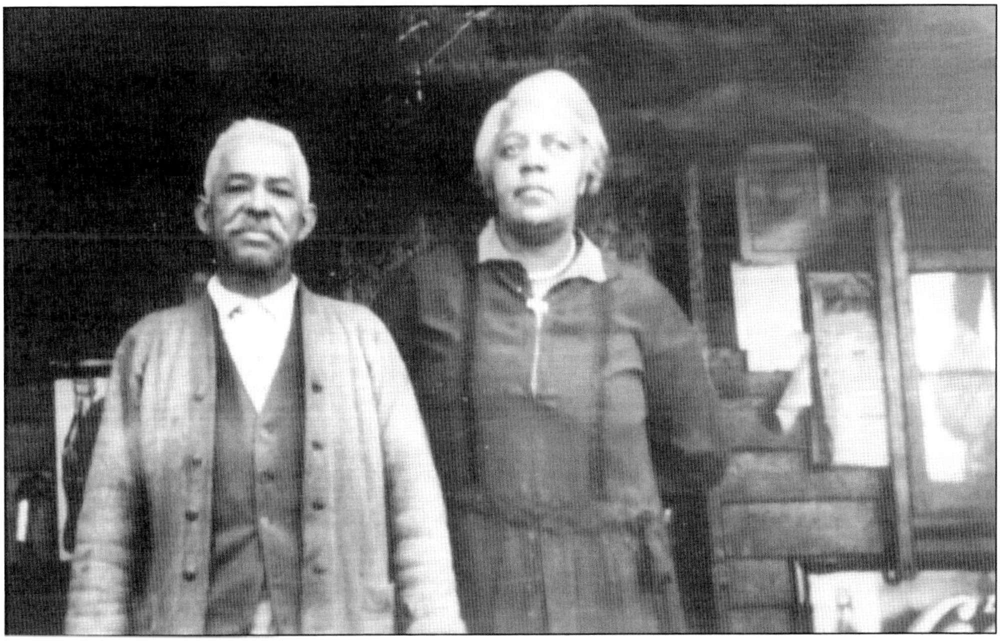

In 1932, there were 15 one- and two-room schools for African American children in Culpeper. Each served local children who lived nearby. One of the schools, the Thompson School, was established around 1927 by local merchants Charles and Amanda Green Thompson (pictured) and served by two teachers—Etta Grayson, who taught fourth through seventh grades, and one of Charles and Amanda's daughters, Lillian Thompson, who taught first through third grades. (Virginia State University Archives.)

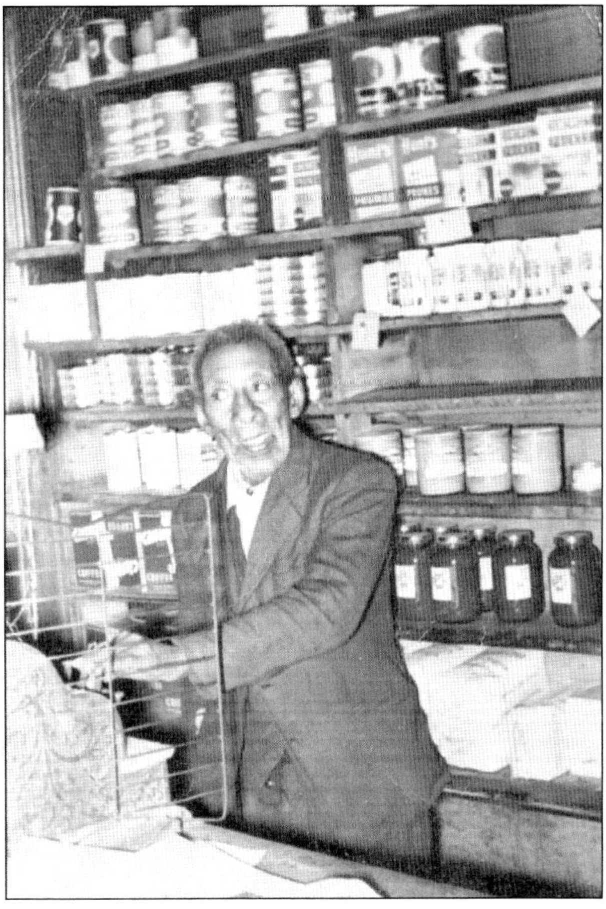

Peter Cypress Christian owned a grocery store in Orange County for more than 20 years. He was born on January 7, 1852, in Louisa County to Toby and Tiny Christian and later married Mary Ellen Johnson. Christian died at 97 years old of complications from tuberculosis on September 2, 1949, and is buried in Woodberry Cemetery in Gordonsville. (Christian family.)

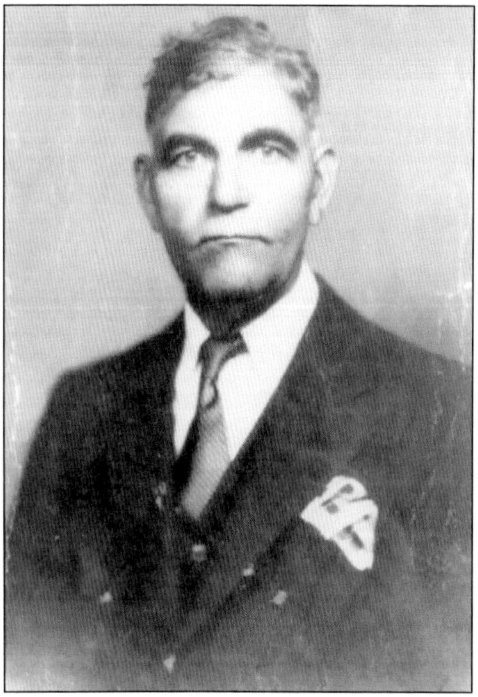

Born in Madison on February 28, 1877, Joseph Clore was the son of Champ and Virginia Jackson Clore. He was a carpenter and married Lula Jackson on April 15, 1905. The couple had 11 known children. He died on June 21, 1964, of heart failure and is buried in Chestnut Grove Baptist Church cemetery in the Brightwood neighborhood of Madison. (Clore family.)

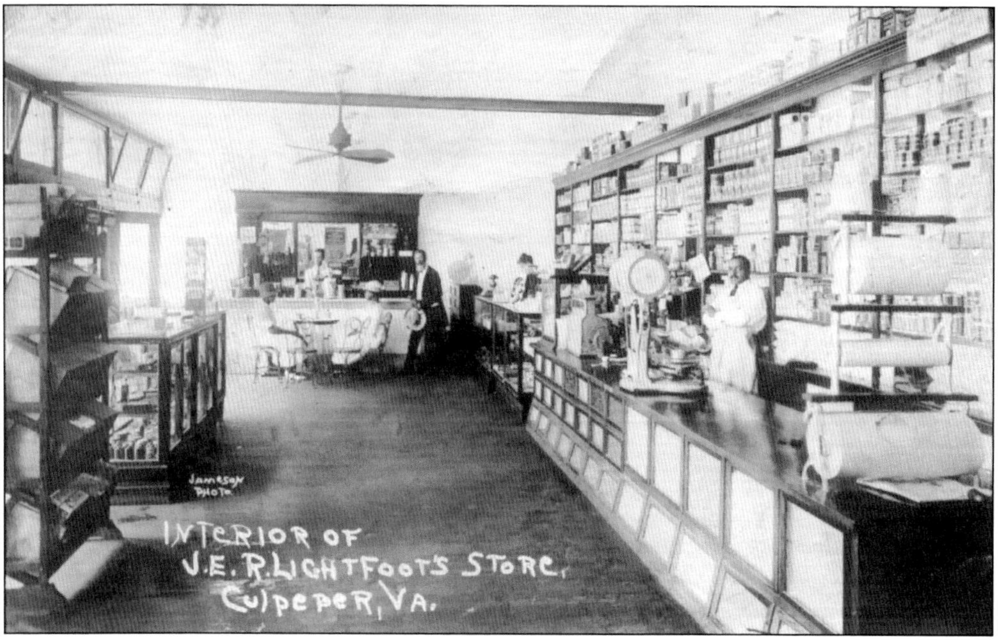

The Lightfoot Store, owned by James Edward Russell "Jesse" Lightfoot, was located on East Davis Street in Culpeper among a community of minority-owned businesses such as Mortimer's Funeral Home and Fred Jackson's barbershop. Jesse Lightfoot was born in 1879 to Henry Clay and Mary Briggs Lightfoot and married Martha Pauline Childs. Lightfoot added a soda fountain so that neighborhood women who worked as domestics had a place to gather, relax, and share information. His store also served as a social mediation location. When his health failed, his son Harrison operated the store until 1943. Lightfoot died on February 28, 1946. (Angela J. Chapman.)

Mary Susan East was born in Orange to William Roger and Susan Shepherd East on December 23, 1909. She was their sixth child. On November 6, 1929, she married Lawrence Wilson Dade Jr., son of Lawrence Sr. and Sarah Walker Dade, and she and her husband made their home in Orange. Mary E. Dade became a midwife but also honed her sewing skills until she became a master seamstress—she was famous throughout the region for making wedding dresses for elite Caucasian clientele. Her devoted husband died on June 30, 1978, and she joined him on October 4 of that same year. They are both buried in West View Cemetery in Orange. (Trumpler family.)

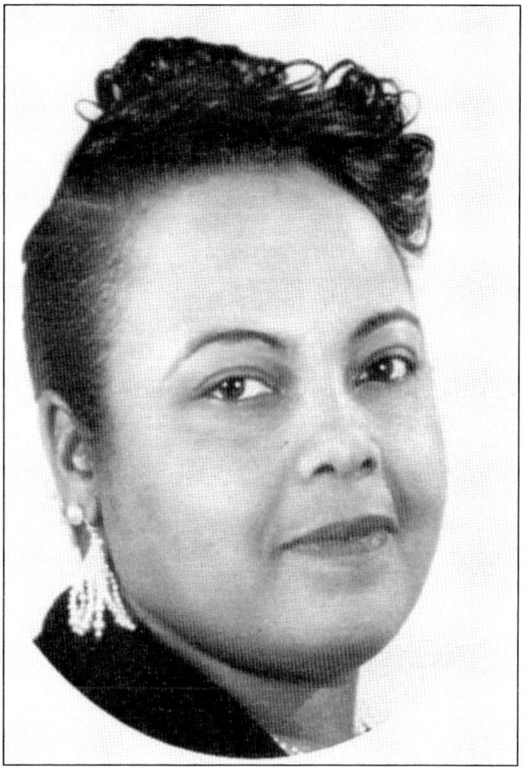

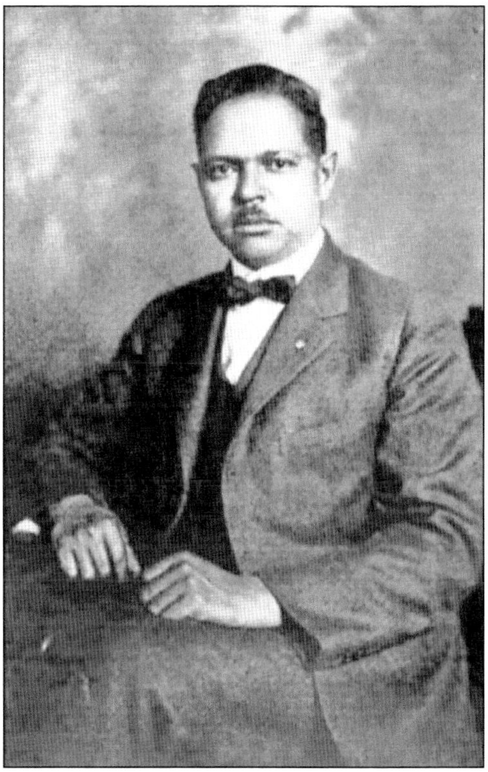

Dr. Isaiah Allen Jackson was born in Orange County on February 2, 1888. By age 23, he had earned a medical degree from the Leonard Medical School at Shaw University in North Carolina. After a brief internship at the Tuskegee Institute, he returned home and opened his practice on November 16, 1911, specializing in ear, nose, and throat ailments. During World War I, he held a commission in the US Army medical corps. His other activities included serving as chairman of the local branch of the Red Cross, state committee and 8th District delegate to the 1920 Republican National Convention in Chicago, and president of the Orange County Colored Horse Show and Racing Association. He died on October 28, 1958. (Lindsay Jackson.)

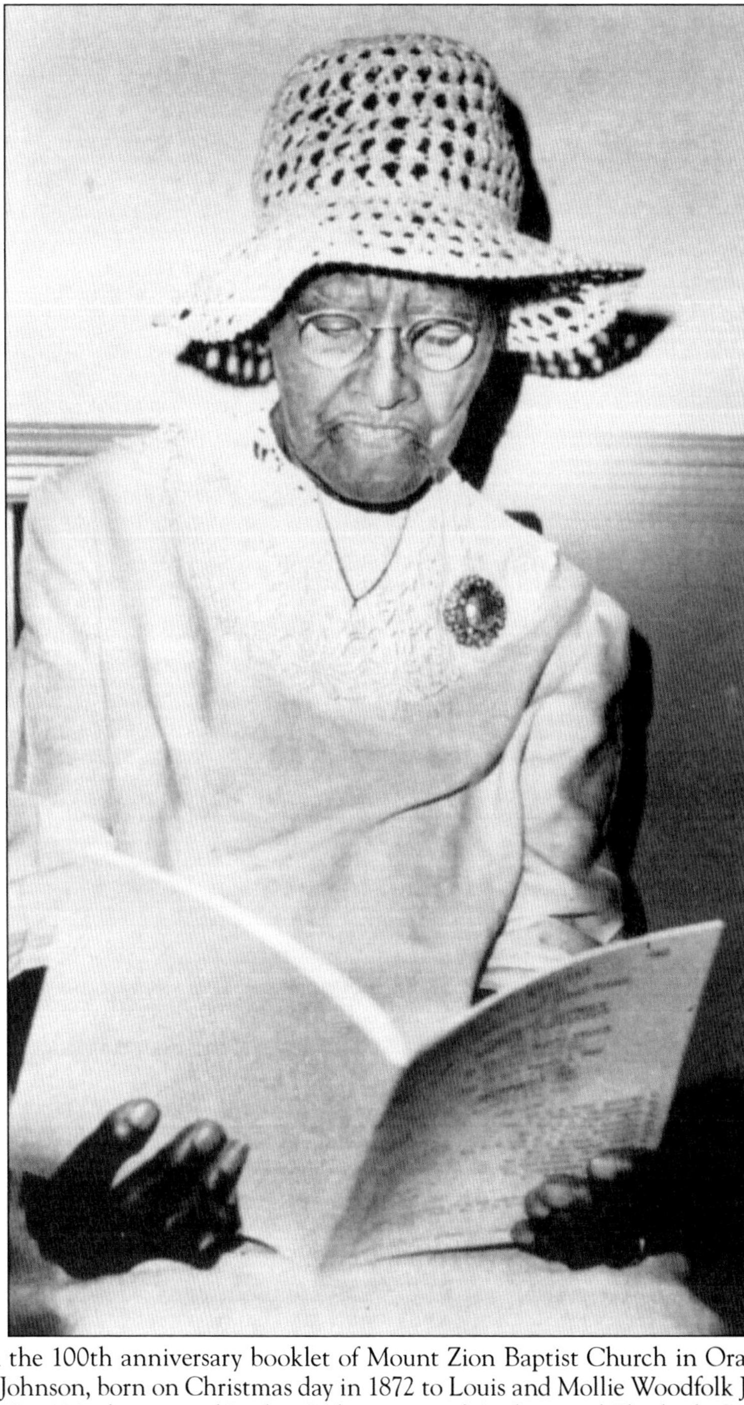

Pictured in the 100th anniversary booklet of Mount Zion Baptist Church in Orange is Mary Magdaline Johnson, born on Christmas day in 1872 to Louis and Mollie Woodfolk Johnson. On September 17, 1890, she married Luther Jackson, son of Andrew and Elizabeth Owen Jackson. She worked as a cook while raising her family. By 1910, she was a widow with three children. She learned midwifery from local doctors in Orange, and for the next 50 years, that was her chosen profession. She remarried to James Daniel, and he died of a stroke on February 1, 1952. She remained single until her death at age 101 on August 21, 1974. (Orange County Historical Society.)

Matthew Alexander Jackson was born in Orange County on August 3, 1879, one of nine children of Allen and Delilah Jackson. He did not follow his brothers into the carpentry business. Instead, in his 20s, he relocated to New York City, where he first worked as a hotel porter and then found work as a shipping clerk for I.S. Wolf & Company on Twenty-fifth Street. His registration card for the First World War notes that he was missing an index finger down to the second joint, which rendered him ineligible for military service. At the time of his death in 1940, he was living on West 138th Street in Manhattan and was still employed by the silk wholesale shipping company. (Lindsay Jackson.)

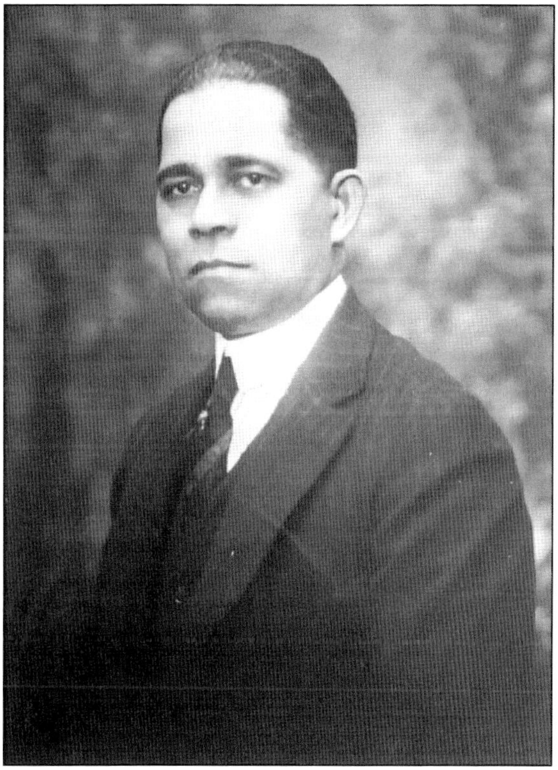

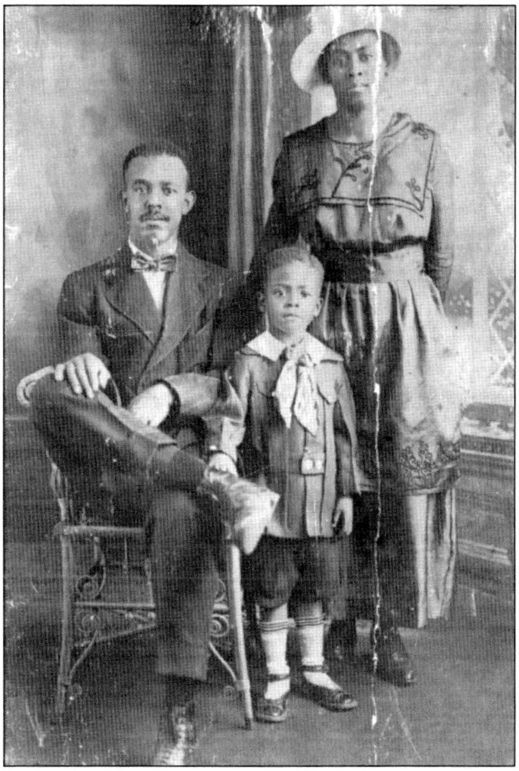

Born in March 1893, Clarence Lewis was the ninth of ten surviving children of Edward Lewis and his wife, Ida Lee Winslow Lewis. His mother died when he was three years old, and he was raised by his older siblings. In 1915, he married Tappahannock, Virginia, native Fannie B. Taylor. The couple briefly relocated to Ardmore, Pennsylvania, before returning to make their home in Culpeper. Pictured here with the couple is their son Clarence Jr., born around 1925. Fannie died in 1963, and Clarence Sr., then a retired truck driver, died in 1966. (George Everett Taylor.)

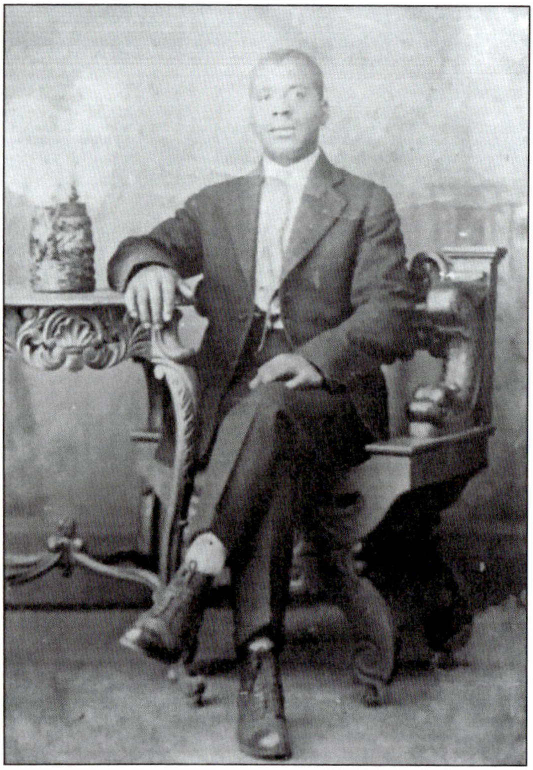

Duke Veney Jackson was the son of David and Caroline Veney Jackson. Veney ancestors were free long before the Civil War. This World War I veteran initially farmed with his father. He later learned the construction trade. He died at age 72 on September 26, 1972, leaving behind a wife (Mary) and several adult children. (Jackson family.)

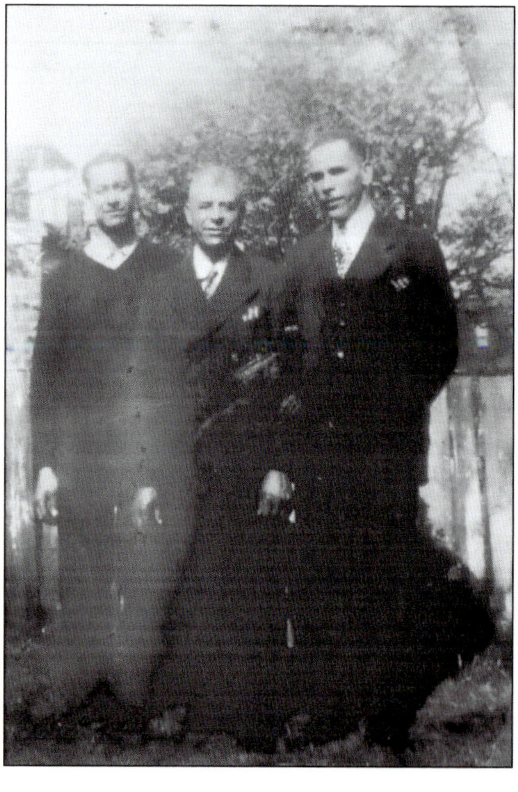

Brothers Carroll (left, 1912–1978), James Clayton (center, 1891–1954), and Richard Lawson (right, 1910–2004) were three of fifteen children born to Hansborough and Estelle Wigginton Lawson of Rappahannock. As they came of age, they relocated to Pennsylvania and worked in the steel industry: Carroll worked in Harrisburg at Central Iron & Steel; James in Steelton at Bethlehem Steel; and Richard in Harrisburg, where he did steel work for a short time. Richard retired from the Pennsylvania Turnpike Commission and was active in civic affairs. (Lawson family.)

Clarence Clifton Tutt was born on June 17, 1890, to Lewis Henry and Mary Willis Jackson Tutt. He married Esther May Ford. In 1917, the couple already had one child, Esther, when Clarence began working as a laborer for his father-in-law's cement company. They worked significantly in the city of Pittsburgh, Pennsylvania. After the death of his first wife in 1943, he remarried to 46-year-old Sarah Elizabeth Jackson, daughter of John Thomas Jackson and Lillie George Jameson. Clarence lived until July 29, 1966, and is buried in the family cemetery. (Tutt family.)

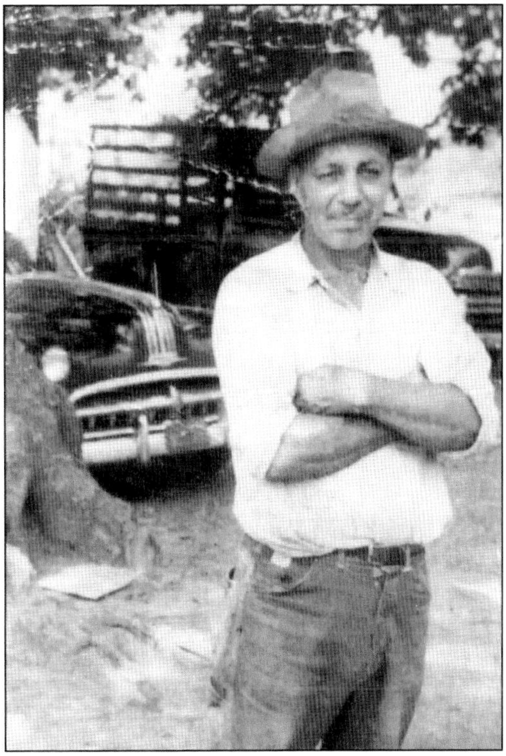

Shown here serving as a waiter for a social event, George "Puggie" Johnson, born in Madison on February 25, 1909, was the son of James Edward and Cora Chivis Johnson. He was the husband of Nettie James, daughter of Isaiah and Rebecca Snyder James of Madison. The couple made their home in Washington, DC. A very public figure, he was an air raid warden with civil defense, ensuring air raid drills were properly performed. He died on January 26, 1990. (Johnson family.)

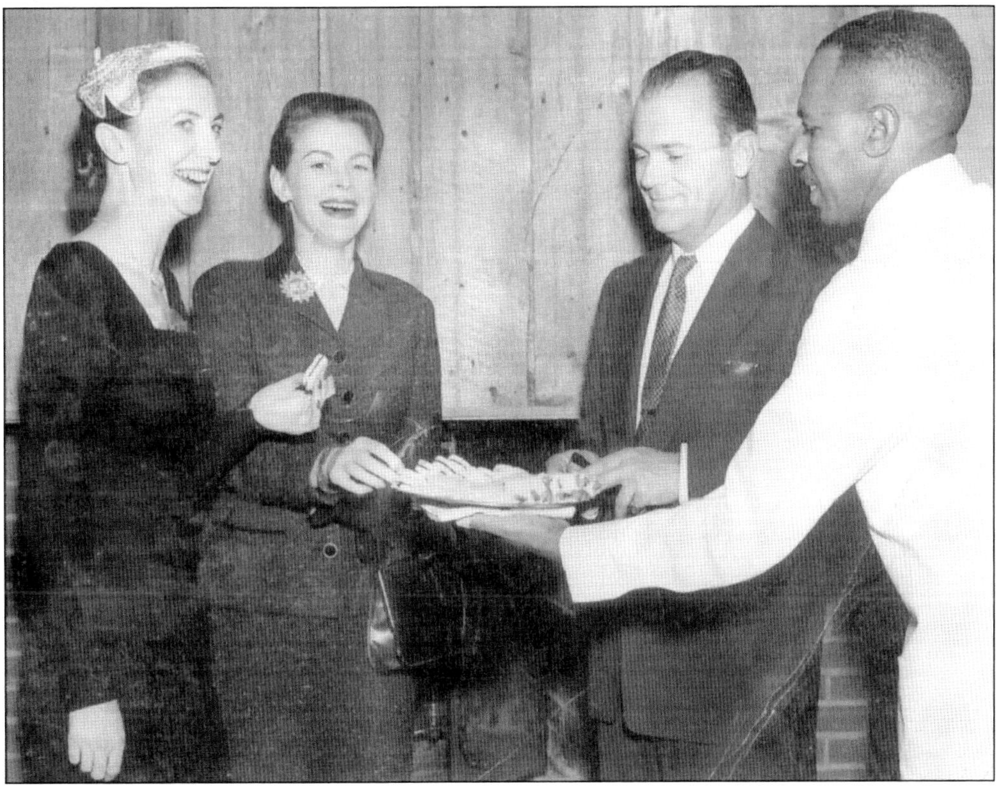

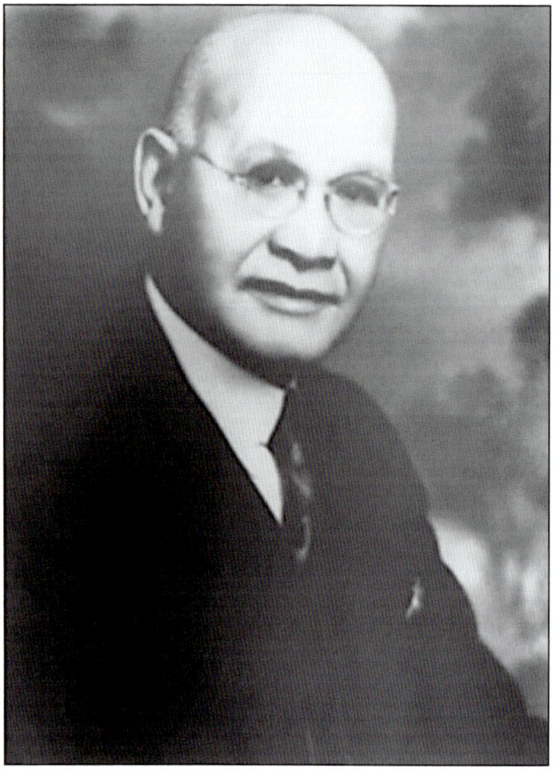

Born in Culpeper in December 1868, George Morton Lightfoot was the seventh child of James T. and Letitia Beck Lightfoot. The year after his father's death, George left the farm and enrolled in Williams College in Massachusetts, where he earned a bachelor of arts degree in 1891. By 1912, he was a professor of Latin at Howard University. With a thesis on Roman satire, he earned a master of arts degree in 1922 from the Catholic University of America. This scholar, husband of Susan Frye, and father of three children died in 1947. (Howard University Archives.)

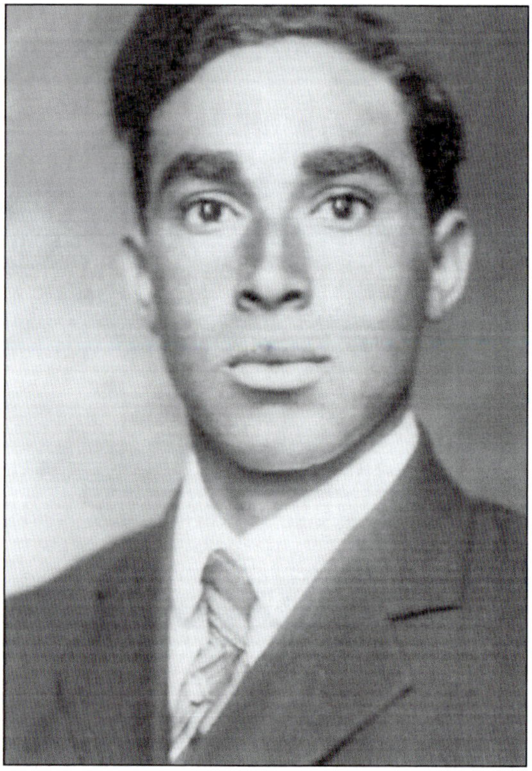

The youngest of three children, John Louis Timbers was born in Rappahannock on September 25, 1893, to Frank Phillip and Mary Hackley Timbers. On December 29, 1915, he married Ethel Fitzhugh, daughter of Berkley and Mildred Fitzhugh. He worked on his family's and other local farms until he decided to relocate his wife and young son, John Henry, to Pittsburgh. He and his wife had a second son, Charles, in 1925. John worked as a general laborer throughout Pittsburgh. His wife was diagnosed with cancer in 1943. The disease overtook her four years later, and she died on Christmas Eve at only 47 years old. He died in October 1974. (Timbers family.)

James E. Walker was born around 1901 to Robert and Lena Wiggenton Walker. The family lived in the Castleton area of Rappahannock. He married Cora Lawson, one of the daughters of Hansbury and Estelle Lawson, on August 20, 1924. The couple moved to Rochester, New York, where Walker took a job in a laundry at a hotel. He died in New York on October 24, 1954. (Lawson family.)

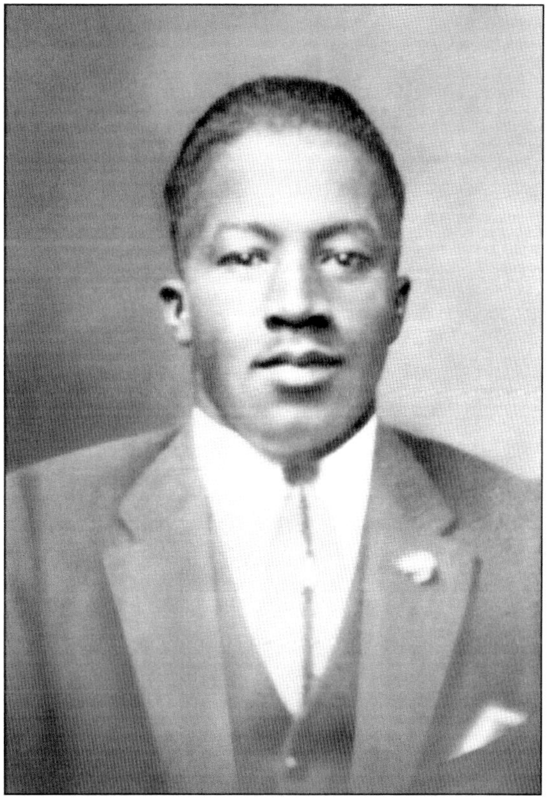

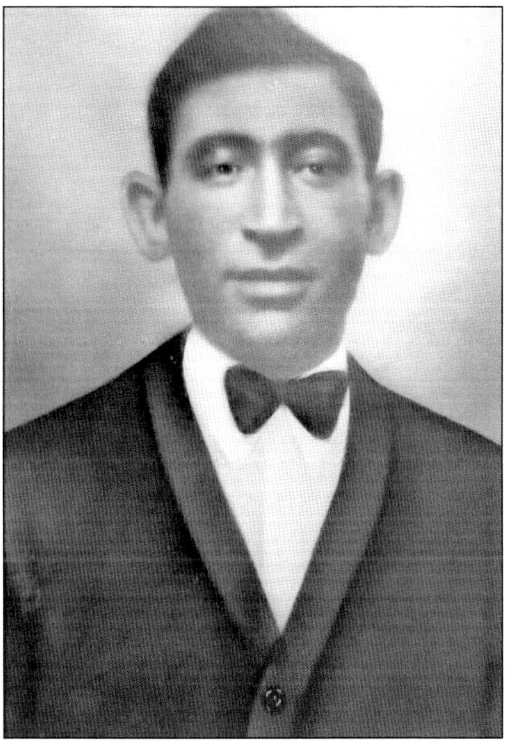

Harry C. Bannister was born in Culpeper to William Lee and Anna Eliza Francis Bannister on May 25, 1890. His mom died in 1913 of cancer. He and his brothers worked a variety of non-farm jobs. He worked as a laborer in a bakery. Tall and slender with gray eyes, he left Virginia for Maryland, where he was employed as a laborer in the US Bureau of Printing and Engraving. He died in 1941. (Bannister family.)

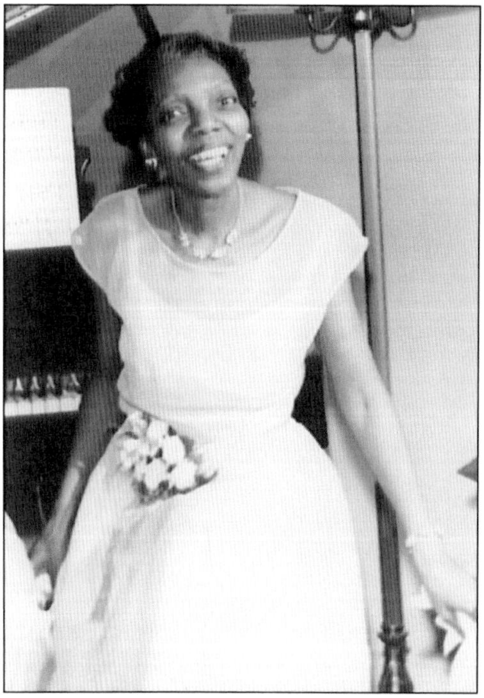

Born in Orange in 1902 to Robert and Lizzie B. Walker Williams, Helen Williams grew up and became a schoolteacher in Washington, DC. She was largely influenced by her maternal grandmother, Ella Walker, whom she often visited in Madison. Helen married John Taylor, an Indiana-born insurance salesman. John was the son of Pullman porter Alfred Taylor and his wife, Martha Hines Taylor. John and Helen had one daughter, Ann, born in 1931. (Taylor family.)

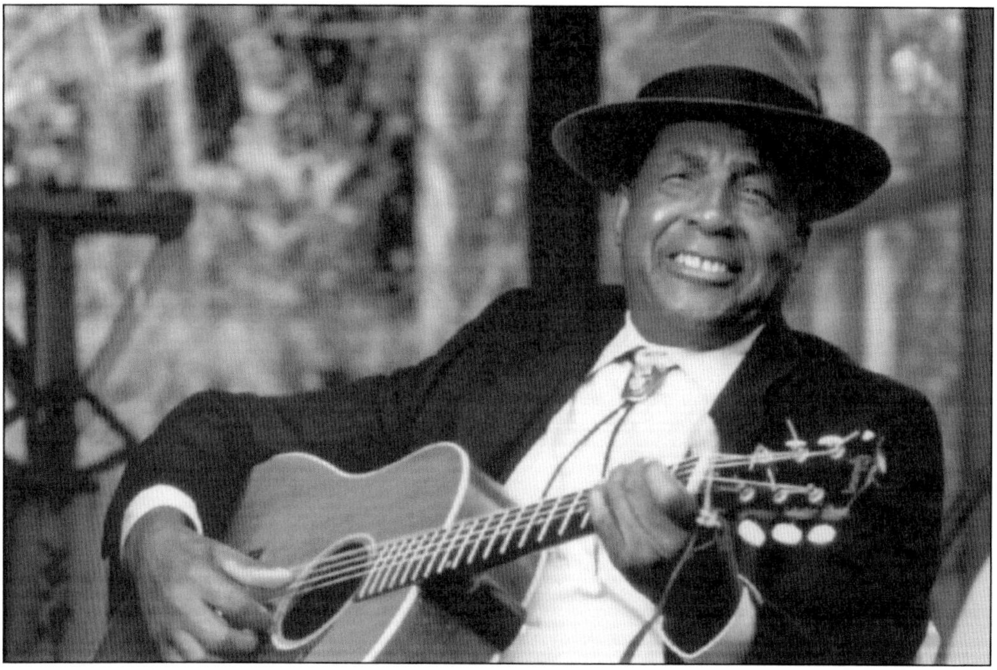

John Jackson played his version of the Piedmont blues on his guitar and entertained audiences all over the world. He was born in Rappahannock to tenant farmers Suddy and Hattie Haney Jackson on February 25, 1924. His father taught him how to play guitar, and in the late 1940s, John relocated to Fairfax County, where his unique sound afforded him invitations and record deals. A historical marker on Zachary Taylor Highway (US Route 522) pays tribute to his contributions to American music. (Smithsonian Institution.)

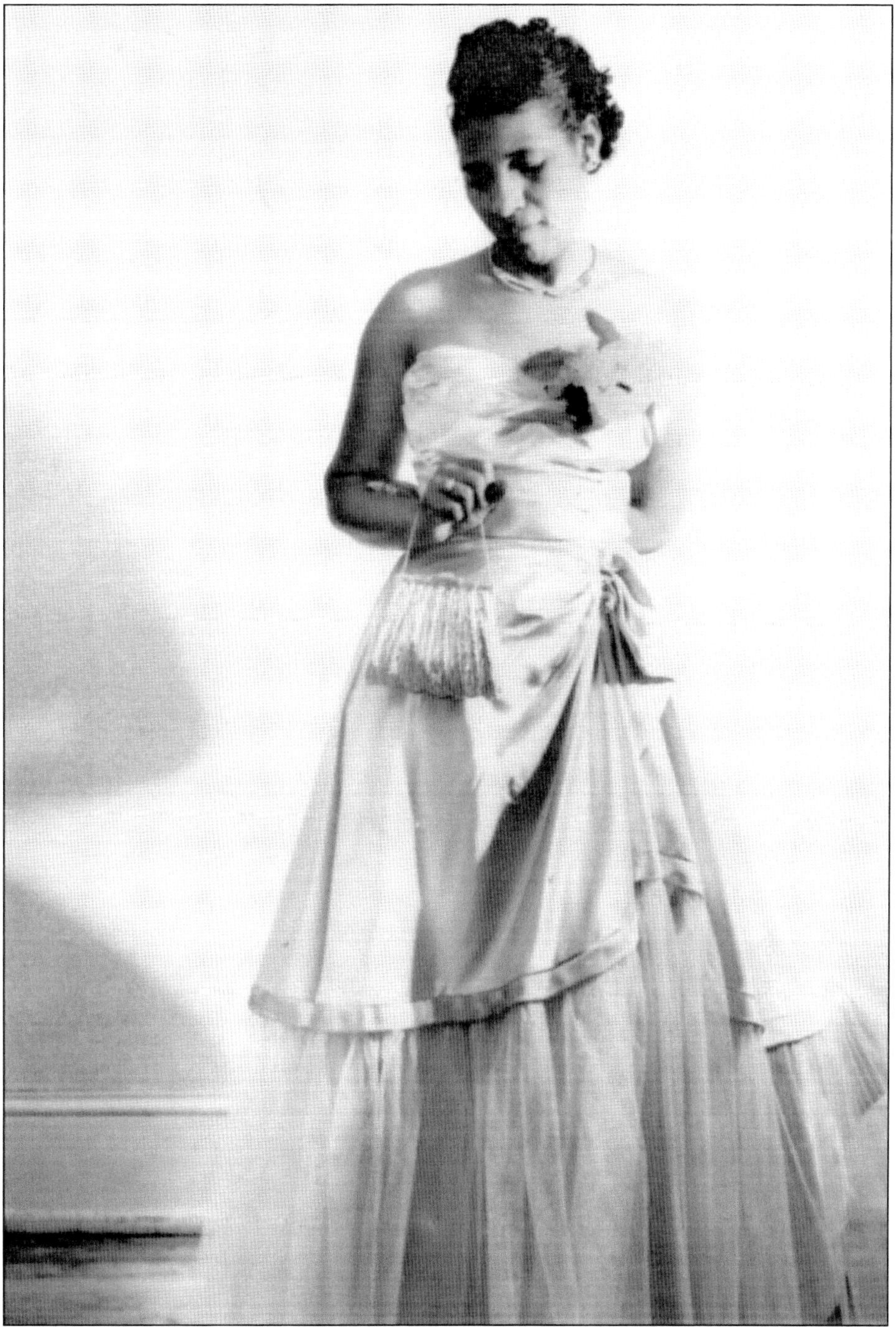

Anna May Frances White was born in the Rixeyville township of Culpeper on June 3, 1910. Her parents were Martin White II and Mary Eliza Nash. She first worked as a maid in Culpeper and married John Thomas Jackson in 1942. After her marriage was annulled, she relocated to Washington, DC, and started a radio career first as an engineer and then as a disc jockey. Along the way, she developed her talent for singing. She and several other women, including two of her sisters, formed a gospel touring group called The Victory Star Quintet. (White family.)

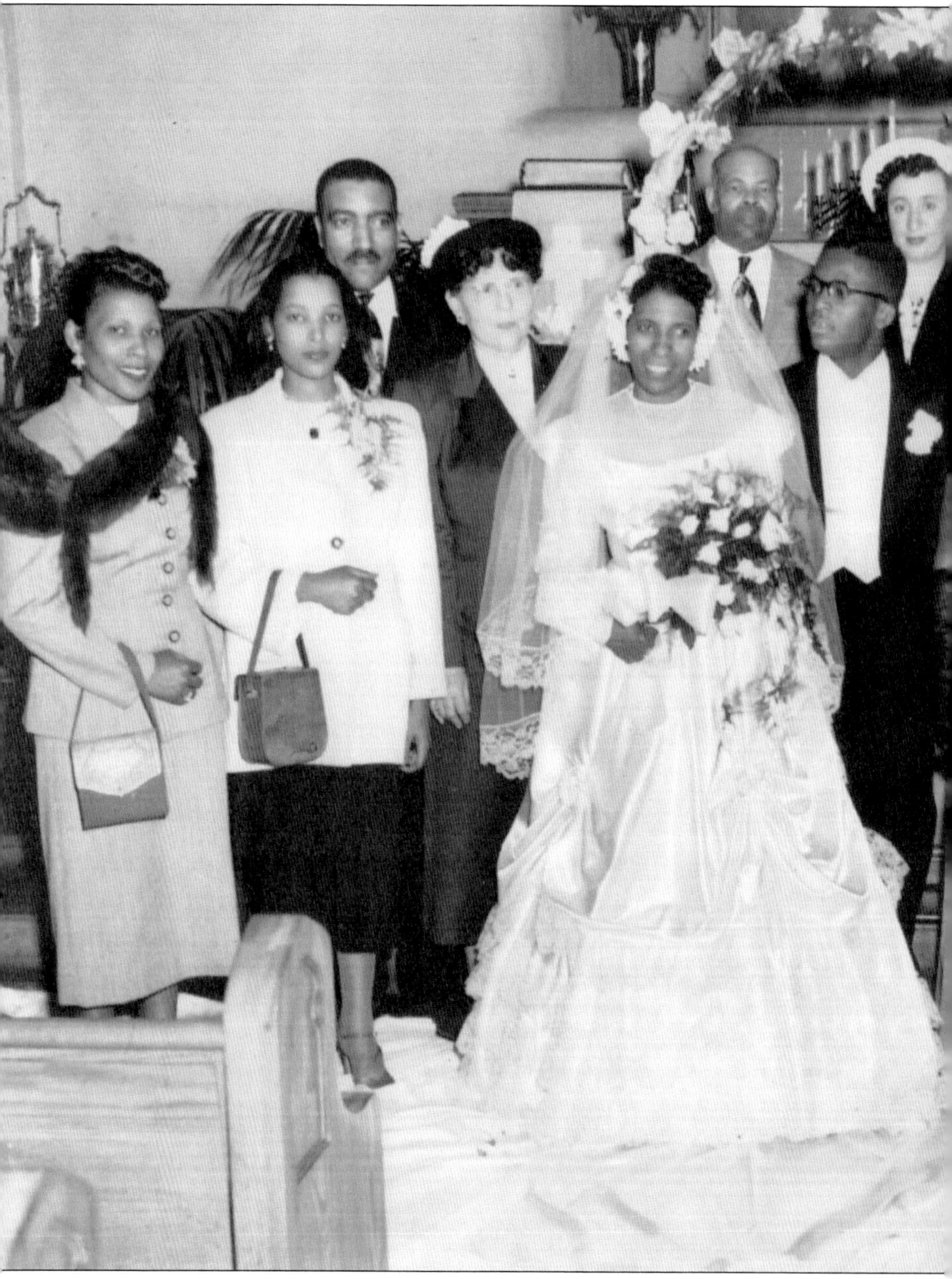

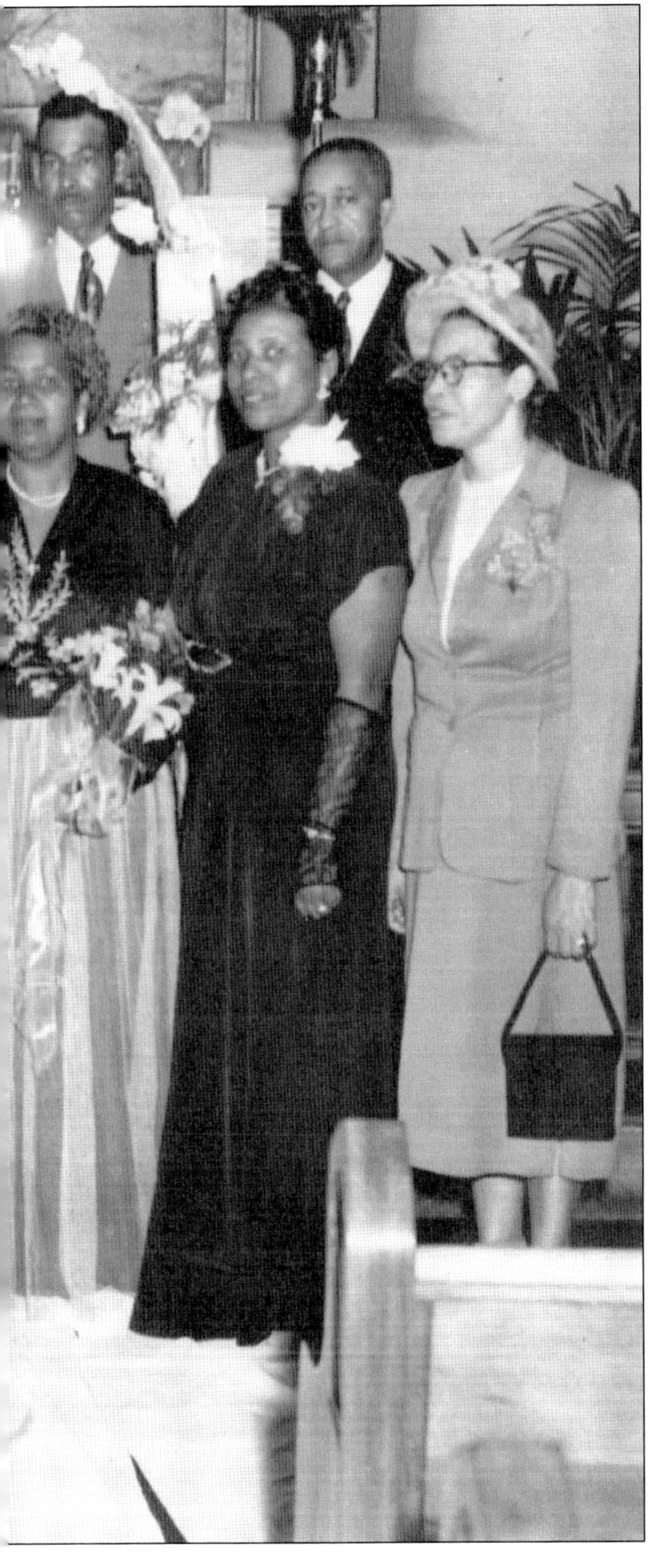

Anna May Frances White remarried on April 20, 1950, to Theodore Kurtz. From left to right are Catherine White Stewart; Thelma White Haywood; Rosslyn Stewart and his wife; bride Frances White; groom Theodore Kurtz; Olberry Nash Jr. and his wife, Ruth (behind the bride and groom); Mary Eliza Nash White; Ed White (behind Mary Eliza); Lucille White Hoffman; Pete Hoffman (behind Lucille); and Ruth Nash. Mary Eliza is Frances' mother. Catherine, Thelma, and Lucille are her sisters. Ed is her brother. Ruth Nash (at farthest right) and Olberry are siblings of Mary Eliza. More than 10 years later, Anna became ill and died on July 11, 1962. She is buried in her family plot in Rixeyville. (White family.)

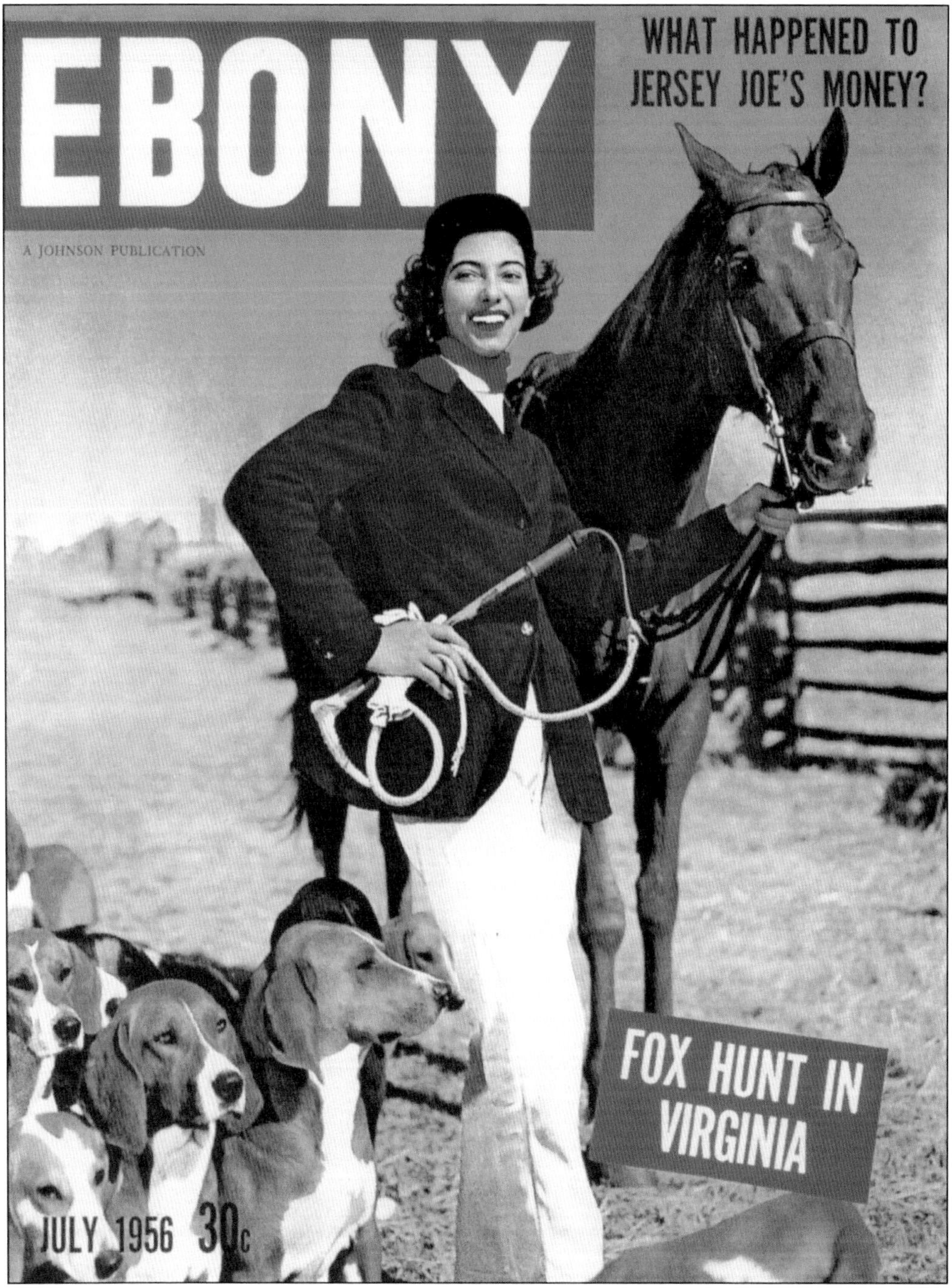

The region is well known for its horse culture, and Orange is usually the first county to be mentioned. Rappahannock and its neighboring county of Fauquier are equally noteworthy. In its July 1956 issue, *Ebony* magazine featured Peggie Ethel Rowe, age 19. Her father, Russell Harry Rowe, was a horse trainer at the John Bentley Estate near Orleans in Fauquier, and her Rappahannock-born mother was Lottie Ethel Brown. (Johnson Publishing Company.)

Six

When They Went to School

In the four counties, a multitude of clapboard one- and two-room elementary schools for minority children were built, often by parents and neighbors, so that the children could have a place to learn from teachers how to read, write, do math, and understand social studies.

With the exception of Orange County, the area did not have the benefit of a high school for African American children, and parents either relocated to towns such as Washington, DC, or sent their children to schools in other Virginia cities such as Manassas or Petersburg.

Economics and the number of children play vital roles in whether a locale can build and support a secondary school, and in 1946, the Virginia legislature voted to allow neighboring counties to develop regional high schools. Initially, African American parents from the five counties of Greene, Rappahannock, Culpeper, Madison, and Orange advocated in their communities to form one regional high school. As time passed, Greene County parents joined with Albemarle, and the remaining parents successfully worked through their churches, local governments, and school officials to build a high school based in Culpeper and financially supported by all four counties.

The George Washington Carver Regional High School was constructed in the valley of Cedar Mountain and opened in October 1948.

This chapter begins with examples of those impacted by the Virginia College for Negroes, as a large proportion of the region's African American teachers were educated there. The institution's name changed several times; it began in 1882 as the Virginia Normal and Collegiate Institute for Negroes, then was renamed Virginia College for Negroes (from 1902 to 1946), then Virginia State College (from 1946 to 1979), and, finally, Virginia State University. Next are some one- and two-room schools, followed by Carver Regional High School and a few members of its dedicated staff. The chapter concludes with a remembrance of two students who were in the first graduating class of 1949.

Although clear photographs of the following people are lost to history, this chapter would be incomplete without the mention of supervisors and lifelong educators such as Harvey A. Fleshmon, Gussie B. Taylor, Arethea Bedford Brown, Carroll Williams, Anne W. Green, Virgelia Price, many generations of the Russell family, and all who had the best intentions for African American students.

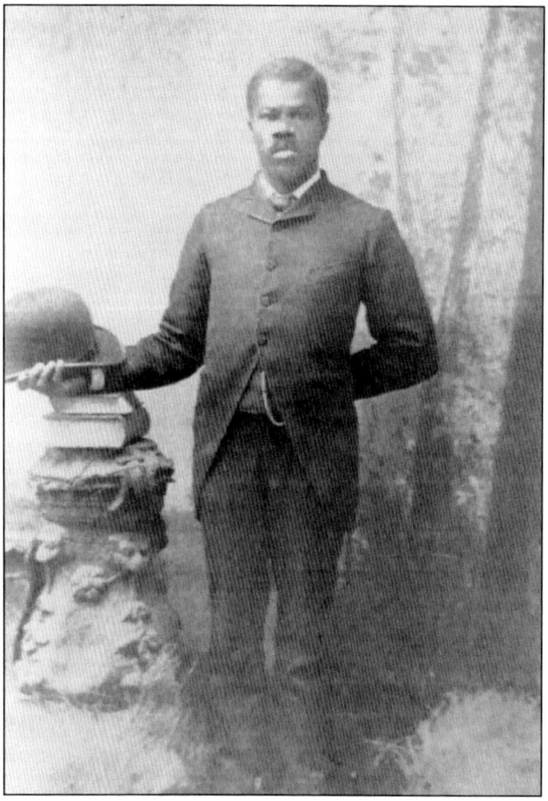

James Henry Beck(s), a teacher in Orange in the 1890s, was the son of Brown and Mary Bannister Beck. He married Fannie Lee Johnson (1871–1959), and both became teachers. They relocated to Orange around 1891, where he taught throughout the county. By the time they both accepted teaching positions in Staunton, six of their eight children had been born in Orange. (Debra Lynn Ashburn.)

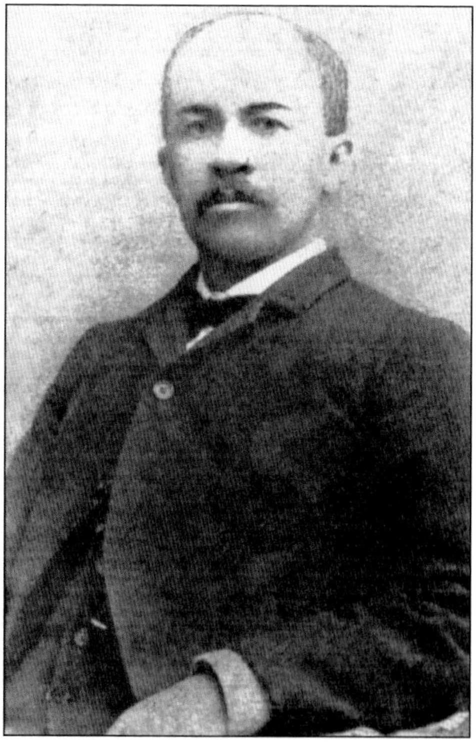

Charles James Daniel was born in Orange County, Virginia, in 1861 to Aaron and Francis Daniel. He studied at Howard University and graduated from the Richmond Institute in 1878. He taught school in Louisa County, Virginia, and from 1882 to 1888, he was principal of a school in Danville. He was then appointed secretary of Virginia Normal and Collegiate Institute and remained in that position until 1916. In addition to being the university secretary, he served as the first librarian. The university gymnasium, erected in 1925, is named in his honor. His son Robert became the fifth president of Virginia State University in 1950. (Virginia State University Archives.)

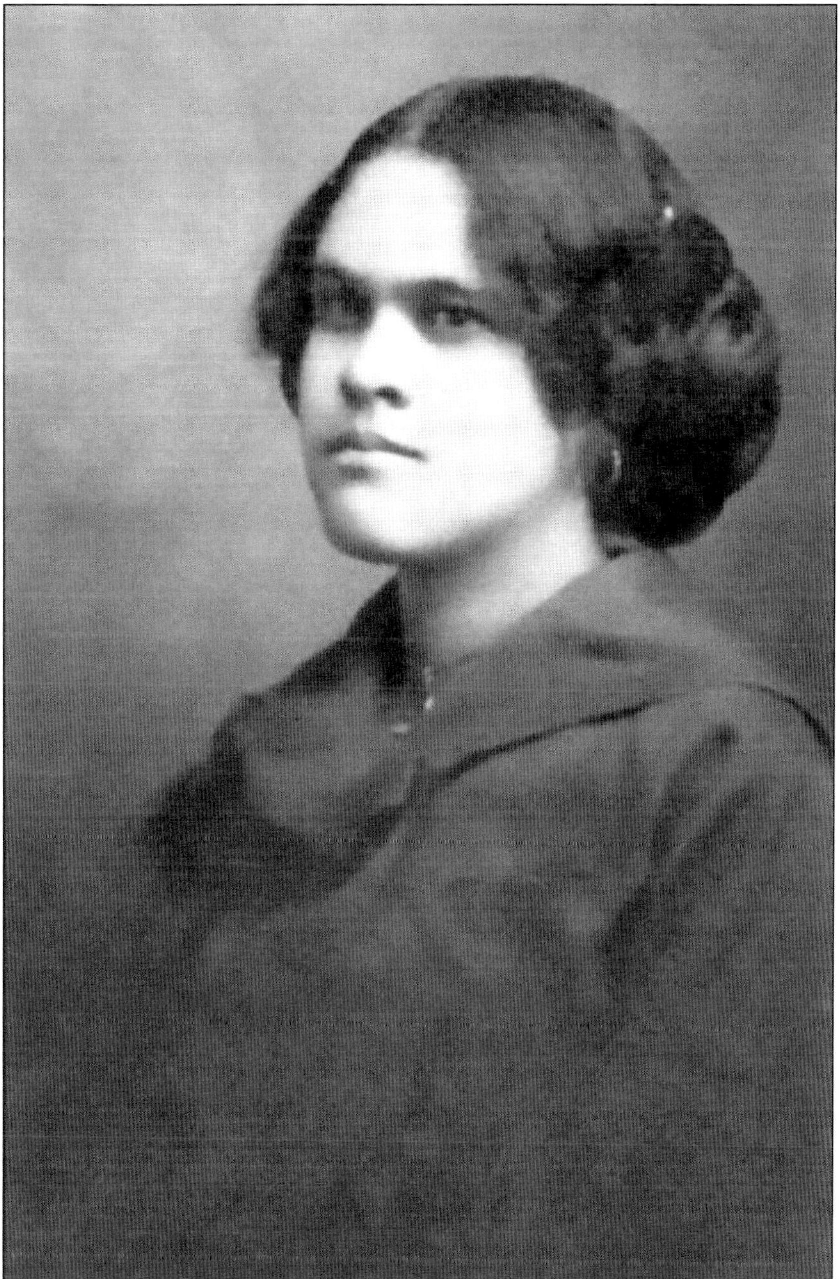

The Madden name is well known in the educational history of Culpeper. Ruth Columbia Madden was born on May 1, 1892, to Thomas Obed Madden Sr. and Landonia Randolph Stokes. Both of Ruth's parents were teachers, but her mother curtailed her own career to care for the household. Her uncle, Rev. Willis J. Madden, was principal of the Culpeper Training School for many years. Ruth, the second of 12 children, graduated from Virginia Normal and Industrial Institute in 1913 (as shown in this photograph), and taught in Henrico, Hanover, and Fauquier Counties. Her husband, educator Marshall Gordon Alexander, died in 1971. She passed away on June 19, 1994. (Virginia State University Archives.)

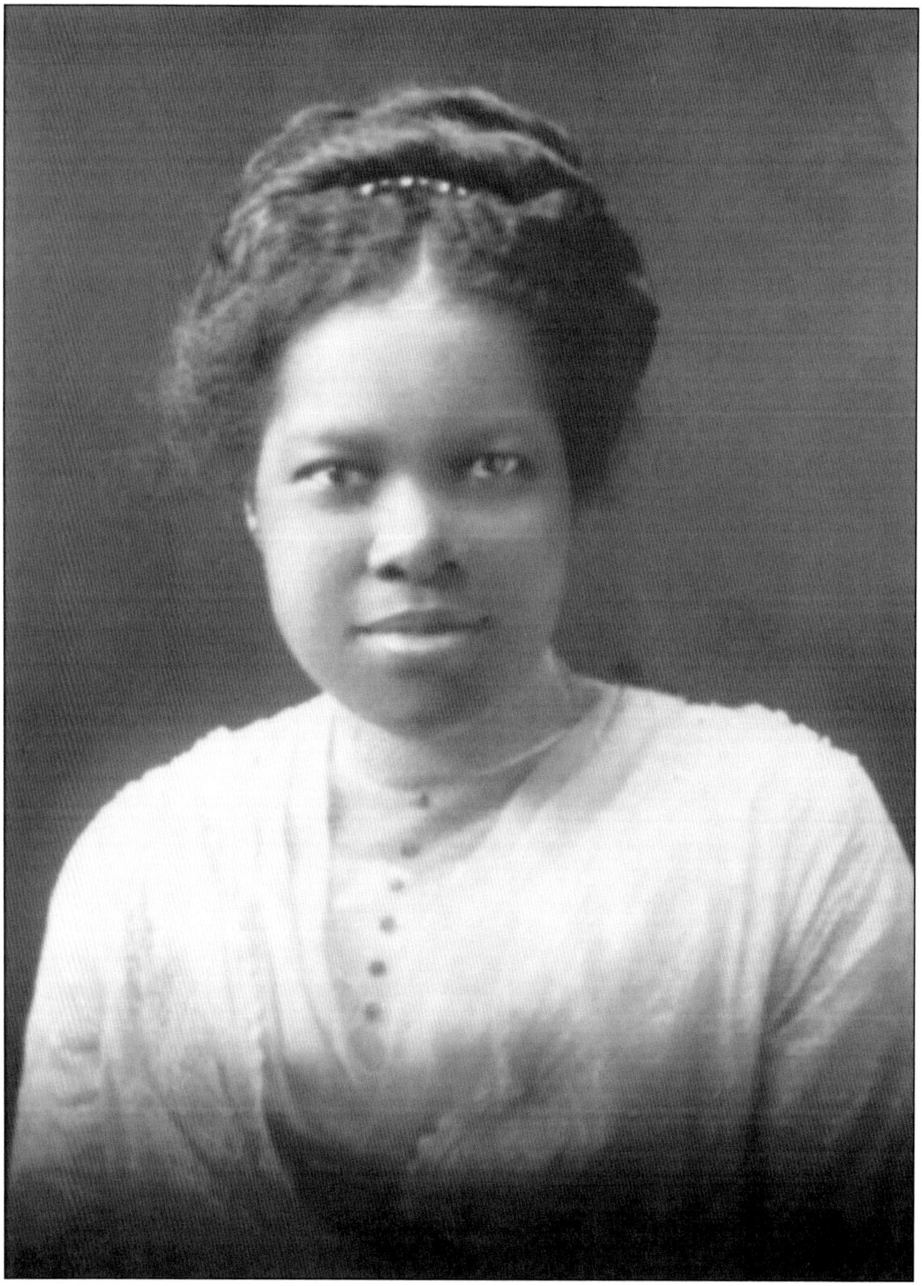

Nannie Helen Burroughs (aka Burruss) was born around 1875 in Orange, was the older daughter of John and Jennie Poindexter Burroughs. Her father became an itinerant preacher, and after his daughter's early education in local schools, he and his wife divorced. By 1900, Jennie Burroughs had relocated with her two daughters to Washington, DC, so that they could benefit from a broader education. After graduating from the M Street School (later Dunbar High School), Nannie sought a teaching position and later a civil service position. Denied both because of her skin color, she decided to start a school of her own. After saving her money and fundraising, in 1909—after the donation of six acres from the Baptist Woman's Convention—she opened the National Training School for Women and Girls. (Library of Congress.)

Born on December 23, 1894, Fannye Tansimore was the fourth child of Lewis and Lucinda Milton Tansimore. In 1915, she married widower, retail merchant, poultry farmer, and US Army captain (ret.) William Roderick Staff, veteran of the Spanish American War. In 1935, she earned her teaching certificate from Virginia Normal and Industrial Institute, and in 1944, she earned a bachelor of science, with distinction, in home economics education from Virginia State College. She taught for 22 years at Lightfoot Training School. In her 23rd year of teaching, at 51 years old, she started at Carver Regional High School. She became caretaker for her husband until his death in 1953. She remarried in 1956 to Charles Warren Reid. After a full life, she died on Valentine's Day in 1976. (Tansimore family.)

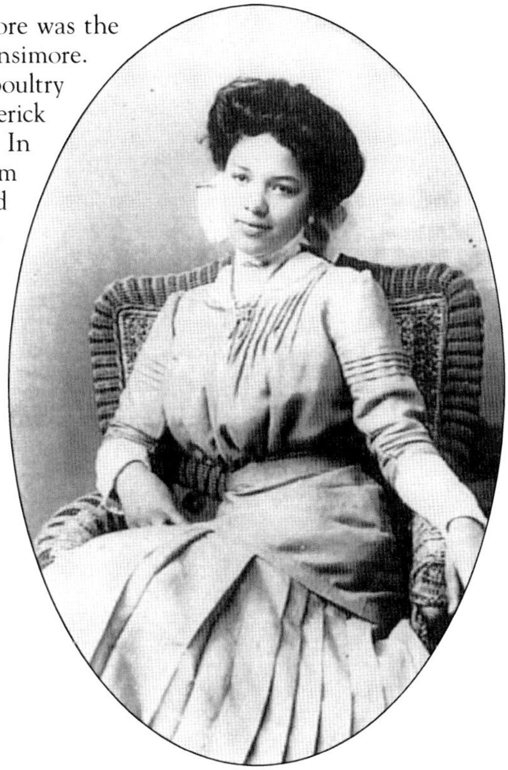

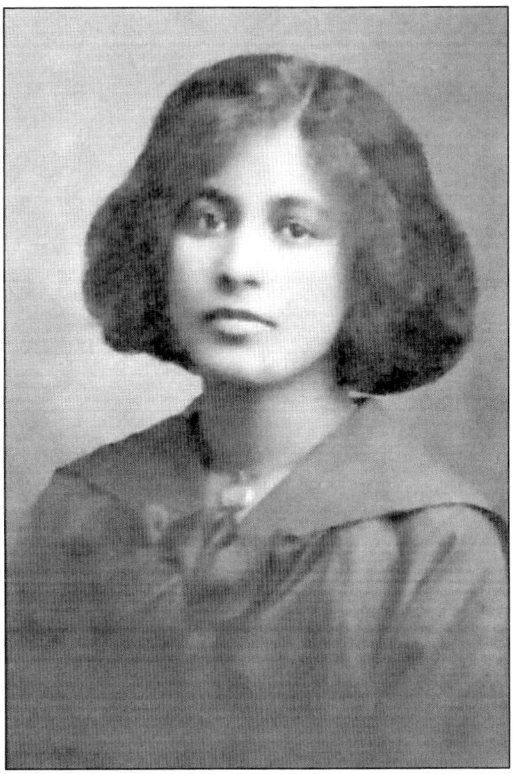

Annie Laura Payne graduated in 1913 with a concentration in business from Virginia Normal and Industrial Institute, where she was vice president of her class. The daughter of Sawney and Cora Lee Lewis (Gatewood) Payne, Annie began her teaching career immediately upon her graduation. Later, in 1936, she was among the first faculty hired for the newly constructed Culpeper Training School. She married building contractor William Montgomery Lovell in 1932 and continued her teaching career. Her husband died in 1973; she lived fully until her death at age 97 on February 15, 1990. (Virginia State University Archives.)

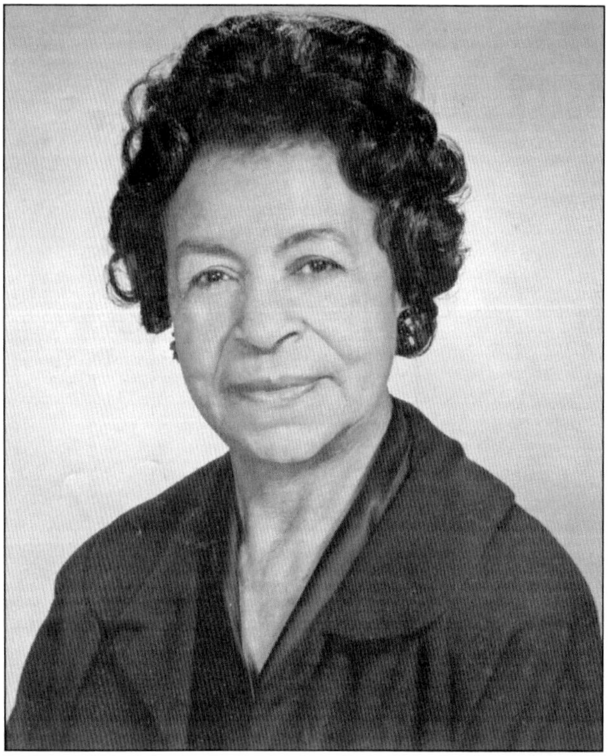

Carrie Welbrock was born to Nannie Hopkins in October 1892 in Albemarle County. By 1900, she was being raised by her widowed grandmother, Mary Hopkins, who was a cook for a private family. In 1910, at about 18 years old, she was already teaching in the Jefferson School in Charlottesville and doing laundry to help her grandmother. On June 5, 1912, she married Humphrey Charles Michie, a station fireman for a company named Home Laundry. She earned both a bachelor's degree and a master of science degree in mathematics. She was one of the inaugural teachers at Carver in 1948 and served as both classroom teacher and assistant principal for many years. She retired in 1963 and died on January 16, 1981. (GWCRHSAA History Committee.)

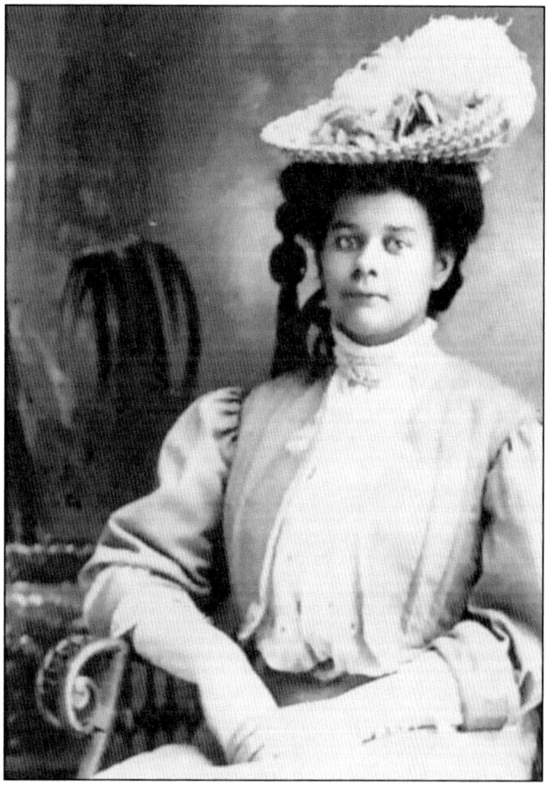

Emma Lacy Wilhoite, born around 1882, was one of eleven children of Laurence and Malinda Wilhoite. In 1907, when she married James Butler Jackson, a carpenter and son of Allen and Delilah Jackson, she was teaching first through seventh grade at the Buena School. She retired from teaching to become a full-time homemaker. Over the years, the couple had five children. Although she no longer taught, she opened her home to young teachers who needed lodging. She died after a brief illness. (Lindsay Jackson.)

Sarah McDaniel Reid (right) taught in Orange for 40 years. She was born there around 1856 to Benjamin and Patsy McDaniel. In the 1870 census, her father was a 70-year-old cobbler with $400 in wealth, and she was a 14-year-old student. Her schooling made her a leader in her community, and she chose teaching as her profession. On October 18, 1877, she married drayman Albert Reid (1839–1913), and the couple had nine known children. At 81 years of age, she died in the home of her daughter Helen Gertrude Reid Galloway (shown here) in Pittsburgh and was brought back to Orange for burial in Westview Cemetery. (McDaniel family.)

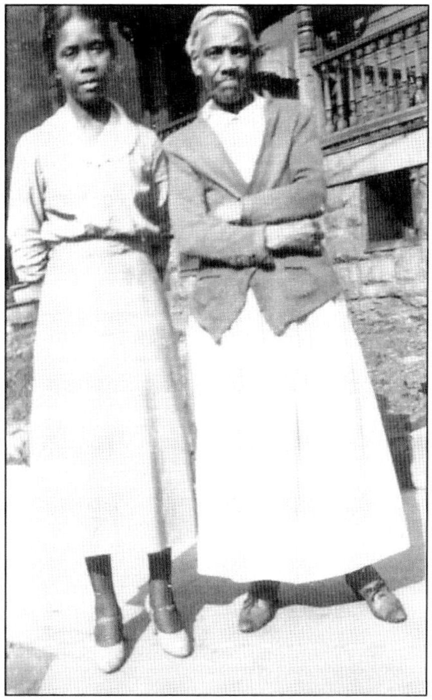

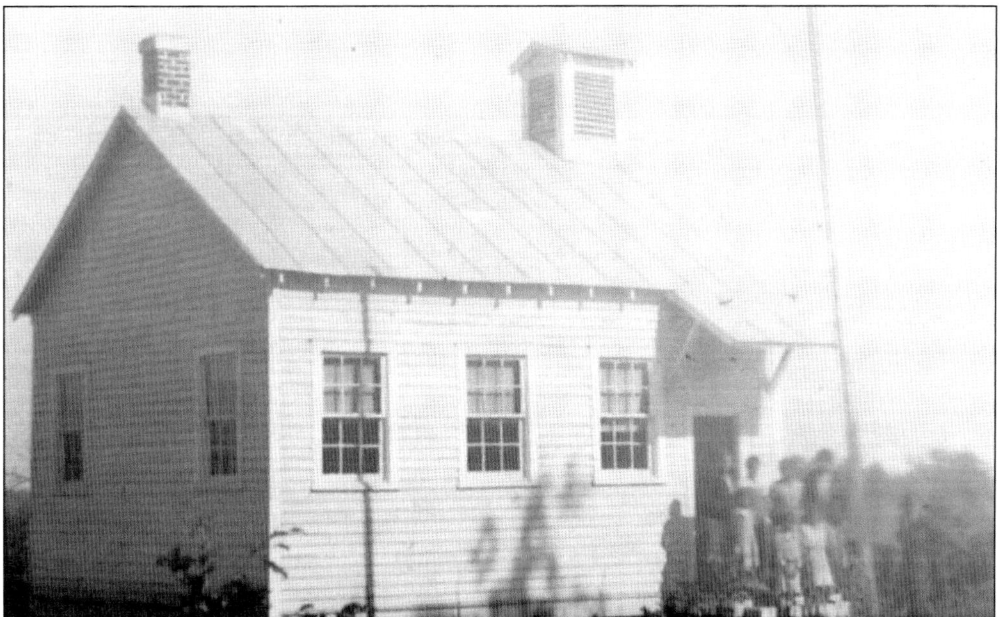

The Perry School was one of many one-room schools in Culpeper for minority children. In this 1932 photograph, the teacher was Olethia S. Thurston, born November 8, 1909, to William Henry and Mary Alice Strother Thurston. After her father's death, Olethia was adopted and raised by her uncle and aunt, Ollie and Emma Thurston. After teaching for many years, she changed careers and became an insurance agent for Southern Aid Insurance Company. She died on Christmas Day in 1981 and is buried in the cemetery of Ebenezar Baptist Church in Lignum. (Virginia State University Archives.)

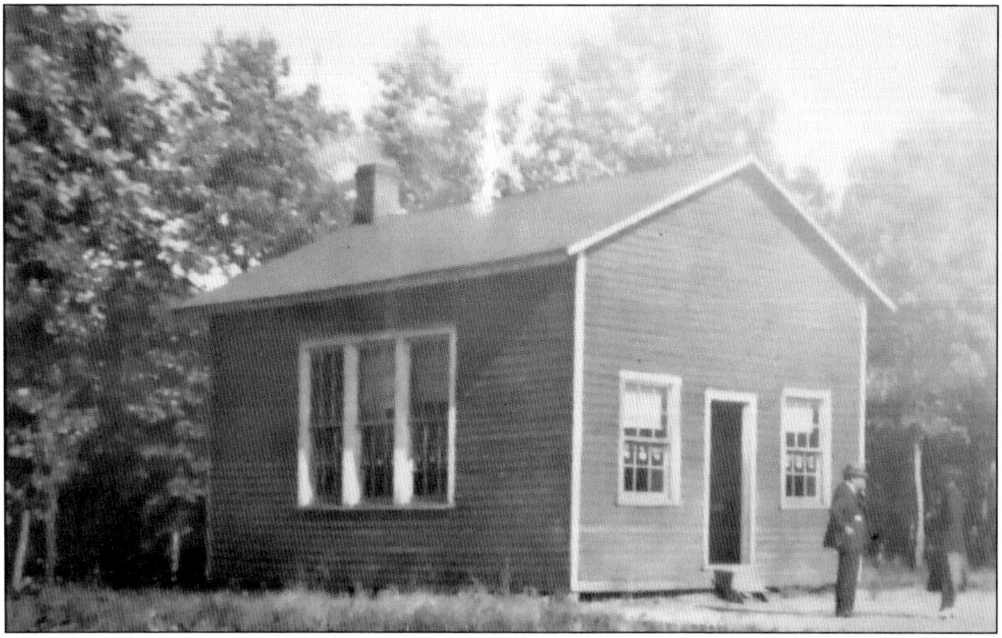

The Brocktown School in Culpeper was located on what is now James Monroe Highway and was rebuilt and enlarged in 1931. The one-room school served students from first through eighth grades and had one instructor. One student who attended was George Everett Taylor, son of Ruth Etta Lewis and George Washington Taylor, who began in the ramshackle building in 1928 before transferring to the new structure shown here. This photograph shows Culpeper Schools superintendent Thomas William Hendrick with teacher Victoria Green. (George Everett Taylor.)

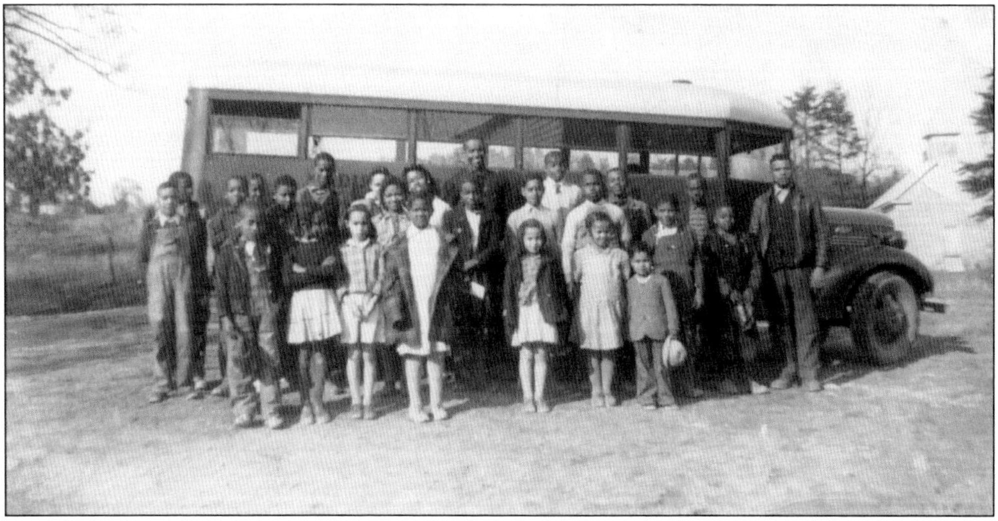

Daniel Washington was born on August 9, 1889, to shoemaker Alfred Washington and his wife, Betty Scott Washington. He married Bessie Blakey, and his family, including six children, lived in the Criglersville village of Madison. In addition to farming his land, Washington (standing at far right) purchased and refitted a bus to transport Madison students to and from local schools. He died on February 1, 1965, and is buried in the cemetery of Second Robertson Church in Madison. (Florence Washington.)

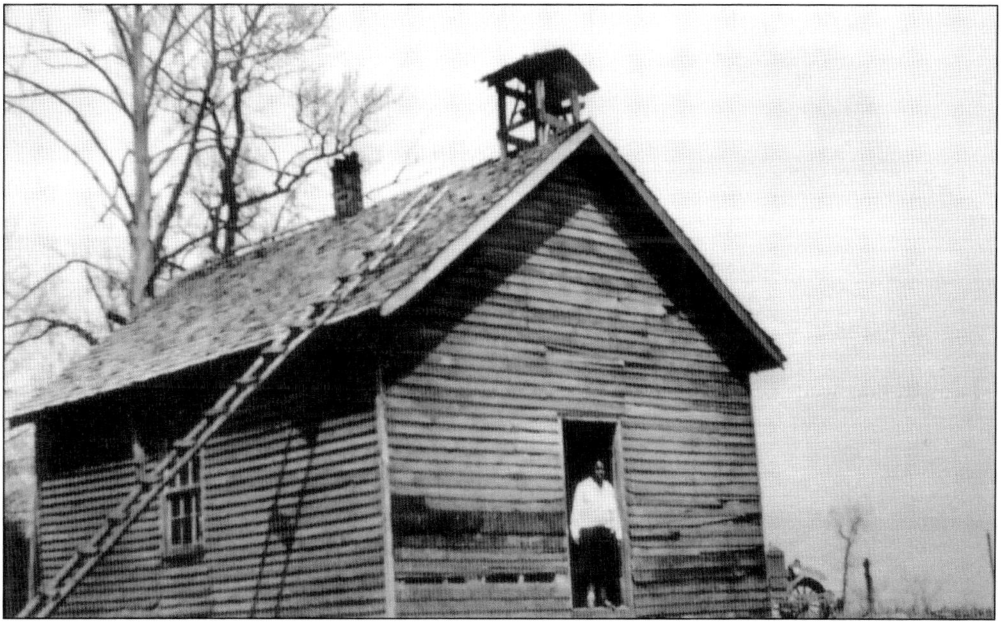

This tattered building for students of color, the Williamsburg School in Madison, was where children in this neighborhood, up to grade seven, were expected to learn. (Virginia State University Archives.)

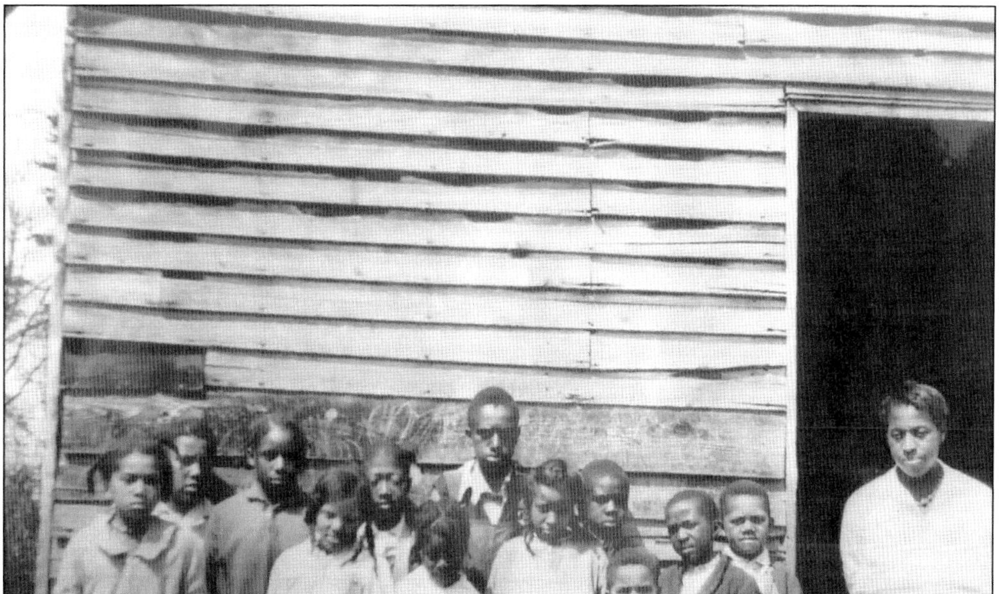

This photograph, taken during the 1930–1931 academic year, shows students at the Williamsburg School in Madison standing with their teacher, Lucille Ellen Barbour Clay. This was her first year teaching in Madison, having received her credentials from the Manassas Industrial Institute several years earlier. One of eight known children, she was born in Charlottesville in 1891 to William and Adell Yeager Barbour. She was married to sawmill laborer Floyd Clay, and the couple adopted and were raising a daughter when Lucille died unexpectedly of heart disease on March 31, 1943, at only 52 years old. (Virginia State University Archives.)

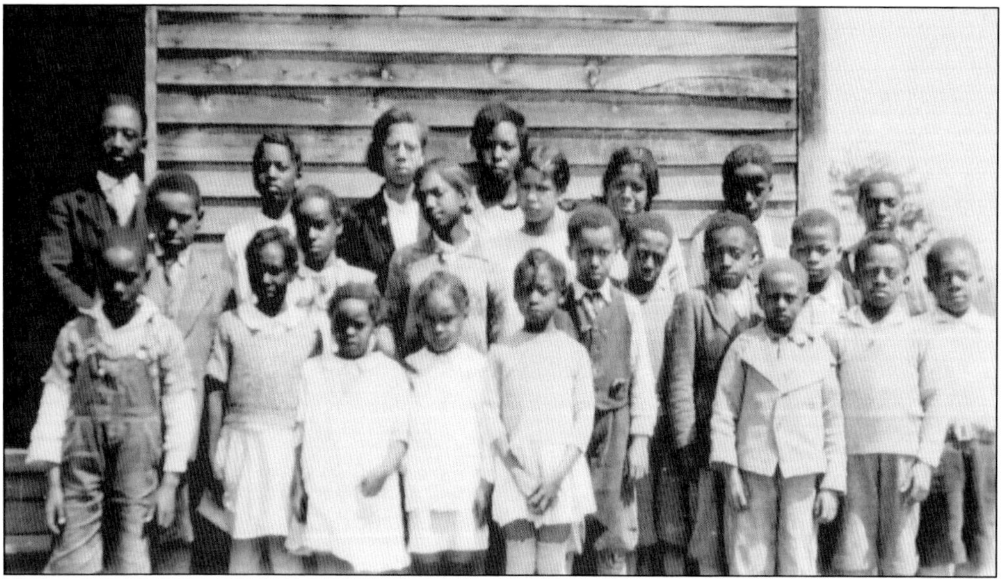

This 1930 photograph of children at Oak Park Elementary School in Madison shows teacher William Fowler. He was a graduate of Coppin State University in Baltimore, Maryland. His first year in Madison was the 1930–1931 academic year, during which he taught first through seventh grades. This school was connected to its church, Oak Park Baptist Church, for the benefit of community children. (Virginia State University Archives.)

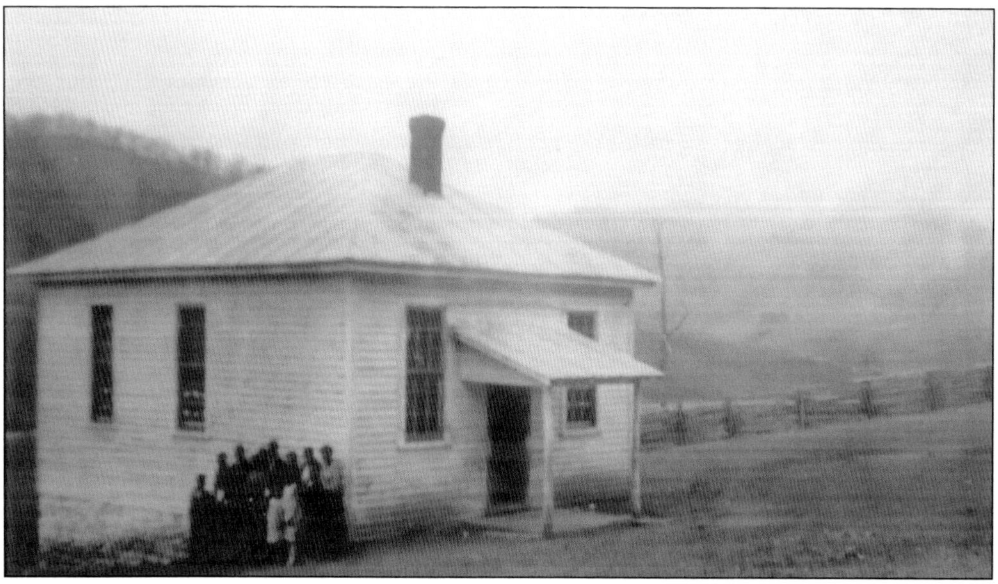

Pleasant Grove School, located in Madison County, is shown here in 1933. (Virginia State University Archives.)

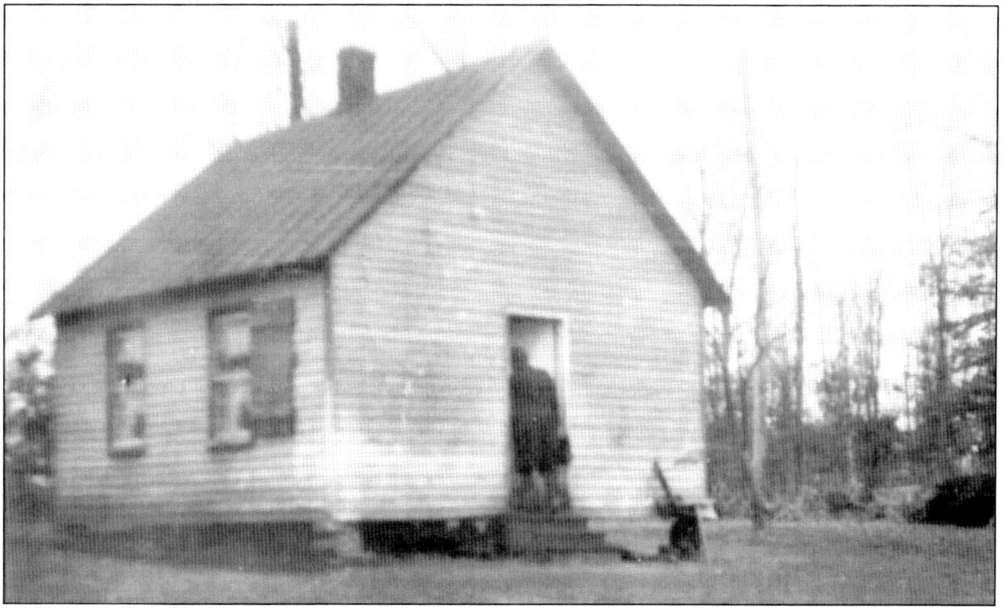

The Peola Mills school was situated in its township and was typical of a one-room clapboard-construction school for minority children in Rappahannock in the 1932–1933 academic year. (Virginia State University Archives.)

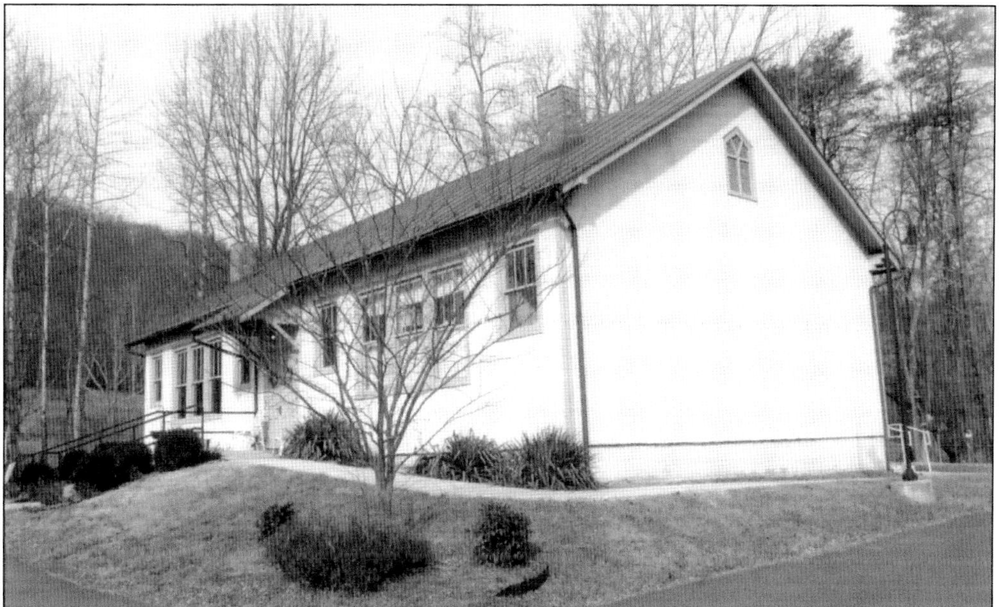

Rappahannock County had three Rosenwald Schools that stood in contrast to the typical one-room schools: Flint Hill, Amissville, and Scrabble. The Scrabble School, opened in 1921 and closed in 1967, is the only one that remains. Abandoned and nearly forgotten after it was closed, the Scrabble School building was reopened in 2009 after an extensive restoration. The building is now the home of the Rappahannock Senior Center. It also houses the Rappahannock African-American Heritage Center, which features an exhibit that tells the story of the school, the community it once served, and its place in local, state, and national history. (Terry Miller.)

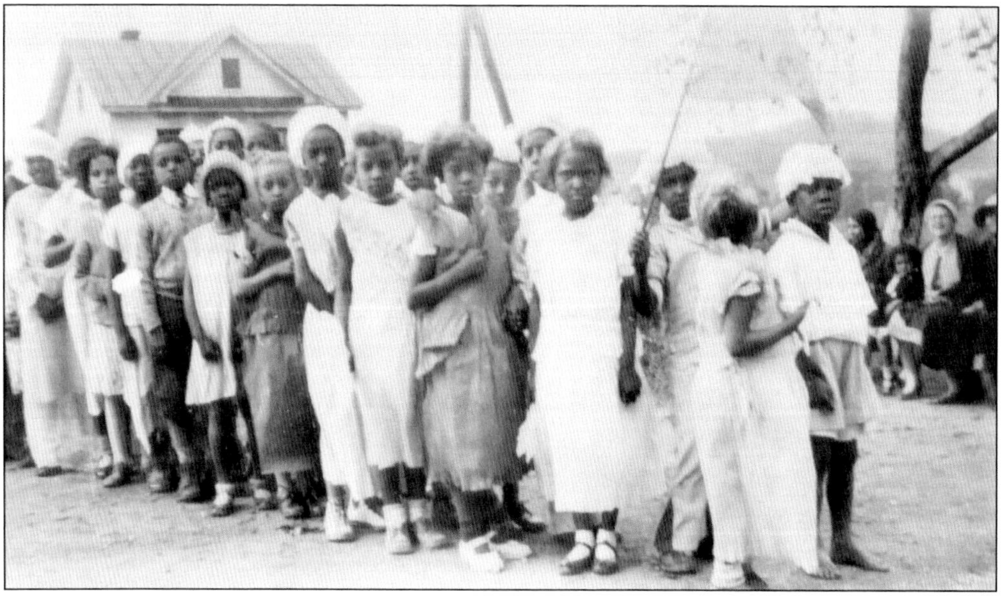

In the month of May, county schools had Exhibit Day, often called a May Day celebration, during which parents, the community, and school administrators visited to enjoy games and demonstrations and to hear the accomplishments of the students. Here, at Exhibit Day in Rappahannock in 1932, costumed elementary students are lining up for their turn at entertaining the crowd. Below are students in higher grades wearing Native American costumes at Little Washington. (Both, Virginia State University Archives.)

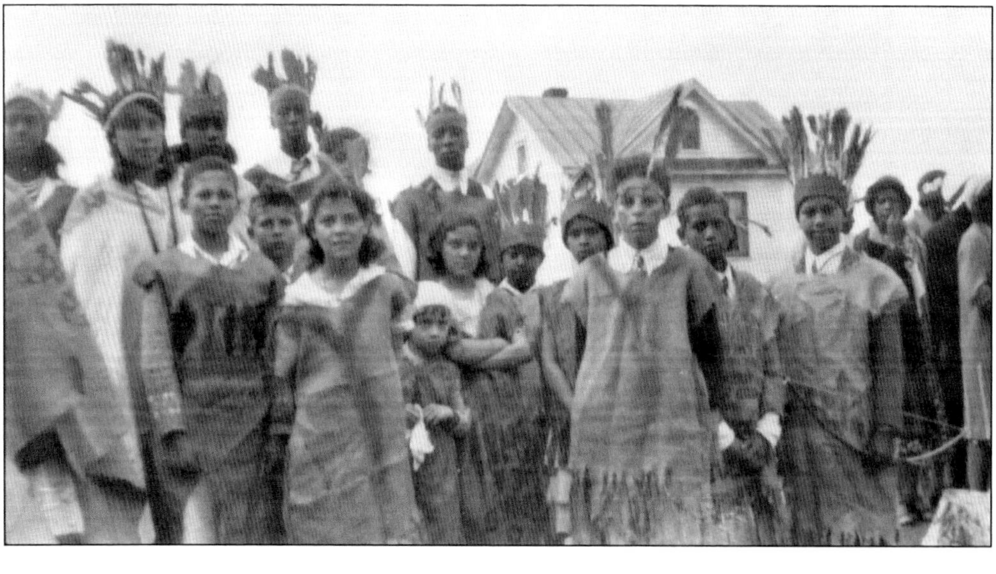

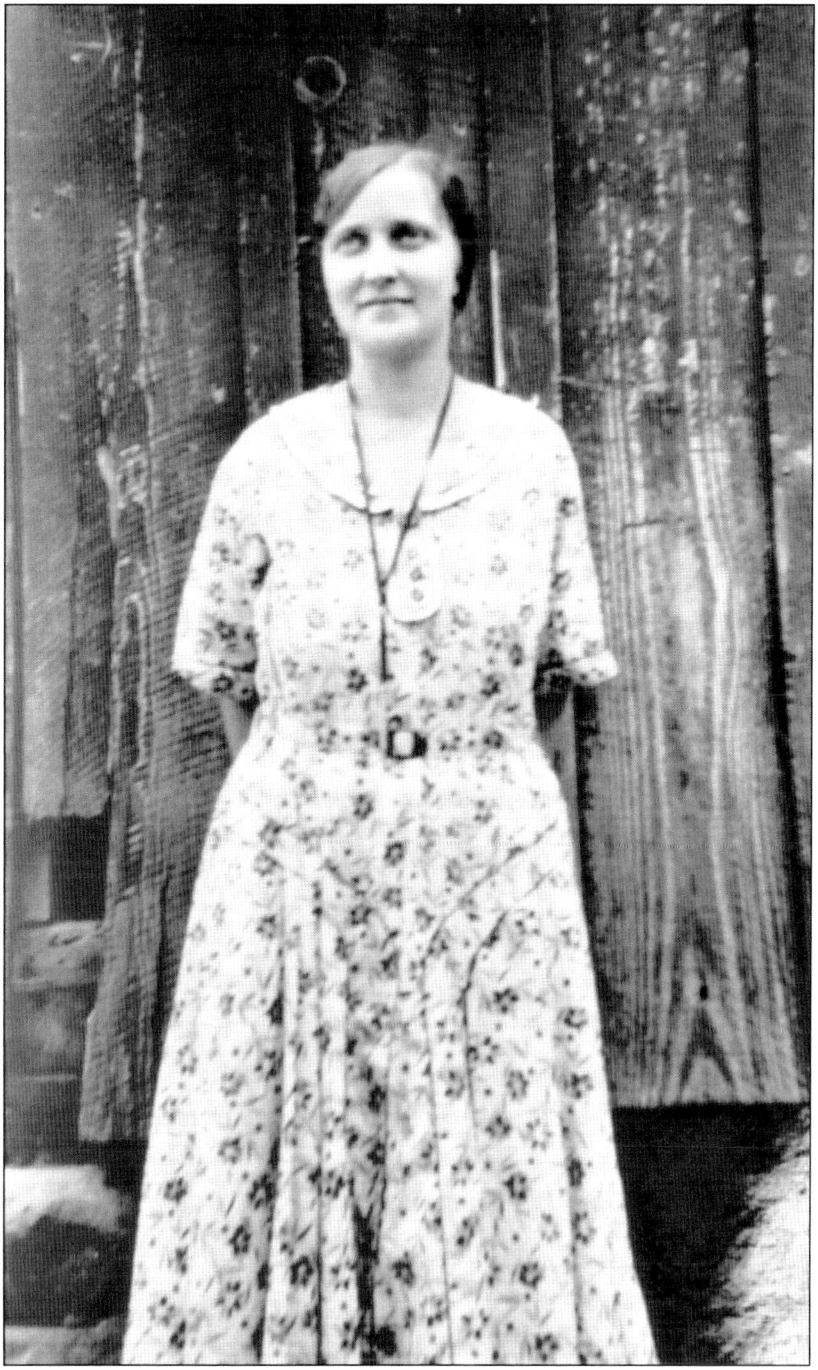

Sadie Louise Dennis was born in Rappahannock on June 13, 1904—she was the youngest of 12 children born to Newton Russell and Gabriella Robinson Dennis (three died as infants). She began teaching at an early age and was assigned to the Norman School in Culpeper. She married Tom Lynn Jones on March 10, 1926; the couple did not have children. Her devoted husband was a homebuilder. After many years, her health failed, and she died on May 31, 1980. She is buried in the cemetery of Shiloh Baptist Church in Woodville. (Virginia State University Archives.)

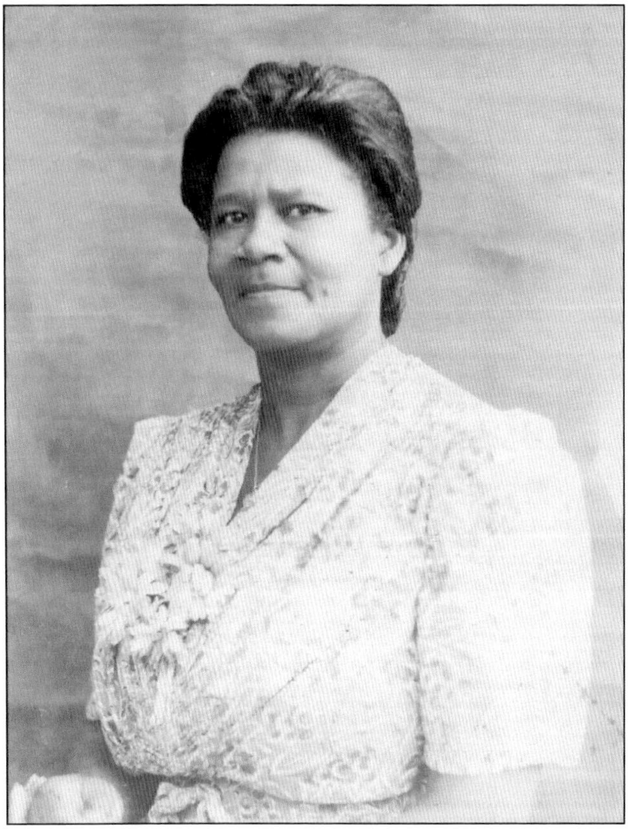

Ruth Robinson was born on January 10, 1898, to Marshall and Lucinda Blackwell Robinson. She earned her teaching certificate from the Manassas Industrial School for Colored Youth. In 1925, she married John Simon Ford, and in 1928, she began teaching in Culpeper schools. She and her husband were the parents of three sons. A believer in lifelong learning, at 47 years old, she earned a bachelor of science from Virginia State College. She was an educator in Culpeper until the mid-1960s. In addition to teaching, she was voted the first female president of the New Wayland Blue Ridge Association. Ruth Robinson Ford died on December 1, 1978, at age 80 and is buried in the National Cemetery in Culpeper next to her husband. (Ruth Renee Lewis.)

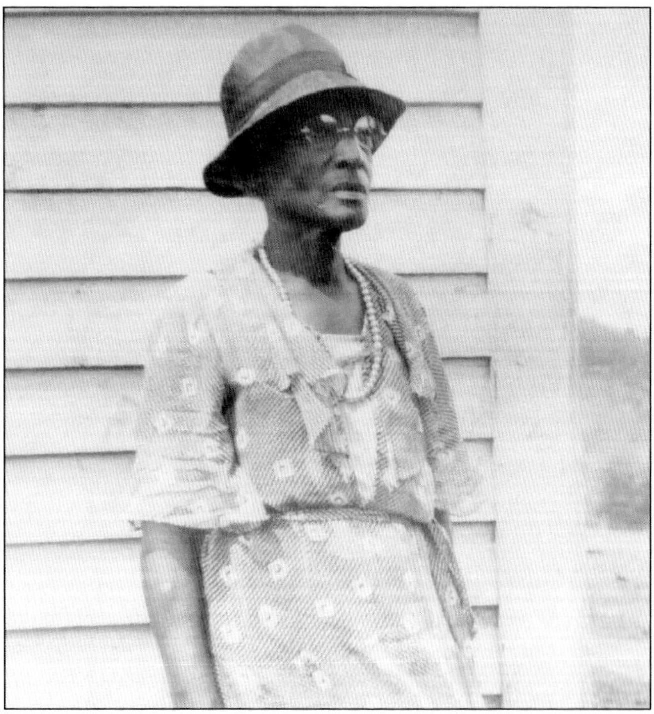

Isabella Miller Lightfoot was born on February 28, 1860, in Centerville, Pennsylvania, to parents whose names are lost to history. She married Orange County native William Lightfoot, and the couple relocated to Virginia. Seeing a need, Isabella started teaching local children. She died on April 4, 1943, of heart disease and is buried in Unionville, Virginia. (Virginia State University Archives.)

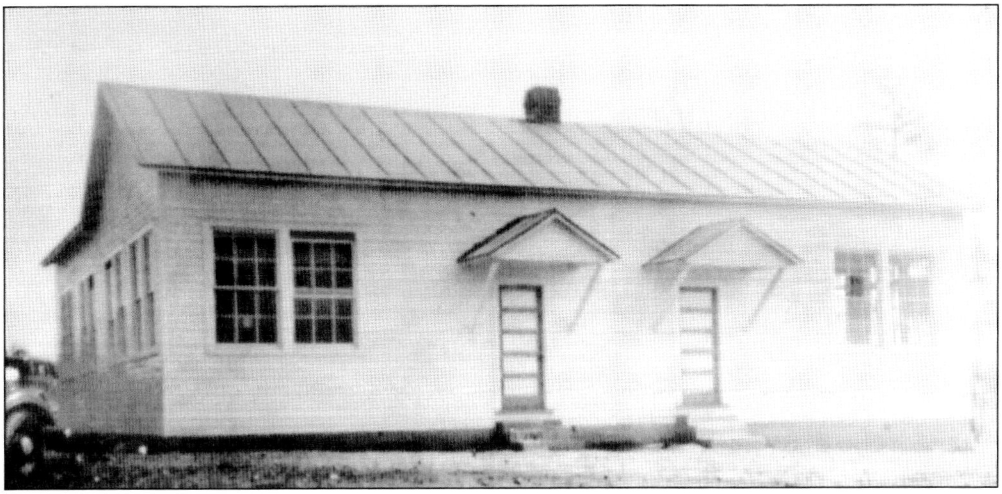

The Orange County Training School for African American high school students was a manifestation of the advanced education system that existed in that county in comparison to the neighboring counties of Culpeper, Madison, and Rappahannock. (Virginia State University Archives.)

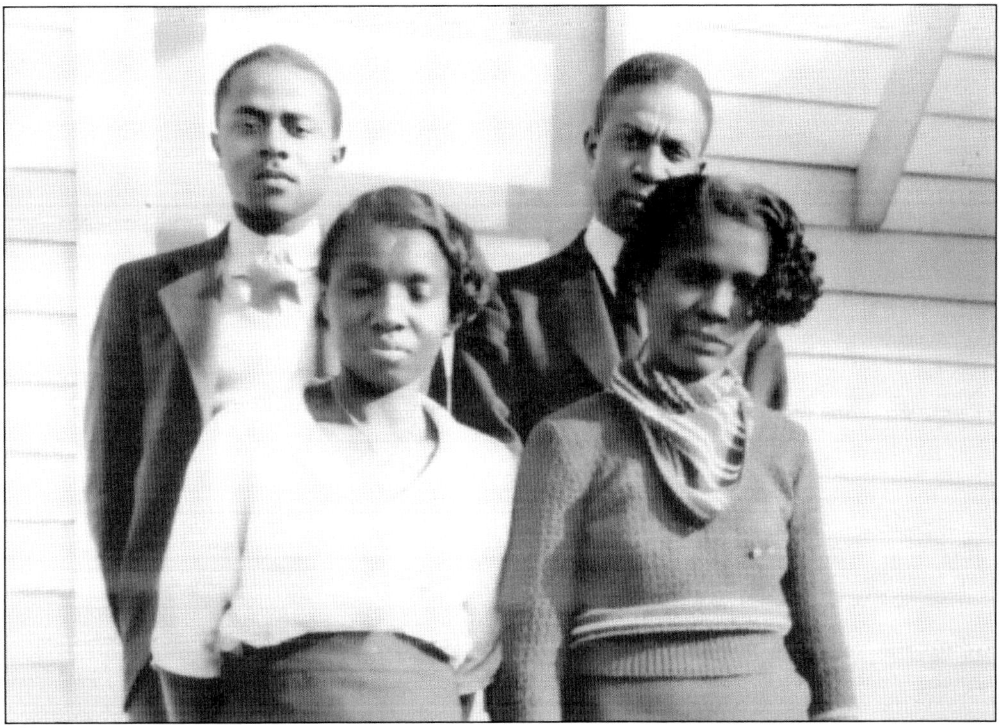

While Archie G. Richardson was the principal at Mecklenburg County Training School and serving as Director of Academics at St. Paul Normal School in Lawrenceville, he traveled throughout Virginia and documented minority teachers and students. This photograph, taken during the 1932–1933 academic year, features new faculty members at the Orange Training School. Although their names are not known, the diverse teachers were recruited from Virginia Union University in Richmond, West Virginia State College in Bluefield, and Morgan College in Baltimore. (Virginia State University Archives.)

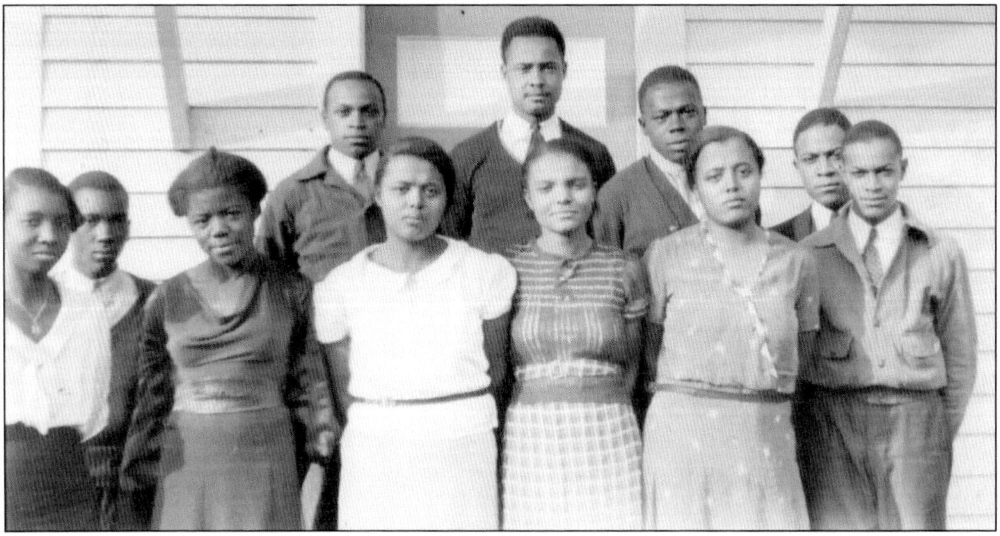

The 1934 Orange County Training School senior class is pictured here. (Virginia State University Archives.)

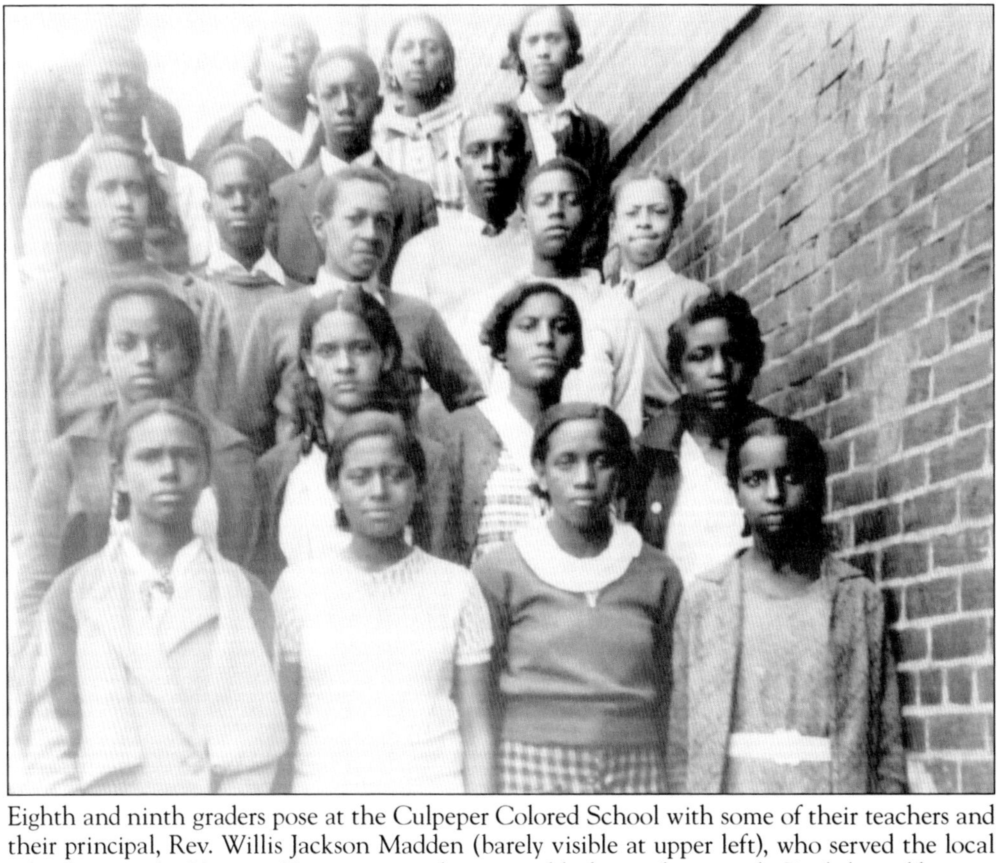

Eighth and ninth graders pose at the Culpeper Colored School with some of their teachers and their principal, Rev. Willis Jackson Madden (barely visible at upper left), who served the local school system for 30 years. He was primarily responsible for teaching math, English, and history. He was in his late 70s when the new Culpeper Training School was built and, thus, was deemed too elderly to handle the new responsibilities. (Virginia State University Archives.)

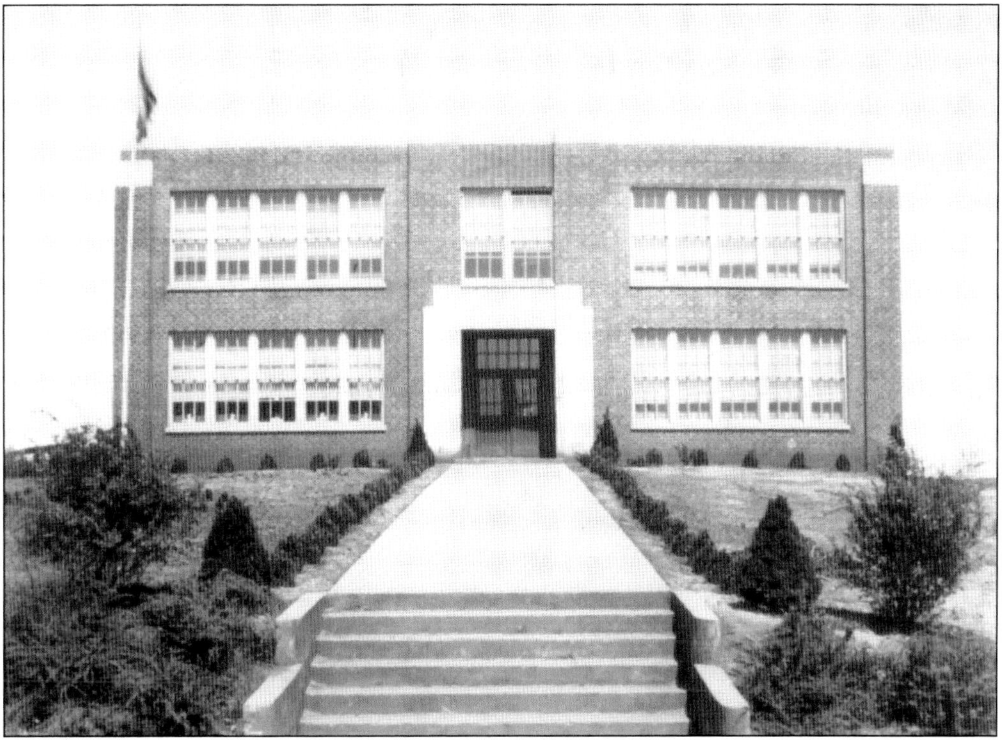

The new, brick Culpeper Training School that opened in the 1930s replaced an old structure that served African American children up to the ninth grade. This photograph was used in the 1939 World's Fair Expedition in New York as representation of the progressive education and modern buildings afforded to the county's African American children. (Library of Virginia.)

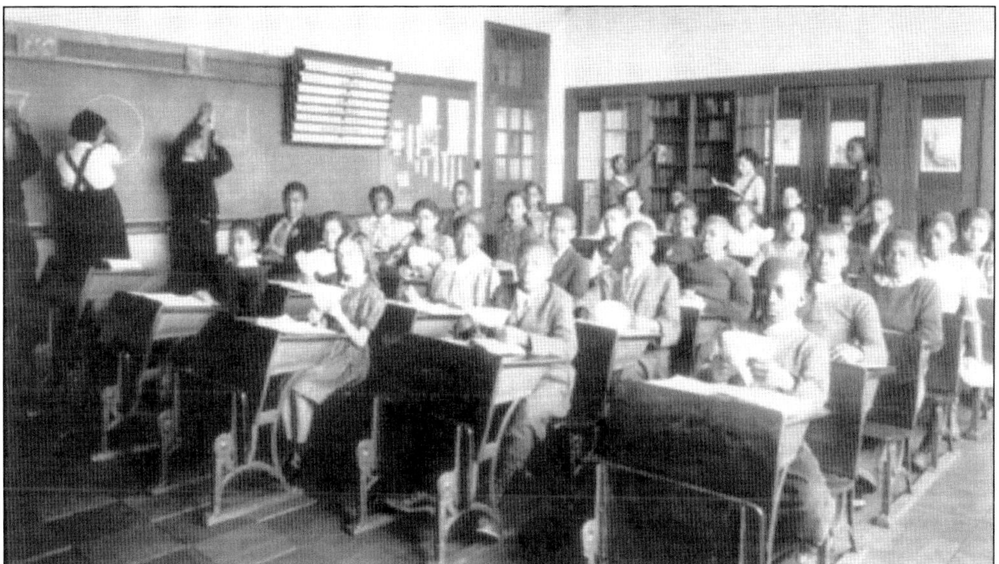

The 1939 New York World's Fair featured this photograph of African American children in the mathematics class of the Culpeper Training School. It was meant to be a representation of the fair's theme, "The World of Tomorrow." (Library of Virginia.)

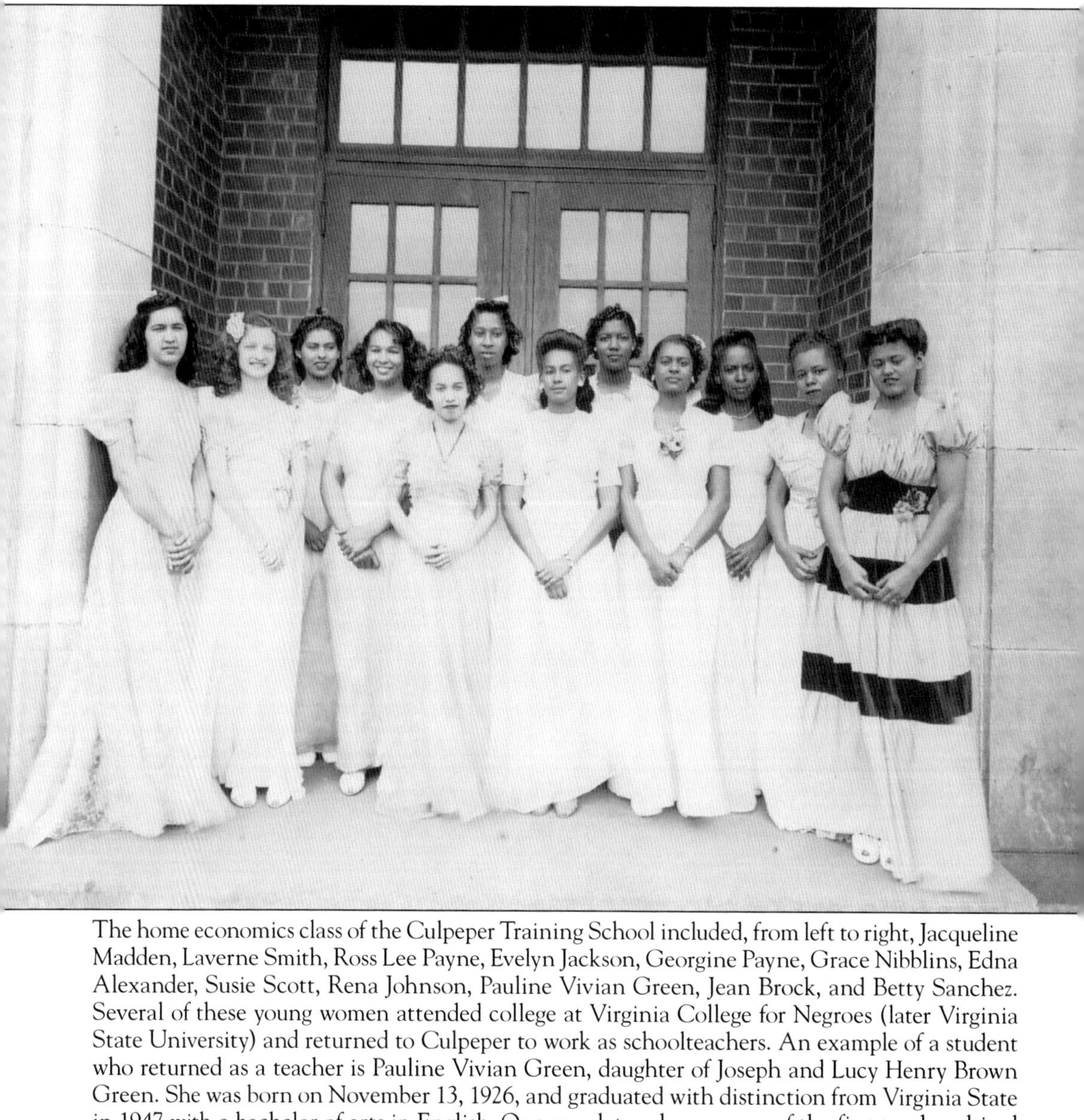

The home economics class of the Culpeper Training School included, from left to right, Jacqueline Madden, Laverne Smith, Ross Lee Payne, Evelyn Jackson, Georgine Payne, Grace Nibblins, Edna Alexander, Susie Scott, Rena Johnson, Pauline Vivian Green, Jean Brock, and Betty Sanchez. Several of these young women attended college at Virginia College for Negroes (later Virginia State University) and returned to Culpeper to work as schoolteachers. An example of a student who returned as a teacher is Pauline Vivian Green, daughter of Joseph and Lucy Henry Brown Green. She was born on November 13, 1926, and graduated with distinction from Virginia State in 1947 with a bachelor of arts in English. One year later, she was one of the first teachers hired at the new Carver Regional High School. She married a native of Charleston, South Carolina—World War II veteran and fellow Virginia State University alumnus John Henry Staggers Jr.—on Christmas Day in 1948. After a few years of teaching at Carver, the couple relocated to Maryland. (Michelle Jameson.)

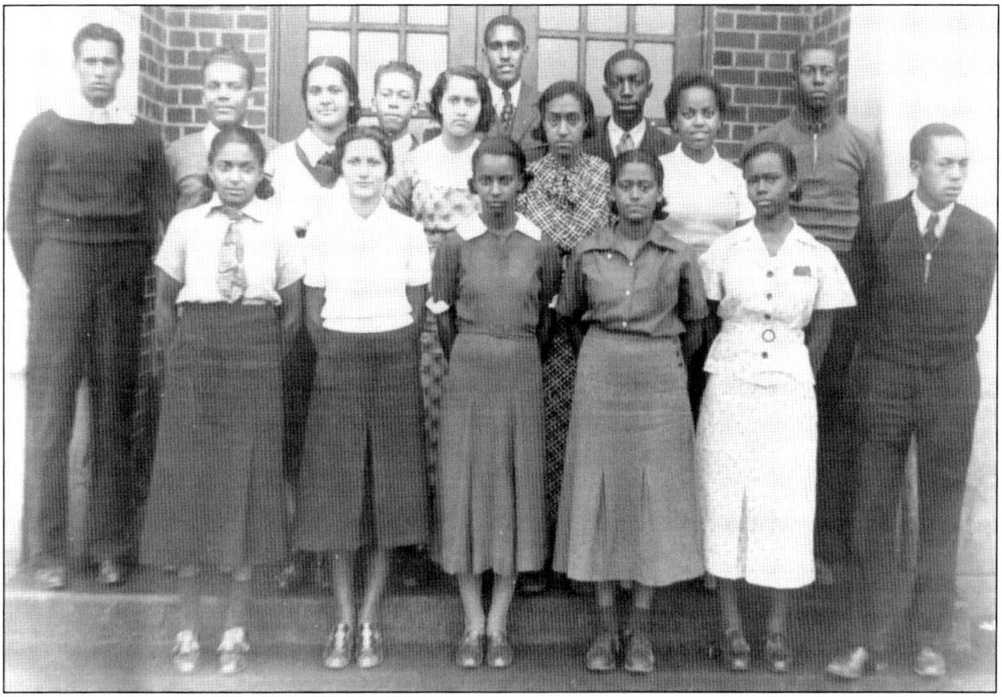

Students matured academically under the leadership of their principal, Tinsley Lee Spraggins (standing at center behind the students), at the Culpeper Training School. This was his last position before he relocated. (Michelle Jameson.)

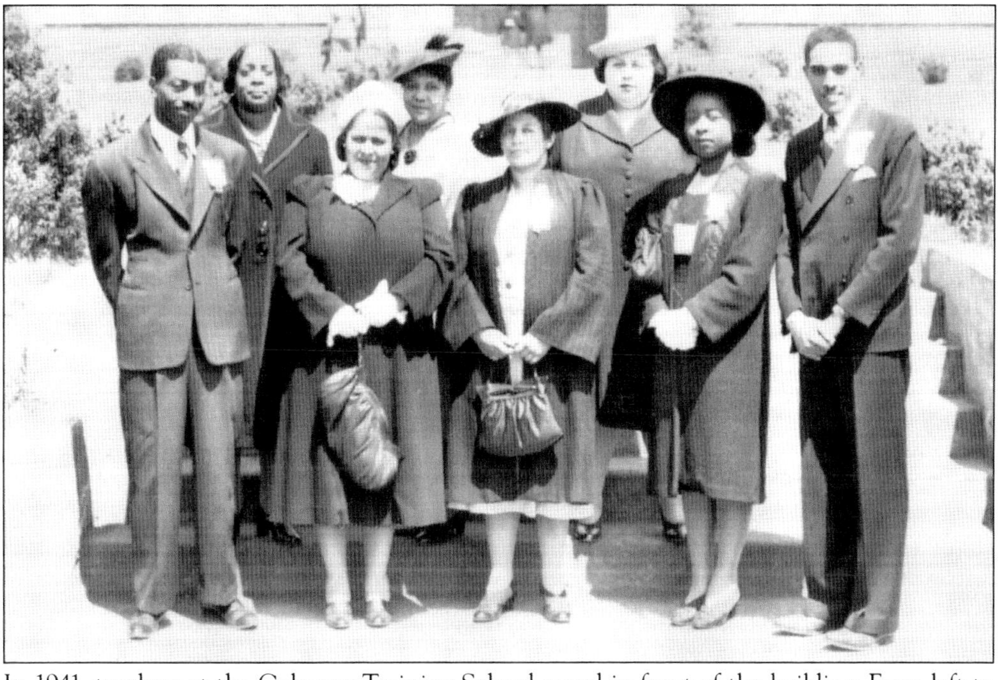

In 1941, teachers at the Culpeper Training School posed in front of the building. From left to right are Cyrus Honesty, Lucy H. Green, Landonia Greenwood, unidentified, Annie P. Lovell, unidentified, E.V. Payne, and Tinsley L. Spraggins (principal). (Angela J. Chapman.)

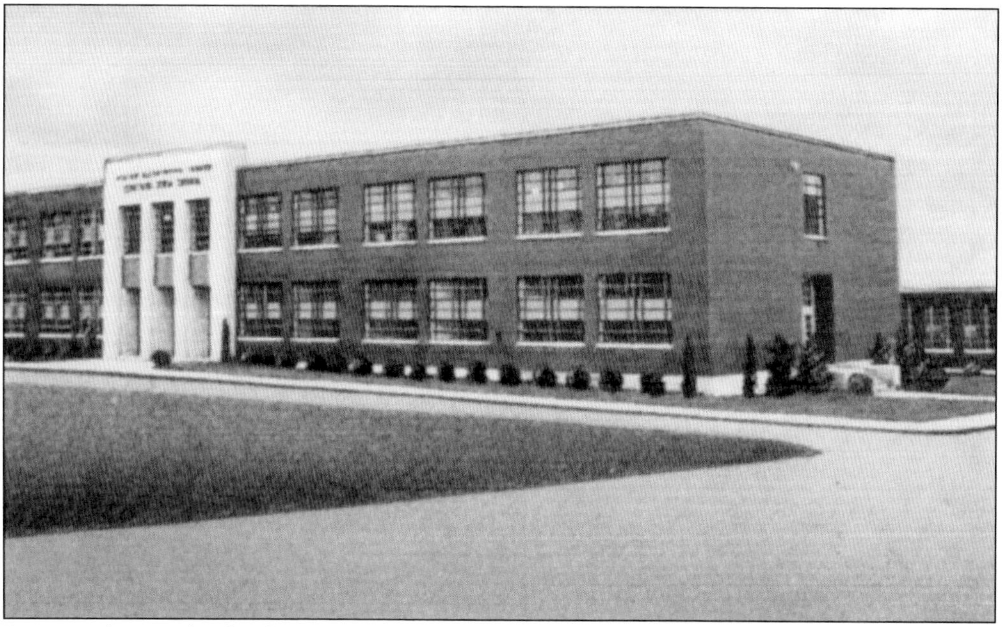

Parents advocated, school superintendents organized, and decisions were made to build a high school for African American students from Culpeper, Orange, Madison, and Rappahannock Counties. Recorded by a deed dated August 31, 1946, African American farmer Noah Price sold 11.5 acres to the collective school boards of the four stated counties for the price of $10 plus other "good and valuable consideration." George Washington Carver Regional High School opened in October 1948 with eighteen teachers, one librarian, one principal, and more than four hundred students. (Terry Miller.)

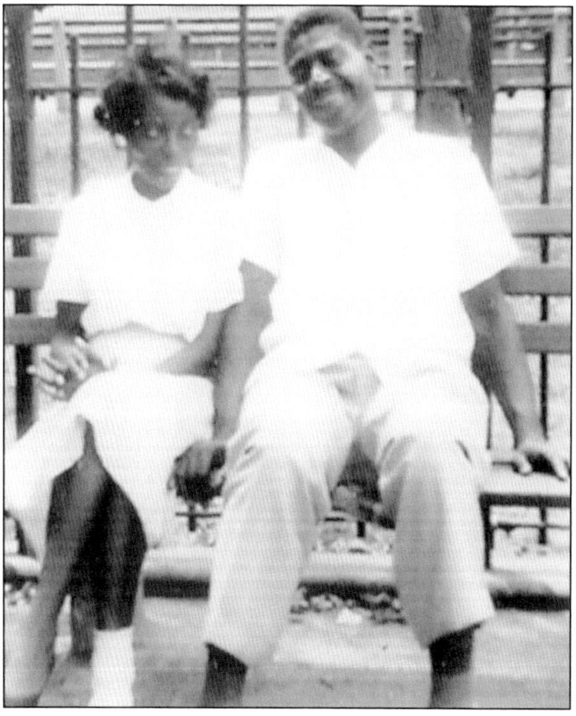

Hiawatha Lorna Smith was born in Albemarle County on July 2, 1926, to blacksmith John R. Smith and his wife, Lara Scott. Hiawatha earned a bachelor of science in library science from Virginia State University in 1948. In addition to establishing the new Carver library, she was a sponsor of the girls' basketball team. She married fellow teacher George Dixon Marshall, and they relocated to Washington, DC, where they made their home, raised a family, and continued to grow professionally. She earned a master of arts from the University of the District of Columbia and retired from DC Public Schools in 1982. George Marshall earned two master of arts degrees—in public administration and in special education. He retired as supervisor of social workers for the DC government. (Marshall family.)

The audience will please stand for the Recessional and Processional

Processional .... Priests' March

Invocation .... Rev. R. L. Harrison

"When I Have Sung My Songs" .... The Glee Club
(By Charles)

Salutatory Address .... Lois Groves
"Confidence for the Challenge"

Valedictory Address .... Virginia Turner
"Onward Into Tomorrow"

"I Shall Not Again Pass This Way" .... The Glee Club
(By Underwood and Durst)

Presentation of Speaker .... Mr. H. A. Fleshmon

Address .... Mr. J. Rupert Picott

"America the Beautiful" .... The Glee Club
(By Ward-Pinney)

Presentation of Class to
Executive Officer of Regional Board .... Mrs. C. W. Michie

Presentation of Diplomas .... Mr. Paul Hounshell

Announcements and Remarks

Recessional .... Priests' March

CLASS MOTTO .... *"Let Us Meet the Challenge"*

CLASS FLOWER ...... *American Beauty Rose*

CLASS COLORS .... *Blue and White*

CLASS OFFICERS

President .... Virginia Elizabeth Turner

Vice-President .... William Richard Stearns

Secretary .... Grace Evangeline Perry

Assistant Secretary .... Lorraine Teresa Dade

Treasurer .... Lois Katherine Groves

CLASS ROLL

The first commencement program for George Washington Carver Regional High School was held on June 10, 1949, in the school's auditorium. The president and treasurer of the class, both Rappahannock natives, were also the valedictorian and salutatorian, respectively. Virginia Elizabeth Turner was born on October 9, 1931, to James A. and Lucy Timbers Turner. Born on April 18, 1932, Lois Katherine Groves was the daughter of Gilbert and Margaret Jackson Groves. (Angela J. Chapman.)

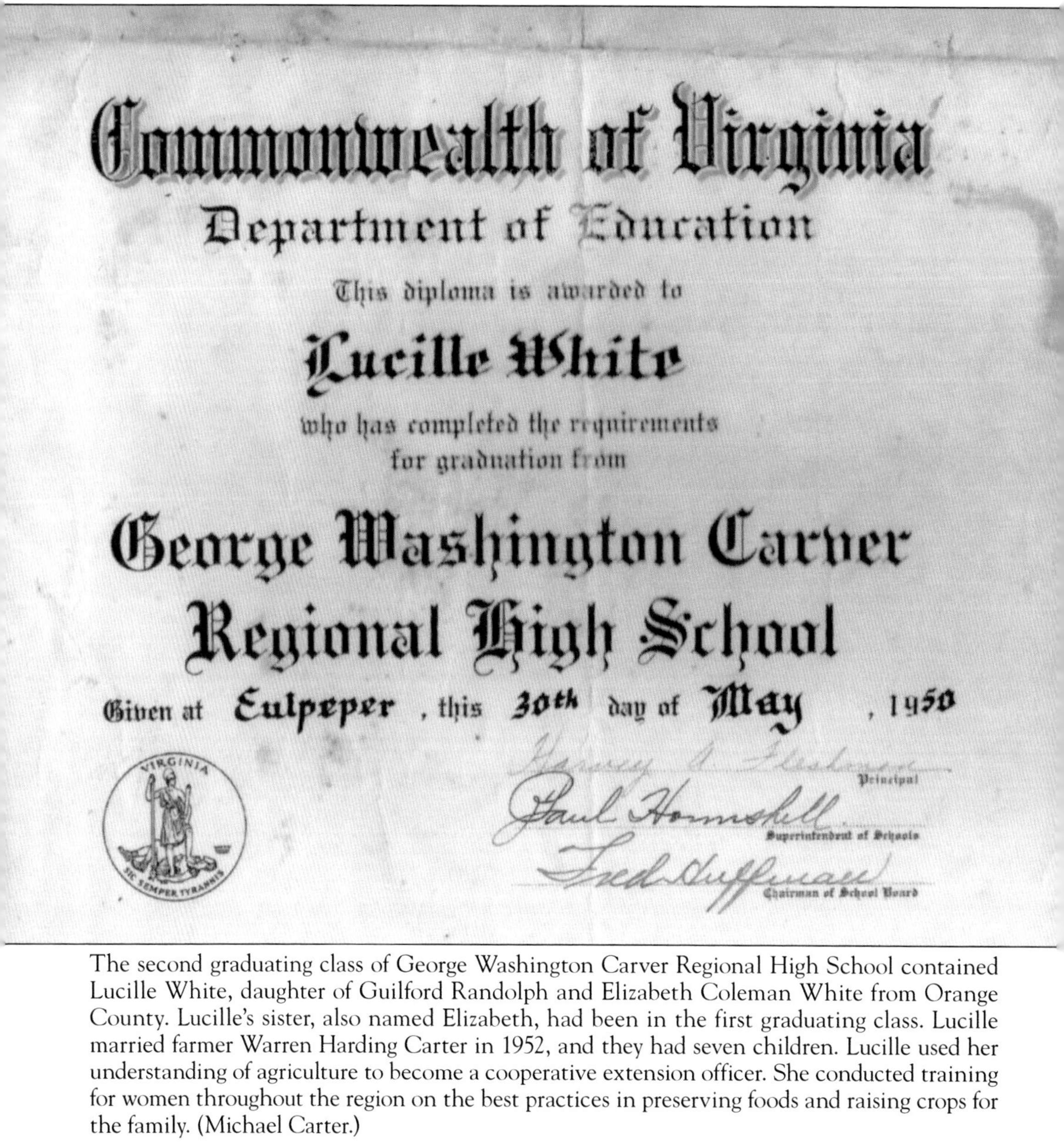

Commonwealth of Virginia

Department of Education

This diploma is awarded to

Lucille White

who has completed the requirements
for graduation from

George Washington Carver
Regional High School

Given at Culpeper, this 30th day of May, 1950

VIRGINIA
SIC SEMPER TYRANNIS

Principal

Superintendent of Schools

Chairman of School Board

The second graduating class of George Washington Carver Regional High School contained Lucille White, daughter of Guilford Randolph and Elizabeth Coleman White from Orange County. Lucille's sister, also named Elizabeth, had been in the first graduating class. Lucille married farmer Warren Harding Carter in 1952, and they had seven children. Lucille used her understanding of agriculture to become a cooperative extension officer. She conducted training for women throughout the region on the best practices in preserving foods and raising crops for the family. (Michael Carter.)

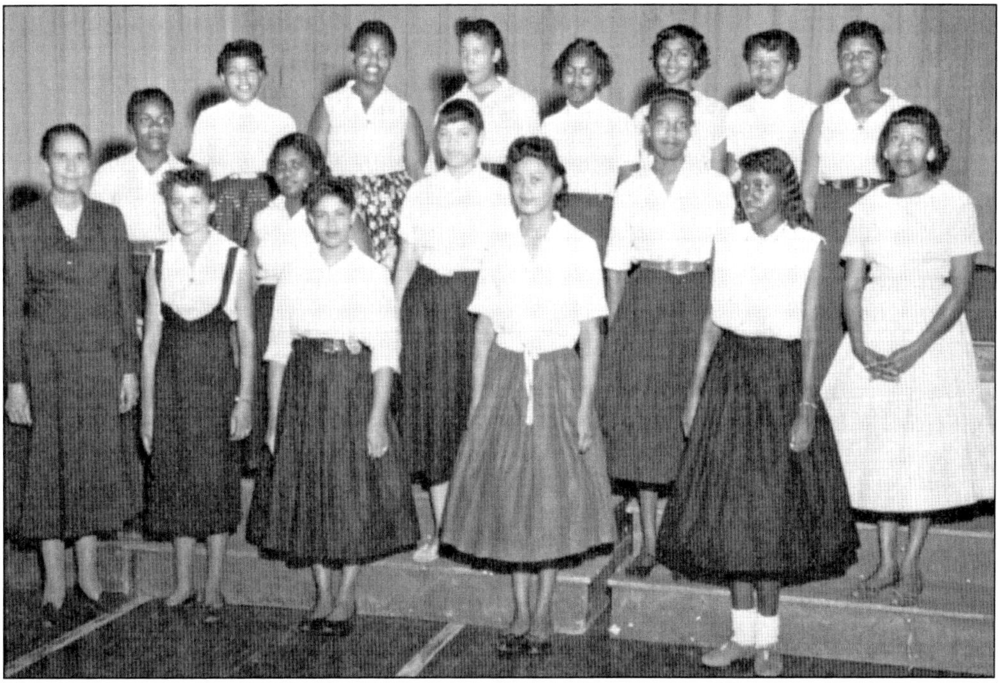

Throughout her years of being a home economics professional, Stella Hairston Fleshmon (at farthest left in the first row) was known for visiting the home of each young lady in her classes. This photograph from the 1952 Carver Regional High School *Hawks* yearbook shows Fleshmon with some of her pupils. Born on March 10, 1906, in Henry County, Virginia, to John L. Hairston and Martha Pannill, she received her high school diploma, bachelor's degree, and master's degree from Virginia State University. She was in Culpeper for nearly all of her teaching career, from 1934 to her retirement. She was married to Harvey A. Fleshmon, principal of Carver Regional High School, and they had two daughters. She died on April 5, 1997, at 91 years old. (Orange County Historical Society.)

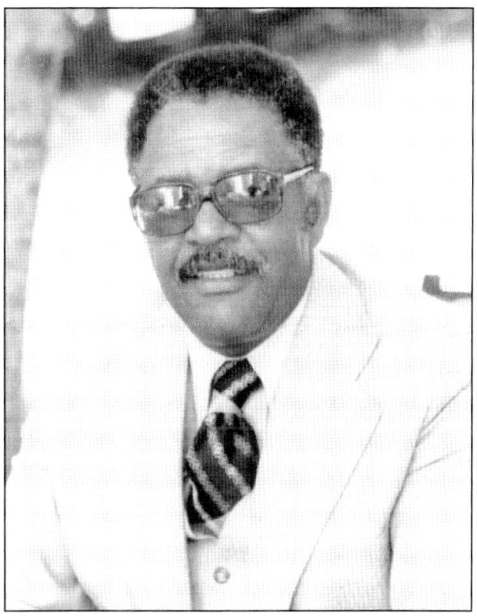

William Henry Lewis was custodian and systems engineer for the entire duration that Carver Regional served as a traditional high school. He remained on staff as the traditional high school transitioned to a vocational training facility after 1968. He was often spoken of as the most trusted member of the staff. Born in Culpeper on April 25, 1923, to Henry and Ella Green Lewis, he was married to Madison-born Mary Helen Gibson Lewis. He died on March 20, 1984, at only 60 years of age and is buried in Fairview Cemetery. (William H. Lewis.)

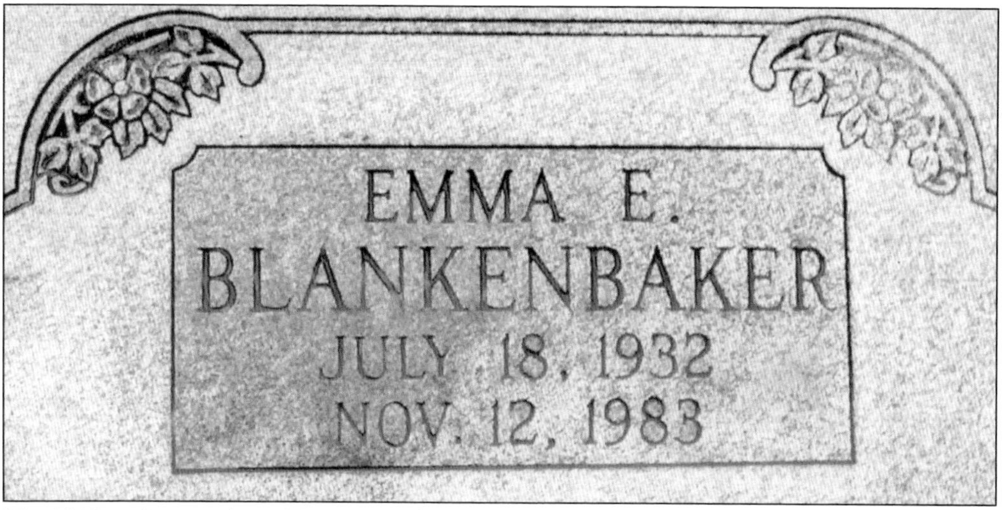

The 1949 graduating class of George Washington Carver Regional High School produced a variety of professionals. One example is Madison-born Emma Elizabeth Tinsley, daughter of Jesse and Marie Lucas Tinsley. When she married Rodman L. Blankenbaker on October 29, 1960, she had already been working as a civilian accounting technician for the US Army. Her husband was a World War II veteran and owner of Blankenbaker Repair Shop. The couple had two children. On November 1, 1983, she died at only 51 years of age from heart disease. (Terry Miller.)

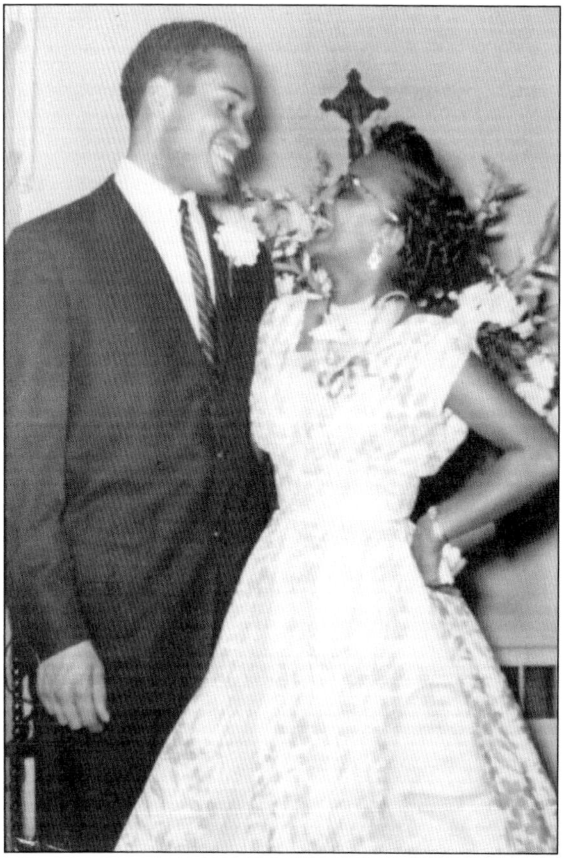

Courtelyou Wellington Payne was born in Culpeper on July 1, 1931, to World War I veteran and barber Harry Lester Payne and his wife, Elizabeth Hansborough Payne. At Carver Regional High School, he was known for his love of music. After he graduated from Virginia State University in 1954, he taught music at Carver and then went to Northern Virginia, where he made a career in Alexandria public schools for more than 30 years before retiring in 1990. He was married to fellow teacher Marcia Johnson of Portsmouth (she died in 2005). He died on November 15, 2008, and is buried in Mount Comfort Cemetery in Fairfax County. (Payne family.)

Seven

When They Prayed

A multitude of African American churches were constructed throughout the counties of Culpeper, Madison, Orange, and Rappahannock from the mid-1800s through the 1950s, the majority of which are Baptist. In addition, countless cemeteries, whether family- or church-based, dot the landscape.

This last chapter pays homage not to individual churches and/or congregants but to those who represent the services that a church provides. Well known are the names of ministers who founded churches and/or led them. Familiar names such as Revs. Leland Warring, Willis Jackson Madden, Fennell Festus Terrell, Lewis Brown, U.B. Johnson, S.A. Sanford, R.L. Banks, George Galloway, and John J. Jackson remind citizens of the struggle to form and maintain houses of worship.

Lesser known are the names of church leaders, sextons, missionaries, and even children. While their photographs may not be accessible, the book aims to state their names or share their contributions. Sextons such as Lewis Morton Ford of Good Hope Baptist Church seemed to know how to mend every brokenness.

Women prepared and served food, taught Sunday school, assisted in baptisms, prepared the bodies of the deceased, wiped weeping eyes, and placed flowers on graves. Among the thousands who performed these important tasks are Ora Scott Ware, Georgia Anna Venney Timbers, and Leola Walker.

Recognizing that they gained much when working together, the New Wayland Blue Ridge Baptist Association, which has been in existence for more than 140 years, continues to be a centralized body whose members share information through regular fellowship. Civic and fraternal organizations, in concert with churches, provided a burial ground for laymen, while the Culpeper National Cemetery continues to be a perpetual-care home for veterans and their beloved ones.

Shared memories for this project end here with a nod and smile to examples of those who were the religious bedrock of their respective communities. To all, a solemn and heartfelt "amen."

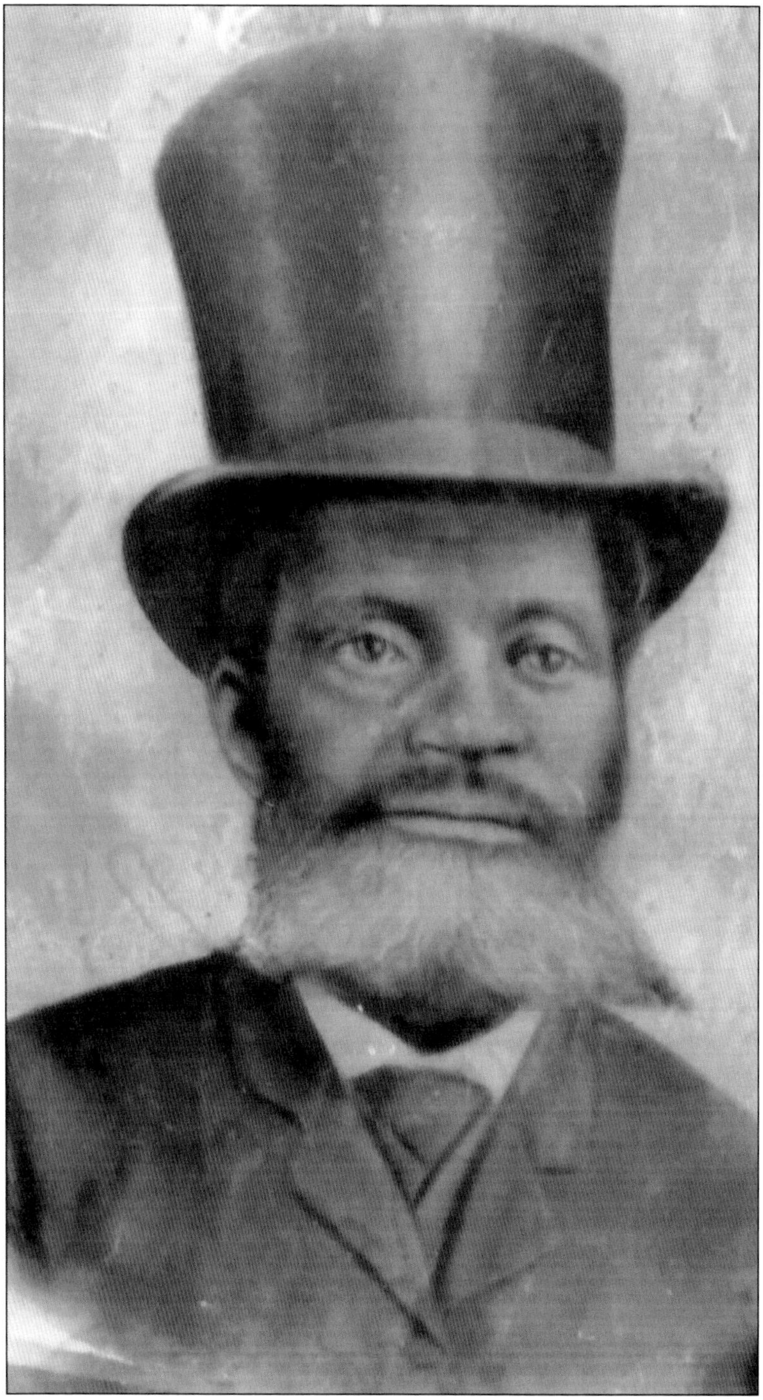

An energetic pastor is important to a vital church. Rev. Wanzer Tibbs proved to be both energetic and evangelistic. This farmer and itinerant minister could claim all four counties in this book as his home, because he founded no less than five churches in the area. His final congregation was Free Union Baptist Church, which many of his family members still attend. He and several family members are buried there. (Elizabeth Tibbs Smith.)

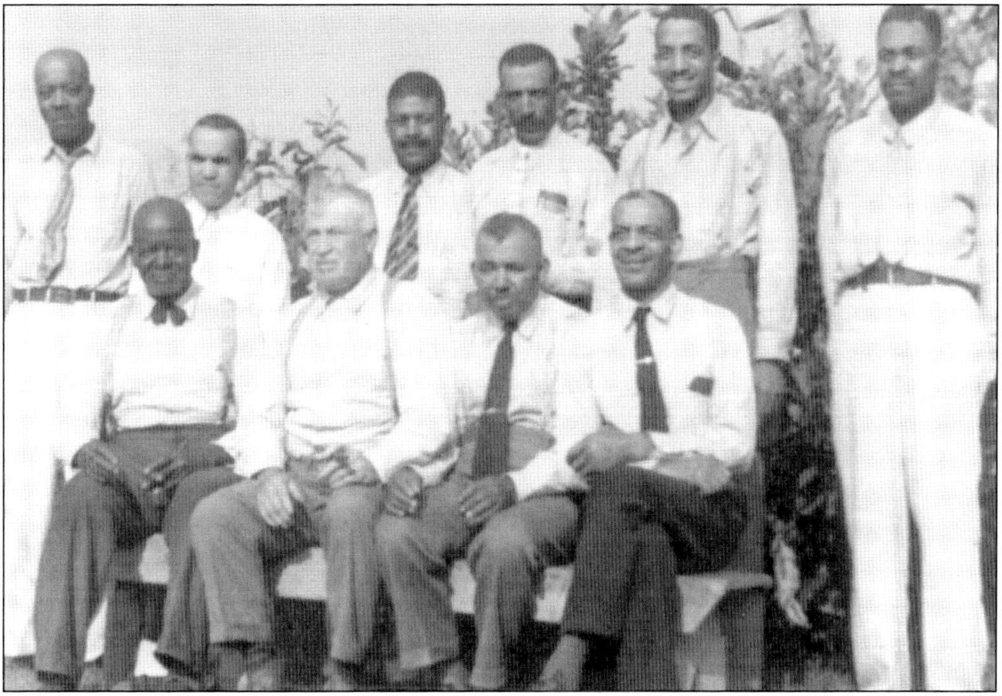

Church buildings exist because people, usually men, construct them. Once the construction is done, they organize ministries that care for the needs of congregants. In addition, those founders take on day-to-day tasks to ensure the church remains vibrant and focused on its mission. Pictured here are the men of Oak Grove Baptist Church in Madison. Seated are, from left to right, William Chivis, Lucien Clore, Edward Johnson, and Isaac Walker. Standing are, from left to right, Shelton Ward, William Evans, William Johnson, James Franklin Walker, William Allen Turner, and Walter Brock. This image is from the Oak Grove Baptist Church anniversary booklet. (Orange County Historical Society.)

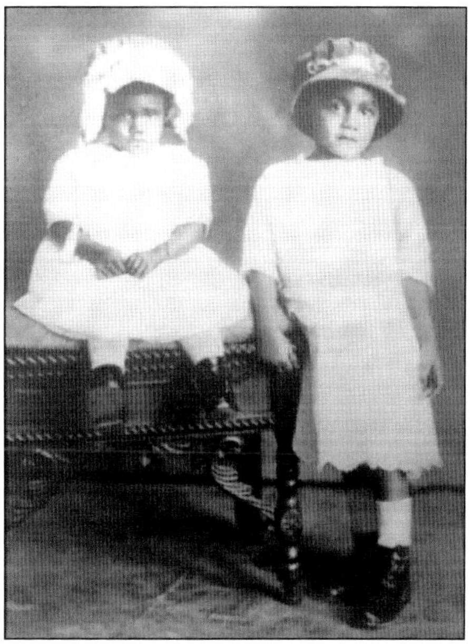

Churches thrive when they have youth who feel valued and, frankly, who can run, play, and feel safe once the religious lessons have been heard. Pictured here are Lillie Earl Johnson (right, b. 1917) and her younger sister Mary (b. 1919), daughters of Russell and Lily Johnson of Culpeper. (Johnson family.)

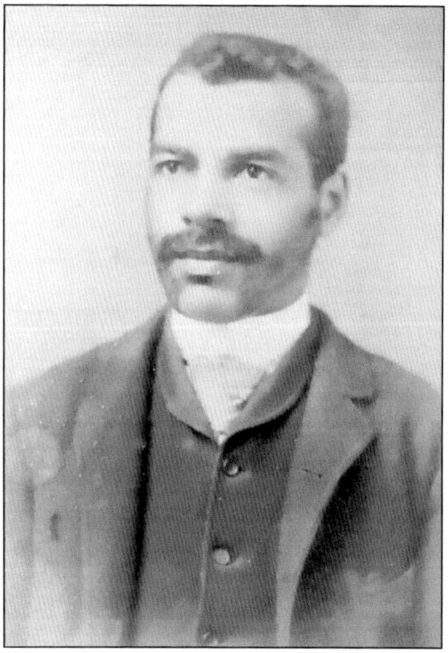

Churches grow when ministers are working together for the benefit of their congregants. One example is Rev. Ernest M. Lovell, born in Madison to William and Mary Young Lovell on September 14, 1857. He worked as a farm laborer until the late 1880s, when he went to Washington, DC, and he graduated from Howard University in 1890. After returning to Madison, he began his career as a minister and was one of the leaders of the newly founded Wayland Blue Ridge Baptist Association. He was the husband of Mary Wilhoite and the father of three children. He died on April 22, 1930, and is buried in the cemetery of Cedar Grove Baptist Church in Buena, Culpeper. (Angela J. Chapman.)

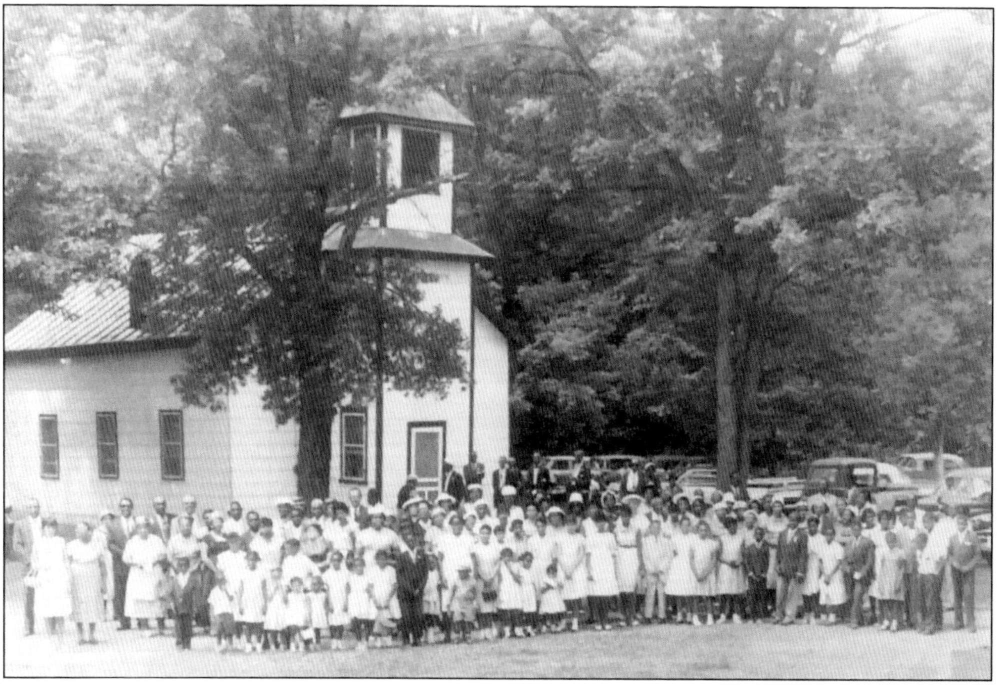

The Wayland Blue Ridge Baptist Association, formed in 1877 as part of the Northern Virginia Baptist Association, supported member churches in carrying out their missions more effectively. Its territory included churches in Alexandria through parts of West Virginia. The first session was held in Culpeper. They reorganized at Antioch Baptist Church (in Culpeper) in 1889 and, with 21 member churches, renamed themselves the New Wayland Blue Ridge Association in honor of the institute in Washington, DC, where many of the ministers were educated. In 1961, they celebrated their 50th anniversary at Blue Hill Baptist Church in Orange, as shown in this photograph. (Hortense Hinton-Jackson.)

Churches and the communities in which they exist thrive because women engage their skills. Beatrice Fleshmon Robinson is illustrative of selfless women throughout the four-county region. Born on Valentine's Day in 1916, she was the daughter of Henry Louis and Mary Jane Harris Fleshmon. After the death of her mother, she was raised by her grandmother, Alice Griffin Fleshmon. She married World War II veteran Ollie Robinson and was the dietician at the George Washington Carver Regional High School, planning and preparing daily meals along with her staff. She also gave freely to her church, Antioch Baptist Church in Culpeper. She died on October 28, 2011, at age 95. (Angela J. Chapman.)

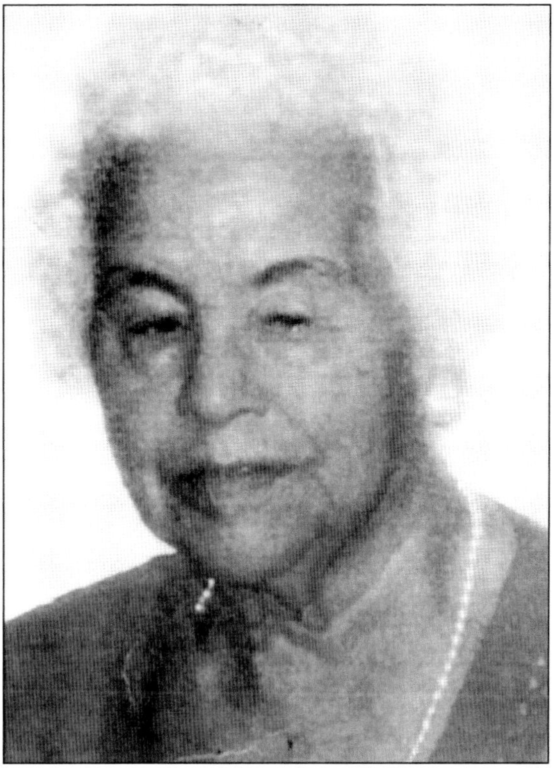

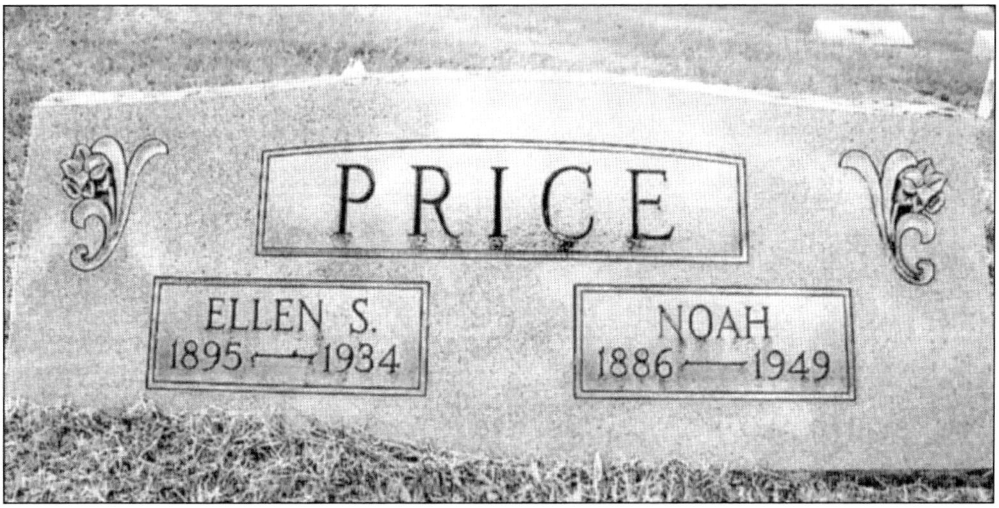

In response to a 1903 Culpeper law that ordered the strict segregation of the cemetery, five fraternal and religious organizations planned and executed the development of a cemetery for Culpeper's minority population. Those organizations were the Grand United Order of Odd Fellows, Sunny Fountain Lodge, Grand United Order of Galilean Fishermen, Summers Tabernacle, and Antioch Baptist Church. The graveyard, initially called Antioch Cemetery, was begun on land adjacent to the white Fairview Cemetery, with the two cemeteries separated by a fence. Sixty-seven years later, the fence was removed and the entire property was called Fairview Cemetery. Shown are the graves of Noah Price and his wife, Ella. Price was the man who sold the land on which the George Washington Carver Regional High School was constructed. (Terry Miller.)

Consistent with our mission to preserve history on a local level, this book was printed in South Carolina on American-made paper and manufactured entirely in the United States. Products carrying the accredited Forest Stewardship Council (FSC) label are printed on 100 percent FSC-certified paper.

MADE IN THE USA